Qualitative
Research
Design

APPLIED SOCIAL RESEARCH
METHODS SERIES

Qualitative Research Design

An Interactive Approach

Joseph A. Maxwell
George Mason University

41 APPLIED SOCIAL RESEARCH METHODS SERIES

Los Angeles | London | New Delhi
Singapore | Washington DC

Los Angeles | London | New Delhi
Singapore | Washington DC

FOR INFORMATION:

SAGE Publications, Inc.
2455 Teller Road
Thousand Oaks, California 91320
E-mail: order@sagepub.com

SAGE Publications Ltd.
1 Oliver's Yard
55 City Road
London EC1Y 1SP
United Kingdom

SAGE Publications India Pvt. Ltd.
B 1/I 1 Mohan Cooperative Industrial Area
Mathura Road, New Delhi 110 044
India

SAGE Publications Asia-Pacific Pte. Ltd.
3 Church Street
#10-04 Samsung Hub
Singapore 049483

Printed in the United States of America

Library of Congress Cataloging-in-Publication Data

Maxwell, Joseph Alex, 1941-

Qualitative research design : an interactive approach / Joseph A. Maxwell. —3rd ed.

p. cm. -- (Applied social research methods ; v. 41)

Includes bibliographical references and index.

ISBN 978-1-4129-8119-4 (pbk.)

1. Research--Methodology. I. Title.

Q180.55.M4M39 2013
001.4′2—dc23   2012012021

This book is printed on acid-free paper.

Acquisitions Editor: Vicki Knight
Associate Editor: Lauren Habib
Editorial Assistant: Kalie Koscielak
Production Editor: Libby Larson
Copy Editor: Codi Bowman
Typesetter: C&M Digitals, Ltd.
Proofreader: Wendy Jo Dymond
Indexer: Molly Hall
Cover Designer: Candice Harman
Marketing Manager: Nicole Elliott
Permissions Editor   Adele Hutchinson

12 13 14 15 16 10 9 8 7 6 5 4 3 2 1

Contents

Preface

A major impetus for a new edition of this book was the opportunity to expand it somewhat beyond the page limits of the Applied Social Research Methods Series, for which it was originally written. However, many readers of the previous editions have said that they appreciated the conciseness of the book, so I didn't want to lose this virtue. Consequently, much of the new material in this edition consists of additional examples of my students' work, including a second example of a dissertation proposal (Appendix B).

Another impetus has been the ongoing development of qualitative research,[1] with a flourishing of new approaches, including arts-based approaches, to how it is conducted and presented. I haven't attempted to deal comprehensively with these, which would have ballooned the book well past what I felt was an appropriate length, as well as taking it beyond an introductory level. If you want to investigate these developments, the *SAGE Encyclopedia of Qualitative Research* (Given, 2008), the *SAGE Handbook of Qualitative Research,* 4th edition (Denzin & Lincoln, 2011), and the journal *Qualitative Inquiry* are good places to start. I've tried to indicate, in Chapters 1 and 3, how I see my approach to design as compatible with some of these developments, in particular with aspects of postmodernism and with the approach known as bricolage, and I have substantially rewritten and expanded my discussion of research paradigms, in Chapter 2.

However, I am also skeptical of some of these developments, particularly those that adopt a radical constructivist and relativist stance that denies the existence of any reality that our research attempts to understand, and that rejects any conception of validity (or related terms) that addresses the relationship between our research conclusions and the phenomena that we study. While I am enough of a postmodernist to believe that every theory and conclusion is our own construction, with no claim to objective or absolute truth, and argue in Chapter 2 that no theory can capture the full complexity of the things we study, I refuse to abandon the goal of gaining a better understanding of the physical, social, and cultural world in which we live, or the possibility of developing credible explanations for these phenomena.

This position is grounded in my third impetus for revising this book: my increasing awareness of how my perspective on qualitative research has been informed by a philosophical realism about the things we study. I have developed this perspective at length in my book *A Realist Approach for Qualitative Research* (Maxwell, 2011b), arguing that the critical realist position I have taken is not only compatible with most qualitative researchers' actual practices, but can be valuable in helping researchers with some difficult theoretical, methodological, and political issues that they face. However, I offer this as a useful perspective among other perspectives, not as the single correct paradigm for qualitative research. As the writing teacher Peter Elbow (1973, 2006) argued, it is important to play both the "believing game" and the "doubting game" with any theory or position you encounter, trying to see both its advantages and its distortions or blind spots. For this reason, I want the present book to be of practical value to students and researchers who hold a variety of positions on these issues. The model of qualitative research design that I develop here is compatible with a range of philosophical perspectives, and I believe it is broadly applicable to most qualitative research.

My greater awareness of the implications of a critical realist stance have led me to revise or expand other parts of the book—in particular, the discussion of theory in Chapter 3; developing (and revising) research questions in Chapter 4; research relationships and ethics, developing interview questions, and data analysis in Chapter 5; the concept of validity in Chapter 6; and the appropriate functions and content of a literature review in a research proposal in Chapter 7. I've also continued to compulsively tinker with the language of the book, striving to make what I say clearer. I would be grateful for any feedback you can give me on how the book could be made more useful to you.

Finally, I realized in revising this work that I had said almost nothing explicitly about how I define qualitative research—what I see as most essential about a qualitative approach. I say more about this in Chapter 2. However, a brief definition would be that qualitative research is research that is intended to help you better understand (1) the meanings and perspectives of the people you study—seeing the world from their point of view, rather than simply from your own; (2) how these perspectives are shaped by, and shape, their physical, social, and cultural contexts; and (3) the specific processes that are involved in maintaining or altering these phenomena and relationships. All three of these aspects of qualitative research, but particularly the last one, contrast with most quantitative approaches to research, which are based on seeing the phenomena studied in terms of variables—properties of things that can vary, and can thus be measured and compared across contexts. (I discuss the difference between variance and process thinking in Chapters 2, 3, and 4.) I see most of the more obvious aspects of qualitative research—its inductive, open-ended approach, its reliance on textual or visual rather than numerical data, and its primary goal of particular understanding rather than generalization across persons and settings—as due to these three main features of qualitative inquiry. (For a more detailed discussion of these issues, see Maxwell, 2011b.)

I want to acknowledge and thank all of the people who have had an influence on this edition. In particular my students at George Mason University, especially the ones who have contributed their work as examples; the editorial staff at SAGE, who contributed a great deal to the final product, especially my editor, Vicki Knight, and Kalie Koscielak, Codi Bowman, Libby Larson, Nicole Elliot, and Amanda Simpson; and the reviewers of the drafts for this edition, whose feedback helped me to see ways to improve the book that I had overlooked:

David Carlone, The University of North Carolina at Greensboro

Sharon L. Caudle, Texas A&M University

Joseph W. Check, University of Massachusetts, Boston

Paula Dawidowicz, Walden University

Mary S. Enright, Capella University

Deborah Gioia, University of Maryland, Baltimore

Gaetane Jean-Marie, University of Oklahoma

David M. Kleist, Idaho State University

William B. Kline, University of Mississippi

Elizabeth Bussman Mahler, EdD, Northeastern University

Eliane Rubinstein, Avila University of Arizona

Anastasia P. Samaras, George Mason University

Ning Jackie Zhang, University of Central Florida

Note

1. Some qualitative practitioners prefer the term "inquiry" to "research," seeing the latter as too closely associated with a quantitative or positivist approach. I agree with their concerns (see Maxwell, 2004a, 2004b), and I understand that some types of qualitative inquiry are more humanistic than scientific, but I prefer to argue for a broader definition of "research" that includes a range of qualitative approaches.

About the Author

Joseph A. Maxwell is a Professor in the Graduate School of Education at George Mason University, where he teaches courses on research design and methods and on writing a dissertation proposal. He has published work on qualitative research and evaluation, mixed method research, sociocultural theory, Native American social organization, and medical education. He has also worked extensively in applied settings. He has presented seminars and workshops on teaching qualitative research methods and on using qualitative methods in various applied fields, and has been an invited speaker at conferences and universities in the United States, Puerto Rico, Europe, and China. He has a PhD in anthropology from the University of Chicago. He can be reached at jmaxwell@gmu.edu.

1

A Model for Qualitative Research Design

In 1625, Gustav II, the king of Sweden, commissioned the construction of four warships to further his imperialistic goals. The most ambitious of these ships, named the *Vasa*, was one of the largest warships of its time, with 64 cannons arrayed in two gundecks. On August 10, 1628, the *Vasa*, resplendent in its brightly painted and gilded woodwork, was launched in Stockholm Harbor with cheering crowds and considerable ceremony. The cheering was short-lived, however; caught by a gust of wind while still in the harbor, the ship suddenly heeled over, foundered, and sank.

An investigation was immediately ordered, and it became apparent that the ballast compartment had not been made large enough to balance the two gundecks that the king had specified. With only 121 tons of stone ballast, the ship lacked stability. However, if the builders had simply added more ballast, the lower gundeck would have been brought dangerously close to the water; the ship lacked the buoyancy to accommodate that much weight.

In more general terms, the *design* of the *Vasa*—the ways in which the different components of the ship were planned and constructed in relation to one another—was fatally flawed. The ship was carefully built, meeting all of the existing standards for solid workmanship, but key characteristics of its different parts—in particular, the weight of the gundecks and ballast and the size of the hold—were not compatible, and the interaction of these characteristics caused the ship to capsize. Shipbuilders of that day did not have a general theory of ship design; they worked primarily from traditional models and by trial and error, and had no way to calculate stability. Apparently, the *Vasa* was originally planned as a smaller ship, and was then scaled up, at the king's insistence, to add the second gundeck, leaving too little room in the hold (Kvarning, 1993).

This story of the *Vasa* illustrates the general concept of design that I am using here: "an underlying scheme that governs functioning, developing, or unfolding" and "the arrangement of elements or details in a product or work of art" (Design, 1984, p. 343). This is the ordinary, everyday meaning of the term, as illustrated by the following quote from a clothing catalog:

> It starts with design. . . . We carefully consider every detail, including the cut of the clothing, what style of stitching works best with the fabric, and what kind of closures make the most sense—in short, everything that contributes to your comfort. (L. L. Bean, 1998)

A good design, one in which the components work harmoniously together, promotes efficient and successful functioning; a flawed design leads to poor operation or failure.

However, most works dealing with *research* design use a different conception of design: "a plan or protocol for carrying out or accomplishing something (esp. a scientific experiment)" (Design, 1984, p. 343). They present "design" either as a menu of standard types of designs from which you need to choose (typical of experimental research), or as a prescribed series of stages or tasks in planning or conducting a study. Although some versions of the latter view of design are circular and recursive (e.g., Marshall & Rossman, 1999, pp. 26–27), all are essentially linear in the sense of being a one-directional *sequence* of steps from problem formulation to conclusions or theory, though this sequence may be repeated. Such models usually have a prescribed starting point and goal and a specified order for performing the intermediate tasks.

Neither typological nor sequential models of design are a good fit for qualitative research, because they attempt to establish in advance the essential steps or features of the study. (See Maxwell & Loomis, 2002, for a more detailed critique of these approaches.) In qualitative research, any component of the design may need to be reconsidered or modified during the study in response to new developments or to changes in some other component. In this, qualitative research is more like sciences such as paleontology than it is like experimental psychology. The paleontologist Neil Shubin (2008) described his fieldwork as follows:

> The paradoxical relationship between planning and chance is best described by General Dwight D. Eisenhower's famous remark about warfare: "In preparing for battle, I have found that planning is essential, but plans are worthless." This captures field paleontology in a nutshell. We make all kinds of plans to get to promising field sites. Once we're there, the entire field plan may be thrown out the window. Facts on the ground change our best-laid plans. (p. 4)

This description also characterizes qualitative research, in which designs are flexible rather than fixed (Robson, 2011), and inductive rather than following a strict sequence or derived from an initial decision. In a qualitative study, "research design should be a reflexive process operating through every stage of a project" (Hammersley & Atkinson, 1995, p. 24). The activities of collecting and analyzing data, developing and modifying theory, elaborating or refocusing the research questions, and identifying and addressing validity threats are usually all going on more or less simultaneously, each influencing all of the others. This process isn't adequately represented by a choice from a prior menu or by a linear model, even one that allows multiple cycles, because in qualitative research, there isn't an unvarying order in which the different tasks or components must be arranged, nor a linear relationship among the components of a design.

Typological or linear approaches to design provide a model *for* conducting the research—a prescriptive guide that arranges the tasks involved in planning or conducting a study in what is seen as an optimal order. In contrast, the model in this book is a model *of* as well as *for* research. It is intended to help you understand the *actual* design of your study, as well as to plan this study and carry it out. An essential feature of this model is that it treats research design as a real entity, not simply an abstraction or plan (Maxwell, 2011b). The design of your research, like the design of the *Vasa,* is real and will have real consequences. Borrowing Kaplan's (1964, p. 8) distinction between the "logic-in-use" and "reconstructed logic" of research, this model can be used to represent the "design-in-use" of a study, the *actual* relationships among the components of the research, as well as the intended (or reconstructed) design. As Yin (1994) stated, "Every type of empirical research has an implicit, if not explicit, research design" (p. 19). Because a design always exists, it is important to *make* it explicit, to get it out in the open where its strengths, limitations, and consequences can be clearly understood.

This conception of design as a model of, as well as for, research is exemplified in a classic qualitative study of medical students (Becker, Geer, Hughes, & Strauss, 1961). The authors began their chapter on the design of the study by stating,

> In one sense, our study had no design. That is, we had no well-worked-out set of hypotheses to be tested, no data-gathering instruments purposely designed to secure information relevant to these hypotheses, no set of analytic procedures specified in advance. Insofar as the term "design" implies these features of elaborate prior planning, our study had none.
>
> If we take the idea of design in a larger and looser sense, using it to identify those elements of order, system, and consistency our procedures did exhibit, our study had a design. We can say what this was by describing our original view of the problem, our theoretical and methodological commitments, and the way these affected our research and were affected by it as we proceeded. (p. 17)

Thus, to design a qualitative study, you can't just develop (or borrow) a logical strategy in advance and then implement it faithfully. You need, to a substantial extent, to *construct* and *reconstruct* your research design, and this is a major rationale for my design model. Qualitative research design, to a much greater extent than quantitative research, is a "do-it-yourself" rather than an "off-the-shelf" process, one that involves "tacking" back and forth between the different components of the design, assessing their implications for one another.[1] It does not begin from a predetermined starting point or proceed through a fixed sequence of steps, but involves interconnection and interaction among the different design components.

In addition, as the architect Frank Lloyd Wright emphasized, the design of something must fit not only its use, but also its environment ("Organic Architecture," n.d.). You will need to continually assess how your design is actually working during the research and how it influences and is influenced by the context in which you're operating, and to make adjustments and changes so that your study can accomplish what you want.

My model of research design, which I call an "interactive" model (I could just as well have called it "systemic"), has a definite structure. However, it is an interconnected and flexible structure. In this book, I describe the key components of a research design, and present a strategy for creating coherent and workable relationships among these components. I also provide (in Chapter 7) an explicit plan for using your design to create a research proposal.

The model I present here has five components, each of which addresses a specific set of concerns:

1. *Goals.* Why is your study worth doing? What issues do you want it to clarify, and what practices and policies do you want it to influence? Why do you want to conduct this study, and why should we care about the results?

2. *Conceptual framework.* What do you think is going on with the issues, settings, or people you plan to study? What theories, beliefs, and prior research findings will guide or inform your research, and what literature, preliminary studies, and personal experiences will you draw on for understanding the people or issues you are studying?

3. *Research questions.* What, specifically, do you want to better understand about the settings or participants that you are studying? What do you *not* know about these that you want to learn? What questions best capture these learnings and understandings, and how are these questions related to one another?

4. *Methods.* What will you actually do in conducting this study? What approaches and techniques will you use to collect and analyze your data? I identify four parts of this component of your design: (a) the relationships that you establish with the participants in your study; (b) your selection of settings, participants, times and places of data collection, and other data sources such as documents (what is often called "sampling," although this term can be misleading for qualitative research, as I discuss in Chapter 5); (c) your methods for collecting your data; and (d) your data analysis strategies and techniques.

5. *Validity.* How might your results and conclusions be wrong? What are the plausible alternative interpretations and validity threats to these results and conclusions, and how will you deal with these? How can the data that you have, or that you could potentially collect, support or challenge your ideas about what's going on? Why should we believe your results?

These components are not substantially different from the ones presented in many other discussions of research design (e.g., LeCompte & Preissle, 1993; Miles & Huberman, 1994; Robson, 2011; Rudestam & Newton, 2007, p. 5). What is innovative is the way the relationships among the components are conceptualized. In this model, the different parts of a design form an integrated and interacting whole, with each component closely tied to several others, rather than being linked in a linear or cyclic sequence. The relationships among these five components are displayed in Figure 1.1.

In this model, in contrast to some other views of research design, the research questions are not the starting point or controlling piece of the design, to which all other components must conform. Instead, they are at the *center* of the design; they are the heart, or hub, of the model, the component that connects most directly to all of the other components. They not only have the most direct influence on the other components, but are also the component most directly affected by the others; they should inform, and be sensitive to, all of the other components. As discussed in more detail in Chapter 4, your research questions are not fixed at the start of the study; they may need to be significantly modified or expanded as a result of changes in your goals or conceptual framework, or because of what you learn while doing the research.

The upper triangle of this model, the half that is more conceptual and usually is the first that you develop, should be a closely integrated unit. Your research questions should have a clear relationship to the goals of your study, and should be grounded in

Figure 1.1   An Interactive Model of Research Design

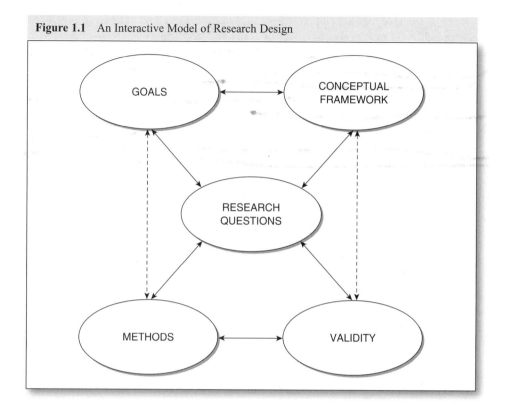

what is already known about the things you are studying and the theoretical concepts and models that can be applied to these. In addition, the goals of your study should be informed by current theory and knowledge, while your decisions about what theory and knowledge are relevant to your study depend on your goals and questions.

Similarly, the bottom triangle of the model, the more operational half of the design, should also be closely integrated. The methods you use must enable you to answer your research questions, and also to deal with plausible validity threats to these answers. Your questions, in turn, need to take into account the feasibility of the methods and the seriousness of particular validity threats, while the plausibility and relevance of particular validity threats, and your ability to deal with these, depend on the questions and methods chosen (as well as on your conceptual framework). Your research questions form the main link between the two halves of the model.

The connections among the different components of the model are not rigid rules or fixed implications; they allow for a certain amount of "give" and elasticity in the design. I find it useful to think of them as rubber bands. They can stretch and bend to some extent, but they exert a definite tension on different parts of the design, and beyond a particular point, or under certain stresses, they will break. This "rubber band" metaphor portrays a qualitative design as something with considerable flexibility, but in which there are constraints imposed by the different parts on one another, constraints which, if violated, make the design ineffective.

I see this interconnection and coherence of a research design as a matter of pragmatic compatibility, not of logical consistency or as derived from some overarching principle or premise. In this way, I think the interactive model I present is compatible with some interpretations of postmodernism, which rejects the idea of universal, overriding metanarratives that define a single correct understanding of something (Bernstein, 1992; Kvale, 1995; Olsson, 2008; Rosenau, 1992). It is also compatible with a currently influential approach to qualitative research known as "bricolage" (Hammersley, 2008; Kincheloe & Berry, 2004; Kincheloe, McLaren, & Steinberg, 2011; Maxwell, 2011a), which rejects the idea of following a preestablished plan or set of methods in favor of a more spontaneous and improvised use of the resources at hand; I discuss bricolage in more detail in Chapter 3.

Many other factors besides these five components influence the design of your study, including your resources, research skills, perceived problems, ethical standards, the research setting, and the data you collect and results you draw from these data during the study. In my view, these are not part of the *design* of a study, but either belong to the *environment* within which the research and its design exist or are *products* of the research. You will need to take these factors into account in designing your study, just as the design of a ship needs to take into account the kinds of winds and waves the ship will encounter and the sorts of cargo it will carry. Figure 1.2 presents some of the factors in the environment that can influence the design and conduct of a study, and displays some of the key linkages of these factors with components of the research design. These factors and linkages will be discussed in subsequent chapters.

Figure 1.2   Contextual Factors Influencing a Research Design

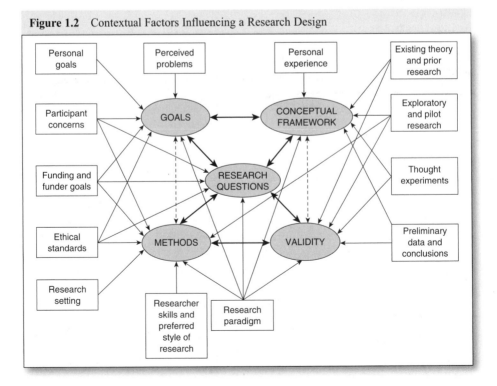

I want to say something specifically about ethics, since I have not identified this as a separate component of research design. This isn't because I don't think ethics are important for qualitative design; on the contrary, attention to ethical issues in qualitative research is being increasingly recognized as essential, not just for ethical reasons but as an integral aspect of the research (Cannella & Lincoln, 2011; Christians, 2011; Fine, Weis, Weseen, & Wong, 2000). I believe that ethical concerns should be involved in *every* aspect of design. I have particularly tried to address these concerns in relation to methods, but they are also relevant to your goals, the selection of your research questions, validity issues, and the critical assessment of your conceptual framework.

As the subtitle of this book indicates, my approach to design is an interactive one. It is interactive in three senses. First, the design model itself is interactive; each of the components has implications for all of the other components, rather than the components being in a linear, one-directional relationship with one another. Second, the design of a qualitative study should be able to change in interaction with the context in which the study is being conducted, rather than simply being a fixed determinant of research practice. (Example 1.1 illustrates both of these interactive processes in the evolution of the design of one study.) Finally, the learning process embodied in this book is interactive, with frequent exercises that enable you to work on the design of your study. This book does not simply present abstract research design principles that you can memorize and then later use in your research. You *will* learn principles that are at least somewhat general, but you'll learn these best by creating a design for a particular qualitative project.

Example 1.1   The Evolution of a Research Design

Maria Broderick began her dissertation study of a hospital-based support group for cancer patients with a theoretical background in adult psychological development and practical experience in the design of such programs; a research interest in discovering how patients' perceptions of support and interaction within the group were related to their developmental level; a plan to use observation, interviews, and developmental tests to answer this question; and the goals of improving such programs and developing a career in clinical practice. However, after her proposal was approved, she lost access to the group she had originally planned to study, and was unable to find another suitable cancer program. She ended up negotiating permission to study a stress-reduction program for patients in a hospital setting, but was not allowed to observe the classes; in addition, the program team insisted on a quasi-experimental research design, with pre- and postintervention measures of patients' developmental level and experiences. This forced her both to broaden her theoretical

(Continued)

(Continued)

framework beyond cancer support programs to behavioral medicine programs in general and to alter her methods to rely primarily on pre- and postinterviews and developmental tests.

As Maria was beginning her research, she herself was diagnosed with a stress-related illness. This had a profound effect on the research design. First, she gained access to the program as a patient, and discovered that it wasn't actually run as a support program, but in a traditional classroom format. This made her extensive literature review on support groups largely irrelevant. Second, she found that her experiences of her illness and what seemed to help her deal with stress differed substantially from what was reported in the literature. These two developments profoundly altered her conceptual framework and research questions, shifting her theoretical focus from ego development to cognitive development, adult learning, and educational theory. In addition, she found that pretesting of the patients was impossible for practical reasons, eliminating the possibility of quasi-experimental assessment of patient changes and shifting her methods and validity checks back toward her original plans.

While Maria was analyzing her data, her gradual creation of a theory that made sense of these patients' (and her own) experiences directed her to new bodies of literature and theoretical approaches. Her increasing focus on what the patients *learned* through the program caused her to see meditation and cognitive restructuring as tools for reshaping one's view of stress, and led her to develop a broader view of stress as a cultural phenomenon. It also reconnected her with her longtime interest in nontraditional education for adults. Finally, these changes led to a shift in her career goals from clinical practice to an academic position, and her goals for the study came to emphasize relating adult developmental theory to empowerment curricula and improving adult education in nontraditional settings.

One way in which the design model presented here can be useful is as a tool or template for conceptually mapping the design of an actual study, as part of the design process or in analyzing the design of a completed study. This involves filling in the circles for the five components of the model with the specific components of that study's design, a strategy that I call a "design map." (This is one use of what is commonly called "concept mapping," discussed in Chapter 3.) I have included two examples of design maps for actual studies. Figure 1.3 is a design map of the eventual structure of Maria Broderick's dissertation research; I created this based on Maria's dissertation. See Maxwell and Loomis (2002) for other such maps.

Figure 1.3   A Design Map of Maria Broderick's Dissertation Research

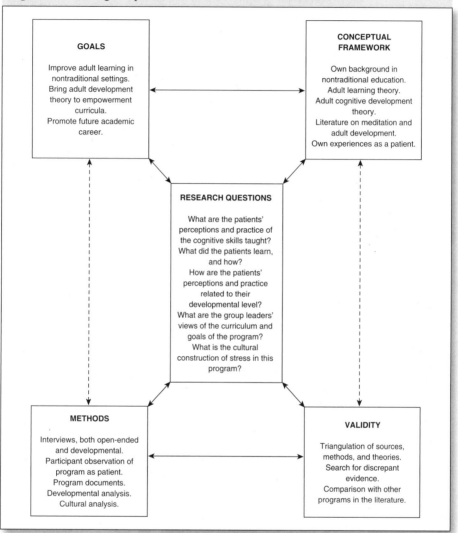

Such a design map is a useful way to display the main parts of your design. However, any such diagram is necessarily a schematic, highly condensed account; it can't substitute for a more detailed explanation of these parts and their connections to one another. It should, therefore, be accompanied by a memo that explains these. Figure 1.4 was created by Karen Kohanowich in planning her dissertation research on the relative advantages and disadvantages of manned and unmanned undersea research; Example 1.2 describes her process in developing this map (my comments to Karen are in brackets).

Figure 1.4 A Design Map for a Study of Manned and Unmanned Undersea Research

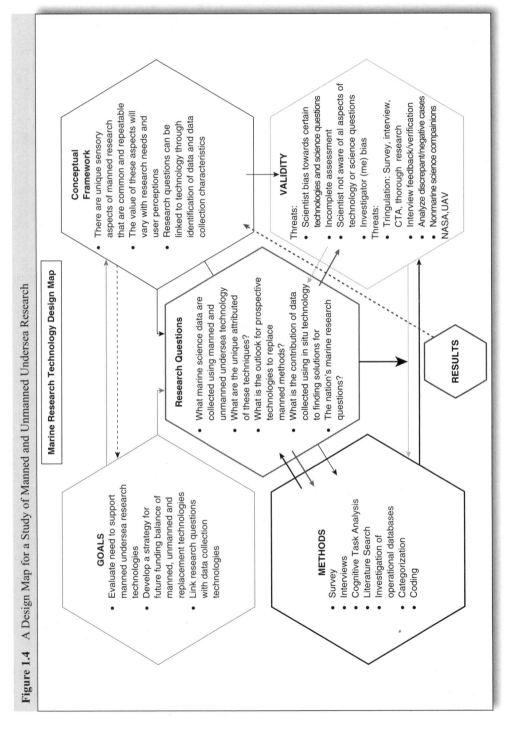

Marine Research Technology Design Map

Conceptual Framework
- There are unique sensory aspects of manned research that are common and repeatable
- The value of these aspects will vary with research needs and user perceptions
- Research questions can be linked to technology through identification of data and data collection characteristics

VALIDITY
Threats:
- Scientist bias towards certain technologies and science questions
- Incomplete assessment
- Scientist not aware of al aspects of technology or science questions
- Investigator (me) bias
Threats:
- Tringulation: Survey, interview, CTA, thorough research
- Interview feedback/verification
- Analyze discrepant/negative cases
- Nonmarine science compainions
- NASA,UAV

Research Questions
- What marine science data are collected using manned and unmanned undersea technology
- What are the unique attributed of these techniques?
- What is the outlook for prospective technologies to replace manned methods?
- What is the contribution of data collected using in situ technology to finding solutions for The nation's marine research questions?

GOALS
- Evaluate need to support manned undersea research technologies
- Develop a strategy for future funding balance of manned, unmanned and replacement technologies
- Link research questions with data collection technologies

METHODS
- Survey
- Interviews
- Cognitive Task Analysis
- Literature Search
- Investigation of operational databases
- Categorization
- Coding

RESULTS

Example 1.2   Memo on Developing the Design Map in Figure 1.4

I knew that there are many personal factors driving my research on undersea technology, both in helpful and potentially biasing ways, so I worked through the Researcher Identity Memo exercise (Exercise 2.1) prior to formulating my design map. This activity was invaluable in a number of ways. I found that just acknowledging a potential personal bias to myself silently had virtually no power when compared to writing it out. By forcing myself to brainstorm goals and questions, and bin them in personal, practical, or intellectual categories, I could extract the personal aspect, respect it for what it is, and put it aside in the "leave for discussion with friends and family" box. This then helped me identify practical goals that had seemed personal, but, now that they were acknowledged in a respectable category that was firewalled from personal influences and distinguished from focused research questions, actually flowed out relatively smoothly as work-related goals that I could relay to the boss in an elevator. With those motivations in their proper places, I could then focus with a clearer mind on the intellectual aspect of the research questions, and target an approach that could be tested in a scholastic construct. Within the design map, the upper-left goal category is described as including all three components by both Maxwell and Loomis (2002) and Maxwell (2005). I actually found it most helpful to use the goal component to represent my practical goals; setting the personal goals to the side as described previously, and integrating the intellectual goals with the research questions.

The resulting design map developed into a more structured process than I expected, with a relatively stable goal/framework core and a more malleable operational component. It is similar to Maxwell's (2005, p. 5) description of upper- and lower-integrated triangles, but with some changes to the feedback mechanisms. The previous exercise showed me that the practical goals really are the core of what I think the study is about, the "why." The conceptual framework follows as the group of assumptions, close to hypotheses, that I'm making about the nature of the forces at work within the study. The more I thought about it, the more important it seemed to keep these components relatively inflexible during the study development to provide a consistent context for the research work. The remaining three components are designed to work together to respond to this framework and provide researched feedback, with the primary link to the goals/framework being the research questions (although there is also a role for input to each from the framework.) I refer to this lower triangle of components "research questions," "methods," and "validity," as a subgroup of *operational components*. Here I recognize and encourage flexibility between components as the study is developed and conducted. I also recognized that there might be indications during the

(Continued)

(Continued)

operational development that the framework should be reconsidered, but felt that continual shifting of the framework based on individual process insights would be counterproductive and threaten the foundation of the research. When I thought, "What type of information would be serious enough to warrant reevaluation of the framework?" I realized that it was, of course, the results (i.e., the product of the operational component interactions). I, therefore, developed a new component—results—which represents the results that emerge from the operational interactions. [This is included in Figure 1.2, as one of the factors influencing a design.]

On the map, solid arrows represent intended influence of one component of the design map on another component, while dotted arrows represent possible post-results adjustments. I added the separate results component for two reasons. First, I consider that the two-way arrows between the three operational components represent intrastudy considerations that occur as a study develops, often as the result of new insights received during the study, but not because of study results per se. I also wanted to emphasize the role of results as the principal force for reconsideration of the fundamental framework and goals. Insights within the operational components may provide temptation to readdress the foundation, but this should be resisted [but not ignored! They may be important enough to overcome the resistance] to allow the process to work. Note that I do not include influence of results on the three operational components. This helps prevent disjointed tinkering with the research design; it does not preclude this consideration, but rather indicates that the framework should be examined first, and the design then considered as a whole system.

As I continue to design my study, I intend to revisit the qualitative and quantitative design elements described by Maxwell and Loomis (2002, Table 9.1) to better describe the contents of each component. I'm looking forward to seeing how this overall construct plays out as my study proceeds.

Karen's map and memo modify my design model in ways that seemed helpful to her, which is fine. I do not believe that there is one right model of, or for, research design; in fact, I don't think there is only one right model of *anything* (see Maxwell, 2011a, 2011b). However, I think that the model that I present here is a *useful* model, for two main reasons:

1. It explicitly identifies as *components* of design the key issues about which you will need to make decisions and which will need to be addressed in any research proposal. These components are, therefore, less likely to be overlooked or misunderstood, and can be dealt with in a deliberate and systematic manner.

2. It emphasizes the *interactive* nature of design decisions in qualitative research, and the multiple connections among design components. A common reason that dissertation or funding proposals are rejected is because they do not make clear the connections among the design components—the *relevance* of decisions about different components for one another. (I discuss this in more detail in Chapter 7.) The model I present here makes it easier to understand and demonstrate these connections.

Matrices as a Strategy for Developing Your Research Design

Matrices (the plural of *matrix*) are another strategy for developing, and displaying, the design of your research. Design maps and design matrices are both useful in creating your design, but they are different, and complementary. Design maps present a schematic picture of the design, keeping the interactive structure of this design. A matrix, in contrast, imposes a more linear ordering of the components, but in doing so, it allows you to develop, and show, the connections between *specific* parts of each component, such as how each research question is related to specific goals, theories, methods and validity issues (see Figure 1.5). Miles and Huberman (1994) were the first to systematically develop and promote such displays in qualitative research; their book contains a wide variety of displays, mostly matrices and what they call "networks," a term that includes both concept maps and flowchart-like diagrams. While their focus was on using displays for qualitative data analysis (I discuss these uses in Chapter 5), displays are valuable in every aspect of qualitative design.

This matrix was developed by Bonnie Sakallaris, a nursing doctoral student, for a study of perceptions of healing in the context of acute illness, and the role of the patient's immediate environment in promoting this. (Her design originally included both qualitative and quantitative methods; I have removed most of the quantitative components because of space limitations.) Her reason for developing this matrix was to address validity issues, but in the process, she created a good display of most of her design; the main thing missing is her conceptual framework.

I provide other examples of matrices developed for different purposes later in this book. Here, I want to emphasize that matrices (and other displays) are multipurpose tools. There is no required structure for these, nor obligatory column headings. You can develop your matrices for whatever purposes you want. (Exercise 5.1 provides guidelines for developing a matrix specifically for connecting your research questions and methods.) The main strength of a matrix is that, by creating rows and columns that address specific components of the design, you can focus on individual cells in the matrix—for example, what analysis strategy you will use for a particular type of data—and the coherence of your design across components within a given row.

The aim of such displays is to help you construct a coherent overall design for your study. A good design for your study, like a good design for a ship, will help it to safely and efficiently reach its destination. A poor design, one in which the components are

(Text continues on p. 18.)

Figure 1.5 A Matrix for a Study of Patients' and Clinicians' Perceptions of Healing

What Do I Need to Know? (Research Questions)	Why Do I Need to Know This? (Goals)	What Kind of Data Will Answer the Questions? (Methods)	Analysis Methods	Potential Conclusions	Alternative Explanations (Validity Threats)	Methods to Investigate Alternative Explanations
What does healing mean to patients experiencing an acute illness?	To understand the meaning of healing from the patient's perspective To inform further inquiry on the existence of healing environments	Interview: Structured and open-ended	Single Case: Coding Cross-Case: Themes Develop matrix with clinicians data	Wholeness Well-being Restoration Transformation Harmony Peace Acceptance	Researcher bias influencing collection and/or interpretation of data Patient feels obligated to provide religious/cultural idealized description that does not reflect personal meaning	Second or third reader/coder Check interpretation with patient Use follow-up clarifying questions, including asking about how they developed their views of healing Collect demographic data and cross reference
What is the patient's perception of the environment of care in	To understand the connection between the environment of care and healing from the patient's perspective.	Interview: Structured and open-ended	Collate descriptors used and measure frequency	Facilitators: Privacy, nature, soothing sounds, social spaces	Patients may not relate their environment to healing, may not notice environment or take it for granted.	Check interpretation with patient Revise Samueli survey to include information from the interviews

14

What Do I Need to Know? (Research Questions)	Why Do I Need to Know This? (Goals)	What Kind of Data Will Answer the Questions? (Methods)	Analysis Methods	Potential Conclusions	Alternative Explanations (Validity Threats)	Methods to Investigate Alternative Explanations
terms of facilitating or hindering their healing?	To inform the healing environment survey		Group responses into themes	Hindrances: Roommate, noise, noxious odors, isolation	Patients may relate information that is not included on the Samueli survey	
What does healing mean to care providers (clinicians) in the context of acute illness?	To understand the meaning of healing from the clinician's perspective To inform further inquiry on the existence of healing environments	Interview: Structured and open-ended	Single Case: Coding Cross-Case: Themes Develop matrix with patient's data	Cure Safety Functional status Well being	Researcher bias influencing interpretation of data Clinician feels obligated to provide religious/cultural idealized description that does not reflect personal meaning. Relationship with interviewer may interfere with responses	Second or third reader/coder Use follow-up clarifying questions Collect demographic data and cross reference Consider not using current or prior places of employment

(Continued)

Figure 1.5 (Continued)

What Do I Need to Know? (Research Questions)	Why Do I Need to Know This? (Goals)	What Kind of Data Will Answer the Questions? (Methods)	Analysis Methods	Potential Conclusions	Alternative Explanations (Validity Threats)	Methods to Investigate Alternative Explanations
What is the clinician's perception of the environment of care in terms of facilitating or hindering patient's healing?	To understand the connection between the environment of care and healing from the perspective of the care provider To inform the healing environment survey	Interview: Structured and open-ended	Collate descriptors used and measure frequency Group responses into themes	Facilitators: Privacy, nature, soothing sounds, social spaces, hand-washing stations, electronic medical record Hindrances: Roommate, noise, noxious odors, isolation, low staffing, poor leadership	Researcher bias Participant desire to please	Check interpretation with clinician
Is there congruence between the described environment of care and the patients' and	To understand factors that facilitate healing from both perspectives To include both perspectives in an assessment of healing environments	Descriptors and themes from interviews and differences	Compare patient and clinician descriptors for similarities Compare Samueli	There will be differences in perception of factors that facilitate healing Clinicians will include		Use information to revise the Samueli survey of Healing Environments Categorize factors for further study:

What Do I Need to Know? (Research Questions)	Why Do I Need to Know This? (Goals)	What Kind of Data Will Answer the Questions? (Methods)	Analysis Methods	Potential Conclusions	Alternative Explanations (Validity Threats)	Methods to Investigate Alternative Explanations
clinicians' descriptions of factors that facilitate healing?			Institute Survey items	environmental factors that to descriptors	promote safety	– Factors that decrease patient stress – Factors that reduce harm or error – Factors that improve social support
Are there differences in the care environment for patients who report a healing experience and patients who do not?	To begin to provide evidence of a healing environment	Samueli Institute's Survey of Healing Environments in Hospitals	Analyze frequency of factors Compare group similarities and differences using statistical analysis	Environments with a higher number of healing factors incorporated into the environment of care will have a higher number of patient's reporting a healing experience.	Healing may be such an individualized experience that there are no healing environments. Differences may be coincidental Responses limited by survey questions	Relate analysis of data back to meaning of healing for patients and clinicians

SOURCE: Bonnie Sakallaris.

not well integrated or are incompatible with their environment, will at best be ineffi-
cient, and at worst will fail to achieve its goals.

THE ORGANIZATION OF THIS BOOK

This book is structured to guide you through the process of designing a qualitative
study. It highlights the issues for which design decisions must be made, and presents
some of the considerations that should inform these decisions. Each chapter in the book
deals with one component of design, and these chapters form a logical sequence.
However, this organization is only a conceptual and presentational device, not a procedure to follow in designing an actual study. You should make decisions about each
component in light of your thinking about all of the other components, and you may
need to modify previous decisions (including your goals) in response to new information or changes in your thinking.

This book takes a Z-shaped path (Figure 1.6) through the components of this model,
beginning with goals (Chapter 2). The goals of your study are not only important, but
also primary; if your reasons for doing the study aren't clear, it can be difficult to make
any decisions about the rest of the design. Your conceptual framework (Chapter 3) is
discussed next, both because it should connect closely to your goals and because the
goals and conceptual framework jointly have a major influence on the formulation of
research questions for the study. Your research questions (Chapter 4) are thus a logical
next topic; these three components should form a coherent unit.

The next component discussed is methods (Chapter 5): how you will actually collect
and analyze the data to answer your research questions. However, these methods and
analyses need to be connected to issues of validity (Chapter 6): how you might be
wrong, and what would make your answers more believable than alternative possible
answers. Research questions, methods, and validity also should form an integrated unit,
one in which the methods for obtaining answers to the questions, and the means for
assuring the credibility of the potential answers in the face of plausible validity threats,
are clearly conceptualized and linked to the research questions. In addition, your goals
and conceptual framework may have direct implications for your methods and validity
concerns, and vice versa.

Finally, Chapter 7 discusses the implications of my model of design for developing
research proposals, and provides a map and guidelines for how to get from your design
to your proposal.

THE EXERCISES IN THIS BOOK

The sociologist C. Wright Mills wrote that

> One of the very worst things that happens to social scientists is that they feel the need to
> write of their "plans" on only one occasion: when they are going to ask for money for a

Figure 1.6   The Organization of This Book

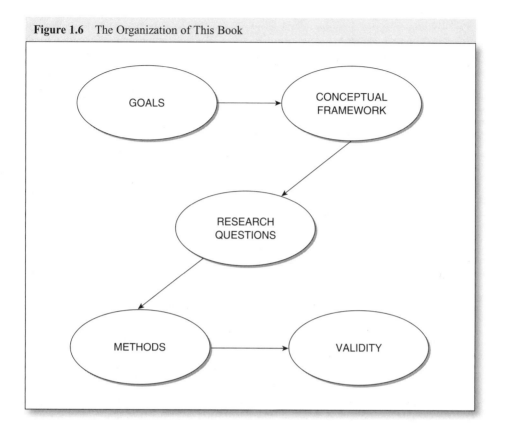

specific piece of work or "a project." It is as a request for funds that most planning is done, or at least carefully written about. However standard the practice, I think this very bad: it is bound in some degree to be salesmanship, and, given prevailing expectations, very likely to result in painstaking pretensions; the project is likely to be "presented," rounded out in some manner long before it ought to be; it is often a contrived thing, aimed at getting the money for ulterior purposes, however valuable, as well as for the research presented. A practicing social scientist ought periodically to review "the state of my problems and plans." (1959, p. 197)

He went on to make an eloquent plea that each researcher write regularly and systematically about his or her research, "just for himself and perhaps for discussion with friends" (Mills, 1959, p. 198), and to keep a file of these writings, which qualitative researchers usually call "memos."

All of the exercises in this book are memos of one sort or another, and I want to briefly discuss the nature of memos and how to use them effectively. Memos (Groenewald, 2008; these are sometimes called "analytic memos") are an extremely versatile tool that can be used for many different purposes. This term refers to any writing that a researcher does in relationship to the research other than actual field notes, transcription, or coding. A memo can range from a brief marginal comment on an interview transcript or a theoretical idea recorded in a field journal to a full-fledged analytic essay. What all of these have in common is that they are ways of getting ideas down on paper (or in a computer), and of using this writing as a way to facilitate reflection and analytic insight. When your thoughts are recorded in memos, you can code and file them just as you do your field notes and interview transcripts, and return to them to develop the ideas further. Not writing memos is the research equivalent of having Alzheimer's disease; you may not remember your important insights when you need them. Peters (1992, p. 123) cited Lewis Carroll's *Through the Looking Glass* on this function of memos:

> "The horror of that moment," the King went on, "I shall never, *never* forget."
> "You will, though," said the Queen, "unless you make a memorandum of it."

Many of the examples used in this book are memos, or are based on memos.[2]

Memos are one of the most important techniques you have for developing your ideas. You should, therefore, think of memos as a way to help you *understand* your topic, setting, or study, not just as a way of recording or presenting an understanding you've already reached; writing is thinking on paper (Howard & Barton, 1988). Memos should include reflections on your reading and ideas as well as your fieldwork. Memos can be written on methodological issues, ethics, personal reactions, or anything else; I wrote numerous memos about research design during the writing and revising of this book. Write memos as a way of working on a problem you encounter in making sense of your topic, setting, study, or data. Write memos whenever you have an idea that you want to develop further, or simply to record the idea for later development. Write *lots of* memos throughout the course of your research project; remember that in qualitative research, design is something that goes on during the entire study, not just at the beginning. Think of memos as a kind of decentralized field journal; if you prefer, you can write your memos in an actual journal.

Whatever form these memos take, their value depends on two things. The first is that you engage in serious reflection, analysis, and self-critique, rather than just mechanically recording events and thoughts. The second is that you *organize* your memos in a systematic, retrievable form, so that the observations and insights can easily be accessed for future examination. I do my memo writing primarily in two forms: on 3 × 5 cards, which I always carry with me for jotting down ideas and which I index by date and topic, and in computer files relating to particular projects, which I use for both brief notes and longer memos. During my dissertation research in an Inuit community in northern Canada, I also kept a field journal, which was invaluable in making sense of my personal responses to the research situation. It can also be very useful to share some of your memos with colleagues or fellow students for their feedback.[3]

Although memos are primarily a tool for thinking, they can also serve as an initial draft of material that you will later incorporate (usually with substantial revision) in a proposal, report, or publication, and I've tried to design most of the memo exercises in this book so that they can be used in this way. However, thinking of memos primarily as a way of communicating to *other* people will often interfere with the kind of reflective writing that you need to do to make memos most useful to you. In particular, beware of what Becker (2007) called "classy writing"—pretentious and verbose language that is intended to impress others rather than to clarify your ideas. A saying among writing instructors is "When you write, don't put a tuxedo on your brain" (Metzger, 1993).

NOTES

1. This tacking back and forth is similar in some ways to the "hermeneutic circle" of textual interpretation (Geertz, 1974). However, I am advocating an interactive rather than a sequential model of research design primarily because I see design as pertaining to the actual relationships of the components of a research study, not because I take an "interpretive" or "humanistic" as opposed to a "scientific" view of research. The interactive model I present here is drawn to a significant extent from research practices in the natural sciences, particularly biology, and is applicable to quantitative as well as qualitative research (Maxwell & Loomis, 2002). In contrast, Janesick (1994), who saw qualitative research design as an interpretive art form analogous to dance, nevertheless, stated that "qualitative research design begins with a question" (p. 210) and presented research design as a sequence of decisions that the researcher will need to make at each stage of the research.

2. For additional discussion and examples of what a memo involves, see Bogdan and Biklen (2003, pp. 114–116, 151–157), Miles and Huberman (1994, pp. 72–75), and Mills (1959). More detailed information on memos can be found in Strauss (1987, Chapters. 1, 5, and 6) and in Corbin and Strauss (2007).

3. See Mills (1959) for advice on how to use memos in developing a research agenda and career.

2

Goals

Why Are You Doing This Study?

In planning, as well as in assessing, ethnographic research, we must consider its relevance as well as its validity.

—Hammersley (1992, p. 85)

Anyone can find an unanswered, empirically answerable question for which the answer isn't *worth* knowing; as Thoreau said, it is not worthwhile to go around the world to count the cats in Zanzibar. In addition, it is easy to become captivated by the stories of your informants, or by what's going on in the setting you are studying, and lose sight of your *reasons* for studying these particular phenomena. Brendan Croskery (1995), reflecting on his dissertation research on four Newfoundland school principals, admitted that

> The study suffered from too many good intentions and too little focused thinking. . . . I painfully discovered that many of the data (though interesting) were not particularly relevant to the core category. (p. 348)

A clear understanding of the goals motivating your work will help you avoid losing your way or spending time and effort doing things that don't advance these goals.

The goals of your study are an important part of your research design. (I am using "goal" in a broad sense to include motives, desires, and purposes—anything that leads you to do the study or that you want to accomplish by doing it.[1]) These goals serve two main functions for your research. First, they help to guide your other design decisions to ensure that your study is *worth* doing, that you, or those you write for, get something of value out of it. Second, they are essential to *justifying* your study, explaining why your results and conclusions matter—a key task of a funding or dissertation proposal or a published article. In addition, as Hammersley (1992, p. 28) noted, your goals inevitably shape the descriptions, interpretations, and theories you create in your research.

They therefore constitute not only important *resources* that you can draw on in planning, conducting, and justifying the research, but also potential *validity threats,* or sources of bias for the research results, that you will need to deal with (see Chapter 6).

PERSONAL, PRACTICAL, AND INTELLECTUAL GOALS

I think it is useful to distinguish among three different kinds of goals for doing a study: personal goals, practical goals, and intellectual (or scholarly) goals. Personal goals are things that motivate *you* to do the study, but are not necessarily important for others. They can include the desire to change or improve some practice or situation that you're involved in, curiosity about a specific issue or event, a preference for conducting a particular type of research, or simply the need to advance your career. These personal goals often overlap with your practical or research goals, but they may also include deeply rooted individual desires and needs that bear little relationship to your "official" reasons for doing the study (see Example 2.1).

Researchers frequently make a sharp separation between their research and the rest of their lives. This practice is harmful to good research in two main ways. First, it creates the illusion that research takes place in a sterile, "objective" environment, subject only to rational and impersonal motives and decisions. This obscures the actual motives, assumptions, and agendas that researchers have, and leads them to ignore the influence of these on their research process and conclusions. It also leads researchers to hide their actual motives and practices when they don't conform to this ideal, feeling that only they are failing to live up to the goal of scientific neutrality and disinterest. Second, this separation cuts the researcher off from a major source of insights, questions, and practical guidance in conducting their research; I discuss this in more detail in Chapter 3. For more on these issues, see C. W. Mills (1959), *The Sociological Imagination*, Appendix, "On Intellectual Craftsmanship."

Two major decisions are often profoundly influenced by the researcher's personal goals. One is the topic, issue, or question selected for study. Traditionally, students have been told to base this decision on either faculty advice or the literature on their topic. However, in many dissertations, personal goals and experiences have also played an important role in these decisions. Strauss and Corbin (1990) argued that

> Choosing a research problem through the professional or personal experience route may seem more hazardous than through the suggested [by faculty] or literature routes. This is not necessarily true. The touchstone of your own experience may be more valuable an indicator for you of a potentially successful research endeavor. (pp. 35–36)

A particularly important advantage of basing your research topic on your own experience is *motivation*. Lack of motivation causes many students to never finish their dissertations, and a strong personal interest in the topic and in answering your research questions can counteract the inevitable interference from work, family obligations, or procrastination. Example 2.1 describes how one student made a substantial change in her dissertation topic as a result of her life experiences and the goals and interests that these created.

Example 2.1   Using Personal Experience to Choose a Dissertation Topic

Carol Kaffenberger, a doctoral student in a counseling program, had carefully planned her dissertation research on the development of conflict resolution skills in children, and was beginning work on her dissertation proposal. However, she found it hard to sustain her interest in this topic. Three years before she began her doctoral work, her youngest daughter, then 12, had been diagnosed with a particularly deadly form of leukemia, was hospitalized for six months and underwent a bone marrow transplant, went into remission and then relapsed, and required a second transplant before recovering three years later. This illness had initiated a family crisis, and caused major changes in the family's roles and responsibilities. Carol quit her job and moved into the hospital with her daughter. Her husband continued to work, maintained the house, and parented their son, who was 15 at the time of the diagnosis. Their older daughter was away at college, but was the donor for the bone marrow transplants.

Initially, Carol had felt that her family was coping well, but as the crisis wore on, she was surprised by the amount of anger and emotional distress expressed by the older siblings, anger that, despite her counseling training, she did not understand. Watching her family recover from this ordeal, she realized that they were never going to be the same. She also realized that her prior assumptions about their experience had been incorrect, and she became very interested in understanding this experience.

At a doctoral student meeting, another student, who knew of Carol's involvement with her daughter's cancer, asked her about her dissertation plans. Carol replied that she would be looking at children's development of conflict resolution skills, and briefly described her plans. The student replied, "What a missed opportunity!" explaining that she thought studying the consequences for families of adolescent cancer would be a terrific topic. After thinking about this, Carol went to her advisor, mentioned the student's idea, and asked, "Is this crazy?" Her advisor replied, "I've been waiting for you to be ready to do this."

Carol did a literature review and found that little was known about the meaning and consequences of adolescent cancer for families, particularly for siblings. She also found that, with increasing survival rates, schools were dealing with many more students who had been affected by a lengthy experience with cancer, as either a survivor or the sibling of a survivor, but had little experience in handling these issues.

(Continued)

(Continued)

Motivated by her interest in this topic, the lack of available information, and the growing importance of this issue, she changed her dissertation to a study of the long-term impact and meaning of adolescent cancer for survivors and their siblings, and its effect on the sibling relationship. She enrolled in my dissertation proposal course in the fall of 1997, defended her proposal in the spring of 1998, and defended her dissertation one year later. She said that she "loved every minute of her dissertation"; she even took her data with her on a vacation to Bermuda when she was finishing her data analysis (Kaffenberger, 1999, personal communication).

A second decision that is often influenced by personal goals and experiences is the choice of a qualitative approach. Locke, Spirduso, and Silverman (1993) argued that "every graduate student who is tempted to employ a qualitative design should confront one question, 'Why do I want to do a qualitative study?' and then answer it honestly" (p. 107). They emphasized that qualitative research is *not* easier than quantitative research, and that seeking to avoid statistics bears little relationship to having the personal interests and skills that qualitative inquiry requires (pp. 107–110). The key issue is the compatibility of your reasons for "going qualitative" with your other goals, your research questions, and the actual activities involved in doing a qualitative study. Alan Peshkin's motives (Example 2.2) for doing qualitative research—that he liked qualitative fieldwork and that it suited his abilities—are perfectly legitimate ones, *if* you choose research questions for which this is an appropriate strategy.

Traditionally, discussions of personal goals in research methods texts have accepted, implicitly or explicitly, the ideal of the objective, disinterested scientist, and have emphasized that the choice of research approaches and methods should be determined by the research questions that you want to answer. However, it is clear from autobiographies of scientists (e.g., Heinrich, 1984) that decisions about research methods are often far more personal than this, and the importance of subjective motives and goals in science is supported by a great deal of historical, sociological, and philosophical work.

The grain of truth in the traditional view is that your personal (and often unexamined) motives as a researcher have important consequences for the validity of your conclusions. If your research questions, selection of settings and participants, data collection, and analysis are driven by your personal desires *without* a careful assessment of the potential impact of the latter on your conclusions, you are in danger of creating a flawed or biased study. King Gustav of Sweden wanted a powerful warship to dominate the Baltic, but this desire led to an ill-considered decision to add a second gundeck to the *Vasa,* causing it to capsize and sink, and thus dealing a severe setback to his goals.

For all of these reasons, it is important that you recognize and take account of the personal goals that drive and influence your research. Attempting to exclude your personal goals and concerns from the design of your research is neither possible nor necessary. What *is* necessary is to be *aware* of these goals and how they may be shaping your research, and to think about how best to achieve these *and* to deal with possible negative consequences of their influence. For example, a strongly held position on some issue may seriously impair an interview with someone who holds an opposing view, or distort your analysis of such an interview, if you haven't explicitly identified your position and considered how to prevent these things from happening. In addition, recognizing your personal ties to the study you want to conduct can provide you with a valuable source of insight, theory, and data about the phenomena you are studying (Marshall & Rossman, 1999, pp. 25–30; Strauss & Corbin, 1990, pp. 42–43); this source will be discussed in the next chapter, in the section titled "Experiential Knowledge." Example 2.2 describes how one researcher's personal goals and values influenced (and were influenced by) a series of qualitative studies.

Example 2.2   The Importance of Personal Values and Identity

Alan Peshkin's personal goals, rooted in his values and identity, profoundly influenced several ethnographic studies he did of schools and their communities (Glesne & Peshkin, 1992, pp. 93–107; Peshkin, 1991, pp. 285–295). In his first study, in a rural town he called Mansfield, he liked the community and felt protective toward it. This shaped the kind of story that he told, a story about the importance of community and its preservation. In contrast, in his second study, an ethnography of a fundamentalist Christian school (which he called Bethany Baptist Academy, BBA) and its community, he felt alienated, as a Jew, from a community that attempted to proselytize him:

> When I began to write . . . I knew I was annoyed by my *personal* (as opposed to research) experience at BBA. I soon became sharply aware that my annoyance was pervasively present, that I was writing out of pique and vexation. Accordingly, I was not celebrating community at Bethany, and community prevailed there no less robustly than it had at Mansfield. Why not? I was more than annoyed in Bethany; my ox had been gored. The consequence was that the story I was feeling drawn to tell had its origins in my personal sense of threat. I was not at Bethany as a cool, dispassionate observer (are there any?); I was there as a Jew whose otherness was dramatized directly and indirectly during eighteen months of fieldwork. (Glesne & Peshkin, 1992, p. 103)

In hindsight, Peshkin realized that if he had been less sympathetic toward Mansfield, he could have told a different, equally valid story about this community, whereas if he had identified with Bethany and wanted to support and perpetuate it, he could legitimately have showed how it was much like Mansfield.

(Continued)

(Continued)

In a third study, this one of an urban, multiethnic and multiracial school and community that he called Riverview, Peshkin resolved at the outset to try to identify the aspects of his identity that he saw emerging in his reactions. He listed six different subjective "I's" that influenced this study, each embodying its own goals. These included the Ethnic-Maintenance I and the Community-Maintenance I that he had discovered in his earlier studies; an E-Pluribus-Unum I that supported the ethnic and racial "mingling" that he saw going on; a Justice-Seeking I that wanted to correct the negative and biased images of Riverview held by its wealthier neighbors; a Pedagogical-Meliorist I that was disturbed by the poor teaching that many minority students received in Riverview and sought to find ways to improve this; and a Nonresearch-Human I that was grateful for the warm reception he and his wife received in Riverview, generated a concern for the people and community, and moderated otherwise sharp judgments he might have made.

Peshkin (1991) strongly recommended that all researchers systematically monitor their subjectivity:

I see this monitoring as a necessary exercise, a workout, a tuning up of my subjectivity to get it in shape. It is a rehearsal for keeping the lines of my subjectivity open—and straight. And it is a warning to myself so that I may avoid the trap of perceiving just what my own untamed sentiments have sought out and served up as data. (pp. 293–294)

Exercise 2.1 is one way to engage in this monitoring.

In addition to influencing his questions and conclusions, Peshkin's personal goals were intimately involved in his choice of methods. As he stated, "I like fieldwork, it suits me, and I concluded that rather than pursuing research with questions in search of the 'right' methods of data collection, I had a preferred method of data collection in search of the 'right' question" (Glesne & Peshkin, 1992, p. 102).

In addition to your personal goals, there are two other kinds of goals (ones that are important for other people, not just for yourself) that I want to distinguish and discuss. These are practical goals (including administrative or policy goals) and intellectual goals. Practical goals are focused on *accomplishing* something—meeting some need, changing some situation, or achieving some objective. Intellectual goals, in contrast, are focused on *understanding* something—gaining insight into what is going on and why this is happening, or answering some question that previous research has not adequately addressed.

Both of these kinds of goals are legitimate parts of your design. However, they need to be distinguished, because while intellectual goals are often a fruitful starting point for framing research questions, practical goals can't normally be used in this straightforward way. Research questions need to be questions that your study can potentially answer, and questions that ask directly about how to accomplish practical goals, such as "How should this program be modified to make it more equitable?" or "What can be done to increase students' motivation to learn science?" are not directly answerable by any research. Such questions have an inherently open-ended nature (expressed by terms such as "can") or value component (expressed by terms such as "should") that no amount of data or analysis can fully address.

On the other hand, research questions such as "What effect has this new policy had on program equity?" or "How did students respond to this new science curriculum?" are not only potentially answerable, but can advance the practical goals implied in the previous questions. For these reasons, you need to frame your research questions in ways that help your study *achieve* your practical goals, rather than smuggling these goals into the research questions themselves, where they may interfere with the coherence and feasibility of your design. A common problem that my students have in developing research questions is that they try to base these questions directly on their practical goals, ending up with questions that not only can't be answered by their research, but fail to adequately guide the research itself. I will discuss this issue more fully in Chapter 4; here, I am simply emphasizing the difference between these two types of goals.

The point is not to eliminate practical goals from your design; in addition to the reasons given previously, practical or policy objectives are particularly important for *justifying* your research. Don't ignore these goals, but understand where they are coming from, their implications for your research, and how they can be productively employed in planning and defending your study.

WHAT GOALS CAN QUALITATIVE RESEARCH HELP YOU ACHIEVE?

Qualitative and quantitative methods are not simply different ways of doing the same thing. Instead, they have different strengths and logics, and are often best used to address different kinds of questions and goals (Maxwell, 2004a; Maxwell & Loomis, 2002). Unfortunately, many research methods textbooks are based (explicitly or implicitly) on a quantitative "mental model" (Greene, 2007, pp. 11–13) for research, privileging quantitative approaches and minimizing or dismissing the key strengths of a qualitative approach. In my view, a key difference between the two approaches is the distinction between "variance theory" and "process theory" as two approaches to explanation (Mohr, 1982). Quantitative researchers tend to see the world in terms of variables; they view explanation as a demonstration that there is a statistical relationship between different variables. Process theory, in contrast, tends to see the world in terms of people, situations, events, and the processes that connect these; explanation is based on an analysis of how some situations and events influence others (Maxwell, 2004a, 2008, 2011b; I say more about this distinction in Chapter 3).

The strengths of qualitative research derive significantly from this process orientation toward the world, and the inductive approach, focus on specific situations or people, and emphasis on descriptions rather than numbers that this requires. I will describe five kinds of intellectual goals for which qualitative studies are especially suited, and three kinds of practical goals to which these intellectual goals can substantially contribute:

1. Understanding the meaning, for participants in the study, of the events, situations, experiences, and actions they are involved with or engage in. I am using "meaning" here in a broad sense, including cognition, affect, intentions, and anything else that can be encompassed in what qualitative researchers often refer to as the "participants' perspective." In my view, these perspectives are part of the reality that you are trying to understand (Maxwell, 2011b; Menzel, 1978).

   Many qualitative researchers have rejected this position, holding that people's beliefs, values, and so on are their *constructions*, rather than part of any reality; they have either seen these constructions as existing entirely separately from the "real" world, or have denied that there *is* any real world outside of our constructions (Schwandt, 1997, p. 134). I don't think this sort of radical constructivism is either philosophically tenable, or that it adequately represents the "theory in use" that most qualitative researchers employ in their actual research. Dealing with this issue in depth is beyond the scope of this book (for a much more extensive discussion, see Maxwell, 2011b); my point is simply that whatever your stance on this issue, it is important to recognize that the meanings, beliefs, and so on of the participants in your study are a major part of what you want to understand. In a qualitative study, you are interested not only in the physical events and behavior that are taking place, but also in how the participants in your study make sense of these, and how their understanding influences their behavior. This focus on meaning is central to what is known as the "interpretive" approach to social science (Bhattacharya, 2008; Bredo & Feinberg, 1982; Geertz, 1974; Rabinow & Sullivan, 1979), a fundamental aspect of most qualitative research and a key difference between qualitative and quantitative research.

2. Understanding the particular contexts within which the participants act, and the influence that this context has on their actions. Qualitative researchers typically study a relatively small number of individuals or situations, and preserve the individuality of each of these in their analyses, rather than collecting data from large samples and aggregating the data across individuals or situations. Thus, they are able to understand how events, actions, and meanings are shaped by the unique circumstances in which these occur (Maxwell, 2004a).

3. Understanding the process by which events and actions take place. Merriam (1988) stated that "The interest [in a qualitative study] is in process rather than outcomes" (p. xii); while this does not mean that qualitative research is unconcerned with outcomes, it does emphasize that a major strength of qualitative research is in getting at the processes that led to these outcomes, processes that experimental and survey research are often poor at identifying (Britan, 1978; Maxwell, 2004a, 2004c; Patton, 1990, p. 94).

4. Identifying unanticipated phenomena and influences, and generating new, "grounded" (Glaser & Strauss, 1967) theories about the latter. Qualitative research has an inherent openness and flexibility that allows you to modify your design and focus during the research to pursue new discoveries and relationships. This flexibility derives from its particularistic, rather than comparative and generalizing, focus, and from its freedom from the rules of statistical hypothesis testing,[2] which require that the research plan not be significantly altered after data collection has begun.

5. Developing causal explanations. The traditional view that only quantitative methods can be used to credibly draw causal conclusions has long been disputed by some qualitative researchers (e.g., Britan, 1978; Denzin, 1970; Erickson, 1986). Miles and Huberman (1984) argued that

> Much recent research supports a claim that we wish to make here: that field research is far *better* than solely quantified approaches at developing explanations of what we call *local causality*—the actual events and processes that led to specific outcomes. (p. 132)

Although the traditional view has been abandoned by some researchers, both qualitative and quantitative (see Maxwell, 2004a, 2004c, in press), it is still dominant in both traditions (Denzin & Lincoln, 2000; Shavelson & Towne, 2002).

Part of the reason for the disagreement has been a failure to recognize that quantitative and qualitative researchers tend to ask different kinds of causal questions. As described previously, quantitative researchers tend to be interested in whether and to what extent *variance* in *x* causes variance in *y*. Qualitative researchers, on the other hand, tend to ask *how x* plays a role in causing *y*, what the *process* is that connects *x* and *y*. Weiss (1994) provided a concrete illustration of this difference:

> In qualitative interview studies the demonstration of causation rests heavily on the description of a visualizable sequence of events, each event flowing into the next. . . . Quantitative studies support an assertion of causation by showing a correlation between an earlier event and a subsequent event. An analysis of data collected in a large-scale sample survey might, for example, show that there is a correlation between the level of the wife's education and the presence of a companionable marriage. In qualitative studies we would look for a process through which the wife's education or factors associated with her education express themselves in marital interaction. (p. 179)

This is not to say that deriving causal explanations from a qualitative study is an easy or straightforward task (Maxwell, 2004c). However, the situation of qualitative research is no different from that of quantitative research in this respect. Both approaches need to identify and deal with the plausible validity threats to any proposed causal explanation; I will discuss this further in Chapter 6.

These intellectual goals, and the inductive, open-ended strategy that they require, give qualitative research a particular advantage in addressing three additional, practical kinds of goals:

1. Generating results and theories that are understandable and experientially credible, both to the people you are studying and to others. Patton (1990, pp. 19–24) gave an example of how the responses to the open-ended items on a questionnaire used to evaluate a teacher accountability system had far greater credibility with, and impact on, the school administration than did the quantitative analysis of the standardized items. Bolster (1983) made a more general argument, that one of the reasons for the lack of impact of educational research on educational practice has been that such research has largely been quantitative, and doesn't connect with teachers' experience of everyday classroom realities. He argued for a qualitative approach that emphasizes the perspective of teachers and the understanding of particular settings, as having far more potential for informing educational practitioners.

2. Conducting research that is intended to improve existing practices, programs, or policies, what is often called "formative evaluation" (Scriven, 1967, 1991; Patton, 2001), rather than to simply assess the impact or value of these. In such research, it is more important to understand the processes by which, and the specific contexts in which, things happen, and how these are understood by participants, than it is to rigorously compare this situation with others or to establish that a change in outcomes occurred as a result of a change in practice (Maxwell, 2004a; Pawson & Tilley, 1997). I discuss the implications for your research questions of the difference between the intellectual goal of understanding these meanings, contexts, and processes, and the practical goal of improving the practice or policy studied, in Chapter 4.

3. Engaging in action, participatory, collaborative, or community-based research with participants in the study. The face credibility of qualitative research, and its focus on particular contexts and their meaning for participants in these contexts, make it particularly suitable for collaborations with these participants (Brydon-Miller, Kral, Maguire, Noffke, & Sabhlok, 2011; Finley, 2008; Jordan, 2008; Pushor, 2008; Somekh, 2008; Tolman & Brydon-Miller, 2001).

Sorting out and assessing the different personal, practical, and intellectual goals that you bring to your study can be a difficult task. In addition, this is not something you should simply do once, when you begin designing the study, and then forget about, as Example 2.2 illustrates. Some of your goals may not become apparent to you until you are well into the research; furthermore, they may change as the research proceeds. Example 2.3 provides an account of how one doctoral student went about identifying her goals in making a decision about her dissertation topic. Exercise 2.1, at the end of this chapter, is what I call a "researcher identity memo"; it asks you to write about the goals and personal identity that you bring to your study, and their potential benefits and liabilities for your research. Example 2.4 is one such memo, written for my qualitative methods class; it shows how one student wrestled with deep and painful issues of her identity and goals in planning for her dissertation research on language curriculum reform in Bolivia. All of the examples in this chapter illustrate some of the advantages that reflection on your goals can provide for your research; in addition, such memos can be valuable in developing your conceptual framework, as described in Chapter 3.

Example 2.3   Deciding on a Dissertation Topic

During her first year of doctoral work, Isabel Londoño, a native of Colombia, enrolled in a qualitative research methods course. For her research project, she interviewed seven women from her country who were working in Boston, exploring their experiences balancing work and family. While working on the project, she also began to read some of the feminist literature available in the United States on women executives, women's psychological development, and women's experience managing work and family. She was excited by the new ideas in this literature, which she had not had access to in her own country, and decided that she wanted to focus on issues of executive women in her country for her dissertation.

At the end of her first year, Isabel took a leave of absence from the doctoral program to work as the chief of staff of her former college roommate, whose husband had just been elected president of Colombia. Among her responsibilities was gathering information on employment, education, and the status of women in her nation. One of the issues that emerged as critical was the need to assess the effect of a recent shift in educational decision making from the national to the local level. In the past, most decisions had been made by the national ministry of education; now, decisions were being shifted downward to the mayors in local municipalities. No one was really sure how this change was being implemented and what its effects were.

Isabel found that investigating an issue that affected the lives of many people in her country changed her perspective, and raised questions about her choice of a thesis topic:

> It became an issue of what was my responsibility to the world. To find out how to solve a personal, internal conflict of executive women? Or was there a problem where I could really be of help? Also, what was more rewarding to me as a person—to solve a problem that affected me personally or solve a problem of the world?

She also felt pressure from others to select a topic that clearly linked to her career goals and showed that she knew what she wanted to do with her life. Coming to a decision about her dissertation research topic forced Isabel to identify and assess her personal and practical goals.

> I thought about why I got into a doctoral program. What I hoped to get out of it personally, professionally, academically. Why did I end up here? Then, I thought about what are the things about the world that move me, that make me sad or happy? I analyzed what that interest was about—people, feelings, institutions. It was important for me to see the themes in common in my interests and motivations. It gave me strength. I also was open to change. Change is the most scary thing, but you have to allow it.

She decided that she would study the decentralization of educational decision making in six municipalities in her country. In making this decision, she chose to disregard others' opinions of her:

> What I have decided is *no,* I am going to do my thesis about something that *moves me inside.* I don't care if I am ever going to work on that topic again because it's something I want to learn about. I don't want to use my thesis as a stepladder for my work, that feels like prostitution. So I believe the interest should be on the thesis topic itself, not on where that is leading you, where you're going to get with it.

(Continued)

(Continued)

One of the things that supported her decision was reading the literature on her topic:

> That was very important because I discovered that what I was interested in was something that had interested a lot of other people before, and was going on in a lot of other places in the world, and was affecting education in other countries. This made my topic relevant. It was very important for me to understand that it was relevant, that I was not just making up a dream problem. I think that's something you always fear, that the problem you see is not really important. I also learned that although other people had done work on the problem, *nobody* had the interest I had—the human impact of implementing a reform in the administration of education.
>
> Writing memos for classes was key, having to put things to paper. I also started keeping a thesis diary and wrote memos to myself in it. The date and one word, one idea, or something that I'd read. Many of the things I've written about have now become the list of what I'm going to do after I do my thesis!
>
> Finally, I think it's important to really try to have fun. I figure, if you don't have fun, you shouldn't be doing it. Of course, sometimes I get tired of my topic and hate it. I sit at the computer and I'm tired and I don't want to do it, but every time I start working, I forget all that and get immersed in my work. And if something has the power to do that, it must be right.

The particular decisions that Isabel made are not necessarily the right ones for everyone; they are unique to her identity and situation. However, the *way* that she went about making the decision—seriously and systematically reflecting on her goals and motives, and the implications of these for her research choices—is one that I recommend to everyone deciding on a major research project.

Exercise 2.1   Researcher Identity Memo

The purpose of this memo is to help you examine your goals, experiences, assumptions, feelings, and values as they relate to your research, and to discover what resources and potential concerns your identity and experience may create. What prior connections (social and intellectual) do you have to the topics, people, or settings you plan to study? How do you think and feel about these topics, people, or settings? What assumptions are you making, consciously or unconsciously, about these? What do you want to accomplish or learn by doing this study?

The purpose is *not* to write a *general* account of your goals, background, and experiences. Instead, describe specifically those experiences, and the beliefs, goals, and expectations that emerged from them, that are most directly relevant to your planned research project, and reflect on *how* these have informed and influenced your research. See Examples 2.2, 2.3, and 2.4 for some of the things you can do with such a memo—not as *models* to mechanically follow, but as *illustrations* of the kind of thinking that this memo requires. If you are just starting your project, you can't be as detailed or confident in your conclusions as some of these researchers were, but try to aim for this sort of exploration of how your identity and goals could affect your study.

The memo is intended to be mainly for *your* benefit, not for communicating to someone else; try to avoid substituting presentation for reflection and analysis. I suggest that you begin working on this memo by brainstorming whatever comes to mind when you think about your prior experiences that may relate to your site or topic, and jot these down without immediately trying to organize or analyze them. Then, try to identify the issues most likely to be important in your research, think about the implications of these, and organize your reflections.

Next are two broad sets of questions that are productive to reflect on in this memo. In your answers to these, try to be as specific as you can.

1. What prior experiences have you had that are relevant to your topic or setting? What beliefs and assumptions about your topic or setting have resulted from these experiences? What goals have emerged from these, or have otherwise become important for your research? How have these experiences, assumptions, and goals shaped your decision to choose this topic, and the way you are approaching this project?

2. What potential advantages do you think the goals, beliefs, and experiences that you described have for your study? What potential disadvantages do you think these may create for you, and how might you deal with these?

Example 2.4   Researcher Identity Memo for a Study of Educational Reform in Bolivia

Barbara Noel

There are several layers of personal interest I hold in the topic of educational reform in Bolivia. Probably the most personal is the bilingual/bicultural nature I share with the profile of the Bolivian population. It wasn't until I was well into my adulthood that I recognized how deeply being bilingual has shaped my life consciously and

(Continued)

(Continued)

unconsciously. Having spent my childhood in Peru and Mexico, with my bicultural parents (Peruvian mother, very Californian father), I was exposed to Spanish yet grew up speaking English at home and at school. When my family moved to Texas I was 11 and shortly after felt the powerful, sneering attitude to everything Latin American. I and the rest of the family quickly, individually, and without any discussion or conscious inner dialogue spent the next few years carving out the Latino in us and successfully assimilating to the mainstream U.S. culture. I continue to observe this inner battle within my siblings and mother. Fourteen years later, I started speaking Spanish again once I realized the futility and extent of destruction from trying to stamp out one culture in favor of another. Since then, I have turned away from a sort of cultural schizophrenia and have begun to identify where I can integrate the two cultures, consciously choosing what I see as the best of both.

In the Bolivian society, I see the same struggle I personally experienced magnified on a very large scale. I see how for most of the nation's history, one dominant culture has sought to eliminate all the others. It is no accident that forced schooling in an incomprehensible language has produced a population where more than half of the adults over 15 years of age are illiterate. The minds of the indigenous people have also been colonized. They passionately fight for their children to speak only Spanish because this, as they see it, is the only vehicle for attaining political voice and economic security. Many of them desperately seek to assimilate and cut out any traces of "cholo" or Indian in them. Even if they or their children understand an indigenous language, they will act as though they don't understand.

I mostly feel angry as I write about these issues. In a way it is this anger and the subsequent passion for justice that drove me to the field of intercultural, bilingual education. Now I find myself inside a whole country wrestling with the same problems my family and I wrestle with. I must be careful to not project my own journey onto my perception of Bolivian society. I need to seek external validation for my perceptions and ongoing theories about this struggle in Bolivia to avoid painting an inaccurate picture. The confusion for me will come from assuming that my inner lens is the same as the lenses of those with whom I speak.

Writing this memo, I have come to see how my personal base could provide a unique contribution to studying this bilingual/bicultural struggle in Bolivia. My own experience will help me capture my interviewees' stories more vividly and sensitively. By having an inside perspective, I can help the people I interview trust me. I need to figure out just how much to share with them in order to open up dialogue and yet not have my experience corrupt their story. This sort of sharing, "I've been there too," may help my interviewees move past the barrier of how I look, a blond "gringa" from an imperialistic nation.

Another layer of interest in this study is the experience of teachers as they undergo making changes the reform asks them to make. They are being told to completely change their mental schemas for teaching, from a transmission approach to a constructivist approach, without any clear guidelines, models, or examples. This leaves the teachers at a loss as to how to begin. Six years after the reform program began they are still confused. I also entered the profession under similar circumstances, when in the U.S. teachers were being told to teach through a whole language approach. It was like being in a dark room not knowing what to grab on to and trying to act as if you have everything under control lest your job be in jeopardy. Had someone interviewed me about this process at that time, my major concern would have been to appear as if everything is wonderful and that the approach was a magic bullet for teaching. I would have been alienated from my colleagues if they had found out I had said anything remotely negative. This experience helps me to understand how vulnerable these teachers might feel and their need for expressing bravado at all costs.

The personal strength I have in this area is also my biggest weakness. My ability to "put myself in their shoes" and view things from behind their lenses can also get confused by my own projection of the situation based on my own experiences. I might also be tempted to move beyond my role as investigator to reformer, provider of "magic bullets." In the past, I have impulsively offered several workshops, at no cost, just because I'd gotten so caught up in the deep needs I've perceived in their practice and their desire to learn. I need to measure my energies so that I can indeed finish what I start out to do. It will be hard to balance this relationship. I don't feel comfortable just going in as an investigator, yet my "save the world" inspirations need to be tempered into a practical approach that meets the dual purposes of helping and investigating. For me, the reform provides hope that a society may start turning around a long history of oppression by valuing its deeply multicultural character in a way I was able to do on a minute scale.

Addendum, July 2000

It is now several months since I wrote this memo. After having read through it again, I notice several things I learned as a result of going through this exercise. Before writing this memo, I knew I felt intensely drawn to the subject but didn't know why. I felt passionate about righting the wrongs but didn't understand where the motivations were coming from or even that they had a personal basis. Had I not identified my motivations for doing research in this area, I would not have realized how strongly my personal experiences could impact my study. I now realize that even though I try to be very aware, my perceptions will be inevitably colored by my personal background.

It would be easy to fault myself as a researcher by thinking that such an emotional attachment would automatically render me unqualified for such a venture. Yet, through the exercise, I was able to turn the coin around and see the strengths that I also bring through a more empathic stance. While my empathy might help me

(Continued)

(Continued)

perceive subtle and important motivations for my informants' responses and behavior, it might also introduce dynamics I unconsciously bring into the situation. I also identified a pattern of behavior I engage in which is to get overly involved with a project so that my emotional connection takes over. I lose my focus and change my role from the one I had objectively started out with. Having identified this pattern, I can, in a way, construct an overhead camera to monitor my actions that might often blink a bright red light to indicate overheating.

What I have come away with from this exercise is clarity of purpose. The real reasons for doing the study. I identified how strongly I felt about the importance of the study personally and professionally. This passion has the possibility, then, to become the engine that sparks my flagging energies and guides me through the blind curves and boring straight stretches of mundane routines during the process of data gathering, transcription, and analysis. I am aware of ways I might possibly corrupt the quality of the information. I also understand how my emotional attachment to the study can be beneficial. This type of reflection helps put in motion a mental machinery that can help monitor my reactions and warn me when I veer off course. Now I see how this memo grounds the rest of the study because it clarifies, energizes, and audits the unique role each researcher brings into the arena.

NOTES

1. I have called these "goals," rather than "purposes," to more clearly distinguish them from the usual meaning of "purpose" in research methods texts—the specific objective of a study, for example, "The purpose of this study is to investigate (understand, explore) _____ " (Creswell, 1994, p. 59). I see this meaning of "purpose" as more closely connected to the research questions of a study, although distinct from these.

2. Although statistical testing of hypotheses is integral to much quantitative research, as a way of dealing with the possibility of chance associations between variables, the usual approach to this, termed "null hypothesis significance testing" or NHST, has been so widely misinterpreted and misused, and so often misrepresented even in textbooks, that many prominent statisticians have argued that it should be completely abandoned (Cohen, 1994, Harlow, Mulaik, & Steiger, 1997; Huck, 2009), particularly since there are now much better alternatives to NHST (Cumming, 2011). Qualitative researchers rarely make use of such tests, but if you plan to do this, you need to be aware of the limitations of NHST, and to know what such tests actually tell you.

3

Conceptual Framework

What Do You Think Is Going On?

Biologist Bernd Heinrich (1984, pp. 141–151) and his associates once spent a summer conducting detailed, systematic research on ant lions, small insects that trap ants in pits they have dug. Returning to the university in the fall, Heinrich was surprised to discover that his results were quite different from those published by other researchers. Redoing his experiments the following summer to try to understand these discrepancies, Heinrich found that he and his fellow researchers had been led astray by an unexamined assumption they had made about the ant lions' time frame: Their observations hadn't been long enough to detect some key aspects of these insects' behavior. As he concluded, "Even carefully collected results can be misleading if the underlying context of assumptions is wrong" (p. 151).

For this reason, the conceptual framework of your study—the system of concepts, assumptions, expectations, beliefs, and theories that supports and informs your research—is a key part of your design (Miles & Huberman, 1994; Robson, 2011). Miles and Huberman (1994) defined a conceptual framework as a visual or written product, one that "explains, either graphically or in narrative form, the main things to be studied—the key factors, concepts, or variables—and the presumed relationships among them" (p. 18).[1] Here, I use the term in a broader sense, to refer to the actual ideas and beliefs that you hold about the phenomena studied, whether these are written down or not; this may also be called the "theoretical framework" or "idea context" for the study. A valuable guide to developing a conceptual framework and using this throughout the research process, with detailed analyses of four actual studies, is Ravitch and Riggan, *Reason & Rigor: How Conceptual Frameworks Guide Research* (2011). (Full disclosure: Sharon Ravitch is a former student of mine, and I wrote the foreword for the book.)

The most important thing to understand about your conceptual framework is that it is primarily a conception or model of what is out there that you plan to study, and of what is going on with these things and why—a tentative *theory* of the phenomena that you are investigating. The function of this theory is to inform the rest of your design—to help you to assess and refine your goals, develop realistic and relevant research questions, select appropriate methods, and identify potential validity threats to your conclusions. It also helps you *justify* your research, something I discuss in more detail in Chapter 7. In this chapter, I discuss the different sources for this theory, and how to use theory effectively in your design. I describe the nature of theory in more detail later in the chapter, in dealing with the uses of existing theory. Here, I want to emphasize that your conceptual framework is a theory, however tentative or incomplete it may be.

What is often called the "research problem" is a part of your conceptual framework, and formulating the research problem is often seen as a key task in designing your study. It is part of your conceptual framework (although it is often treated as a separate component of a research design or proposal) because it identifies something that is *going on* in the world, something that is itself problematic or that has consequences that are problematic. Your research problem functions (in combination with your goals) to justify your study, to show people why your research is important. In addition, this problem is presumably something that is not fully understood, or that we don't adequately know how to deal with; therefore, we want more information about it. Not every study will have an explicit statement of a research problem, but every good research design contains an implicit or explicit identification of some issue or problem, intellectual or practical, about which more information is needed. (The justification of "needed" is where your goals come into play.)

Many writers identify the part of a research design, proposal, or published paper that deals with the conceptual framework of a study as the *literature review*. This can be a dangerously misleading term. In developing your conceptual framework, you should not simply review and summarize some body of theoretical or empirical publications, for three reasons:

1. It can lead to a narrow focus on the literature, ignoring other conceptual resources that may be of equal or greater importance for your study. As Locke, Spirduso, and Silverman (1993) pointed out, "In any active area of inquiry the current knowledge base is not in the library—it is in the invisible college of informal associations among research workers" (p. 48). This knowledge can be found in unpublished papers, dissertations in progress, and grant applications, as well as in the heads of researchers working in this field. Locke, Spirduso, and Silverman emphasized that "The best introduction to the current status of a research area is close association with advisors who know the territory" (p. 49). In addition, an exclusive orientation toward the literature leads you to ignore your own experience, your speculative thinking (discussed later in the section titled "Thought Experiments"), and any pilot and exploratory research that you've done.

2. It tends to generate a strategy of "covering the field" rather than focusing specifically on those studies and theories that are particularly *relevant* to your research (for more on this, see Maxwell, 2006). Literature reviews that lose sight of this need for relevance often degenerate into a series of "book reports" on the literature, with no clear connecting thread or argument. The relevant studies may be only a small part of the research in a defined field, and may range across a number of different approaches and disciplines.[2] The most productive conceptual frameworks are often those that bring in ideas from *outside* the traditionally defined field of your study, or that integrate different approaches, lines of investigation, or theories that no one had previously connected. Bernd Heinrich used Adam Smith's *The Wealth of Nations* in developing a theory of bumblebee foraging and energy

balance that emphasized individual initiative, competition, and a spontaneous division of labor, rather than genetic determination or centralized control (Heinrich, 1979, pp. 144–146; 1984, p. 79).

3. It can lead you to think that your task is simply descriptive—to report what previous researchers have found or what theories have been proposed. In constructing a conceptual framework, your purpose is not only descriptive, but also critical; you need to understand (and clearly communicate in your proposal or research paper) what *problems* there have been with previous research and theory, what contradictions or holes you have found in existing views, and how your study can make an original contribution to our understanding. You need to treat the literature not as an *authority* to be deferred to, but as a useful but fallible source of *ideas* about what's going on, and to attempt to see alternative ways of framing the issues. For good examples of this attitude, see Example 3.2 and the "Context" section of Martha Regan-Smith's proposal (Appendix A).

Another way of putting this is that a conceptual framework for your research is something that is *constructed*, not found. It incorporates pieces that are borrowed from elsewhere, but the structure, the overall coherence, is something that you build, not something that exists ready-made. It is important for you to pay attention to the existing theories and research that are relevant to what you plan to study, because these are often key sources for understanding what is going on with these phenomena. However, these theories and results are often partial, misleading, or simply wrong. Bernd Heinrich (1984) found that many of the ideas about ant lions in the literature were incorrect, and his subsequent research led to a much more comprehensive and well-supported theory of their behavior. You will need to critically examine each idea or research finding to see if it is a valid and useful module for constructing a theory that will adequately inform your study.

This idea that existing theory and research provide "modules" that you can use in your research was developed at length by Becker (2007, pp. 141–146). As he stated,

> I am always collecting such prefabricated parts for use in future arguments. Much of my reading is governed by a search for such useful modules. Sometimes I know I need a particular theoretical part and even have a good idea of where to find it (often thanks to my graduate training in theory, to say a good word for what I so often feel like maligning). (1986, p. 144)

Before describing the sources of these modules, I want to discuss a particularly important part of your conceptual framework—the philosophical and methodological paradigm(s) that you can draw on to inform your work.

THE VALUE (AND PITFALLS) OF RESEARCH PARADIGMS

The concept of paradigm was largely drawn from Thomas Kuhn's (1970) influential book *The Structure of Scientific Revolutions*. In his postscript to the second edition of this work, Kuhn described a paradigm as "the entire constellation of beliefs, values, techniques, and so on shared by the members of a given community" (p. 175). Despite this broad definition, Kuhn focused mainly on the substantive theories and methods of such communities.

In contrast, participants in the methodological "paradigm wars" in the social sciences focused on the philosophical beliefs and assumptions of different methodological communities, and mostly saw these philosophical positions as foundational for research practices, implying specific methodological strategies. At the most abstract and general level, examples of such paradigms are philosophical positions, such as positivism, constructivism, realism, pragmatism, and postmodernism, each embodying very different ideas about reality (ontology) and how we can gain knowledge of it (epistemology). At a somewhat more specific level, paradigms that are relevant to qualitative research include interpretivism, critical theory, feminism, queer theory, and phenomenology, and there are even more specific traditions within these. It is well beyond the scope of this book to describe these paradigms and how they can inform a qualitative study; useful discussions of these issues can be found in Creswell (2006) and Schram (2003); the *SAGE Encyclopedia of Qualitative Research Methods* (Given, 2008) has entries covering each of the terms listed previously, as well as numerous other approaches.

Since the previous edition of this book was published, I have become increasingly critical (see Maxwell, 2011a) of the way paradigms are typically invoked in discussions of research. Part of this concern is informed by the work of the sociologist Andrew Abbott (2001, 2004). Abbott argued, on the basis of numerous examples from a range of the social sciences, that philosophical positions, rather than being unified sets of premises that strongly shape the practices of particular communities of scholars, function instead as heuristics, conceptual and practical resources that are used to solve specific problems in theory and research. He stated, "The idea of heuristics is to open up new topics, to find new things. To do that, sometimes we need to invoke constructivism. . . . Sometimes we need a little realism" (2004, p. 191; see also Seale, 1999, pp. 24–29). Wimsatt (2007) has provided a detailed philosophical justification for such a heuristic approach, and applied this approach to numerous issues in biology, and Hacking (1999) has shown how particular phenomena (mental illness, child abuse, nuclear weapons, rocks) can be usefully seen both as real and as social constructs.

This view is quite consistent with bricolage as an approach to qualitative research, which I mentioned in Chapter 1. The term "bricolage" was taken from the work of the French anthropologist Claude Levi-Strauss (1968), who used it to distinguish mythological from scientific thought. (In current French usage, bricolage means "do-it-yourself," and is used to refer to stores such as The Home Depot; see "Bricolage," n.d.) Levi-Strauss described the bricoleur as someone who uses whatever tools and materials are at hand to complete a project. The key idea is that rather than developing a logically consistent plan in advance and then systematically using the materials and tools that the plan and the norms of the community prescribe (as science is widely, though I think somewhat incorrectly, believed to do), the bricoleur spontaneously adapts to the situation, creatively employing the available tools and materials to come up with unique solutions to a problem. This concept was applied to qualitative research methods by Denzin and Lincoln (2000), and developed more extensively by Kincheloe and Berry (2004; Kincheloe et al., 2011). It closely resembles the model of research design that I presented in Chapter 1, and challenges the idea of paradigms as logically consistent systems of thought on which research practices are based.

As I described in the Preface to this edition, my approach to qualitative research has increasingly been informed by the philosophical position generally called critical realism. This position, which has gained widespread acceptance in the philosophy of science, can itself be seen as an example of bricolage, since it combines two common-sense perspectives that have often been seen as logically incompatible. The first of these perspectives is ontological realism: the belief that there is a real world that exists independently of our perceptions and theories. This world doesn't accommodate to our beliefs; believing that global warming is a hoax will not keep the Earth from warming. (For some powerful cautionary examples of how a society's ignorance of, or false beliefs about, the environmental consequences of its actions can lead to its demise, see Jared Diamond's 2011 book *Collapse*.)

The second perspective is epistemological constructivism: Our understanding of this world is inevitably our construction, rather than a purely objective perception of reality, and no such construction can claim absolute truth. This is widely recognized both in science (Shadish, Cook, & Campbell, 2002, p. 29) and in our everyday lives; we recognize that what people perceive and believe is shaped by their assumptions and prior experiences as well as by the reality that they interact with. From this perspective, every theory, model, or conclusion (including the model of qualitative research design presented here) is necessarily a simplified and incomplete attempt to grasp something about a complex reality.

I have found this combination of perspectives extremely useful in thinking about a wide range of issues in qualitative research (for a detailed exploration of this view and its implications for qualitative research, see Maxwell, 2011b), but have also combined this perspective with insights from additional diverse philosophical positions, including pragmatism and postmodernism. I have done so, not to create a unified supertheory of qualitative research, but to benefit from a dialogue between the different perspectives, taking what Greene (2007; see also Koro-Ljungberg, 2004) has called a dialectical approach, one that combines divergent mental models to expand and deepen, rather than simply confirm, one's understanding.

For these reasons, I want to make several points that are relevant to using paradigms in your research design:

1. Although some people refer to "the qualitative paradigm," there are many different paradigms within qualitative research, some of which differ radically in their assumptions and implications (cf. Denzin & Lincoln, 2011; Pitman & Maxwell, 1992). It will be important to your research design (and your proposal) to make explicit which paradigm(s) your work will draw on, since a clear philosophical and methodological stance helps you explain and justify your design decisions. Using an established paradigm allows you to build on an accepted and well-developed approach to research, rather than having to construct (and explain) all of this yourself.

2. You can combine aspects of different paradigms and traditions, as described previously; although if you do this, you will need to assess the compatibility of the modules that you borrow from each, and what each will contribute to your study. Schram (2003, p. 79) gave a valuable account of how he combined the ethnographic and life history traditions in conducting his dissertation research on an experienced teacher's adjustment to a new school and community.

3. Your decisions about paradigm issues are not entirely a matter of free choice. You have already made many assumptions about the world, your topic, and how we can understand these, even if you have never consciously examined these. Thus, what is important is to be *aware* of the basic assumptions that you hold about reality and about how we can understand the things we study. For example, do you believe that the concept of "cause" is valid in qualitative research, or in the social sciences generally, and if so, how do you understand this concept? This is currently a controversial issue within qualitative research (Anderson & Scott, in press; Donmoyer, in press; Howe, 2011; Maxwell, 2004c, in press), and has important implications for the types of conclusions you will draw from your study. Choosing a paradigm or tradition (or combining several of these) should involve assessing which paradigmatic views best fit with your assumptions and methodological preferences (Becker, 2007, pp. 16–17), as well as what insights and productive approaches these views might provide for your study.

Trying to work within a paradigm (or theory) that doesn't fit your actual beliefs is like trying to do a physically demanding job in clothes that don't fit—at best you'll be uncomfortable, at worst it will keep you from doing the job well. Such a lack of fit may not be obvious at the outset; it may emerge only as you develop your conceptual framework, research questions, and methods, since these should also be compatible with your paradigmatic stance. Writing memos is a valuable way of revealing and exploring these assumptions and incompatibilities (see Becker, 2007, pp. 17–18).

There are four main sources for the modules that you can use to construct a conceptual framework for your study: (1) your experiential knowledge, (2) existing theory and research, (3) your pilot and exploratory research, and (4) thought experiments. I will begin with experiential knowledge, because it is both one of the most important conceptual resources and the one that is most seriously neglected in works on research design. I will then deal with the use of existing theory and research in research design, in the process introducing a technique, known as concept mapping, that can be valuable in developing a conceptual framework for your study. Finally, I will discuss the uses of your pilot research and thought experiments in generating preliminary or tentative theories about your subject.

EXPERIENTIAL KNOWLEDGE

Traditionally, what you bring to the research from your own background and identity has been treated as *bias*, something whose influence needs to be *eliminated* from the design, rather than a valuable component of it. This has been true to some extent even in qualitative research, despite the fact that qualitative researchers have long recognized that in this field, the researcher *is* the instrument of the research. In opposition to the traditional view, C. Wright Mills (1959), in a classic essay, argued that

> The most admirable scholars within the scholarly community . . . do not split their work from their lives. They seem to take both too seriously to allow such dissociation, and they want to use each for the enrichment of the other. (p. 195)

Separating your research from other aspects of your life cuts you off from a major source of insights, hypotheses, and validity checks. Alan Peshkin, discussing the role of subjectivity in the research he had done, concluded that

> The subjectivity that originally I had taken as an affliction, something to bear because it could not be foregone, could, to the contrary, be taken as "virtuous." My subjectivity is the basis for the story that I am able to tell. It is a strength on which I build. It makes me who I am as a person and as a researcher, equipping me with the perspectives and insights that shape all that I do as a researcher, from the selection of topic clear through to the emphases I make in my writing. Seen as virtuous, subjectivity is something to capitalize on rather than to exorcise. (Glesne & Peshkin, 1992, p. 104)

Anselm Strauss (1987) emphasized many of the same points in discussing what he called "experiential data"—the researcher's technical knowledge, research background, and personal experiences. He argued that

> These experiential data should not be ignored because of the usual canons governing research (which regard personal experience and data as likely to bias the research), for these canons lead to the squashing of valuable experiential data. We say, rather, "mine your experience, there is potential gold there!" (p. 11)

Students' papers and proposals sometimes seem to systematically ignore what their authors know from their own experience about the settings or issues they have studied or plan to study; this can seriously impair their ability to gain a better understanding of the latter, and can threaten a proposal's credibility. Carol Kaffenberger's dissertation research on the effects of childhood cancer on the families of cancer survivors, discussed in Chapter 2, was substantially informed by her family's experience with her daughter's cancer.

Both Peshkin (Glesne & Peshkin, 1992) and Strauss (1987) emphasized that this is not a license to uncritically impose one's assumptions and values on the research. Reason (1988, 1994) used the term "critical subjectivity" to refer to

> a quality of awareness in which we do not suppress our primary experience; nor do we allow ourselves to be swept away and overwhelmed by it; rather we raise it to consciousness and use it as part of the inquiry process. (1988, p. 12)

The explicit incorporation of your identity and experience in your research has gained wide theoretical and philosophical support (e.g., Berg & Smith, 1988; Denzin &

Lincoln, 2000; Jansen & Peshkin, 1992). The philosopher Hilary Putnam (1987, 1990) argued that there cannot, even in principle, be such a thing as a God's-eye view, a view that is the one true objective account. *Any* view is a view *from some perspective*, and is therefore shaped by the location (social and theoretical) and lens of the observer.

Philosophical argument does not, however, solve the problem of how to incorporate this experience most productively in your research design, or how to assess its effect on your research. Peshkin's account of how he became aware of the different "I's" that influenced and informed his studies was discussed in Chapter 2, and Jansen and Peshkin (1992) and Grady and Wallston (1988, pp. 40–43) provided valuable examples of researchers using their subjectivity and experience in their research. At present, however, there are few well-developed and explicit strategies for doing this.

The technique that I call a *researcher identity memo*, which was introduced in Chapter 2 for reflecting on your goals and their relevance for your research, can also be used to explore your assumptions and experiential knowledge. I originally got the idea for this sort of memo from a talk by Robert Bogdan, who described how, before beginning a study of a neonatal intensive care unit of a hospital, he tried to write down all of the expectations, beliefs, and assumptions that he had about hospitals in general and neonatal care in particular, as a way of identifying and taking account of the perspective that he brought to the study. This exercise can be valuable at any point in a study, not just at the outset. Example 3.1 is part of one of my identity memos, written while I was working on a paper on diversity, solidarity, and community, trying to develop a theory that incorporated contact and interaction, as well as shared characteristics, as a basis for community. (A more recent version of this paper is Chapter 4 in Maxwell, 2011b.) Example 3.2 is a memo in which the researcher used her experience to refocus a study of women's use of breast self-examination. Example 2.4, in the previous chapter, deals in part with the author's prior experiences and how these influenced her understanding of educational reform in Bolivia, as well as her goals.

Example 3.1   Identity Memo on Diversity

I can't recall when I first became interested in diversity; it's been a major concern for at least the last 20 years. . . . I do remember the moment that I consciously realized that my mission in life was to make the world safe for diversity; I was in Regenstein Library at the University of Chicago one night in the mid-1970s talking to another student about why we had gone into anthropology, and the phrase suddenly popped into my head.

However, I never gave much thought to tracing this position any further back. I remember, as an undergraduate, attending a talk on some political topic, and being struck by two students' bringing up issues of the rights of particular groups to retain their cultural heritages; it was an issue that had never consciously occurred to me.

And I'm sure that my misspent youth reading science fiction rather than studying had a powerful influence on my sense of the importance of tolerance and understanding of diversity; I wrote my essay for my application to college on tolerance in high school society. But I didn't think much about where all this came from.

It was talking to the philosopher Amelie Rorty in the summer of 1991 that really triggered my awareness of these roots. She had given a talk on the concept of moral diversity in Plato, and I gave her a copy of my draft paper on diversity and solidarity. We met for lunch several weeks later to discuss these issues, and at one point, she asked me how my concern with diversity connected with my background and experiences. I was surprised by the question, and found I really couldn't answer it. She, on the other hand, had thought about this a lot, and talked about her parents emigrating from Belgium to the US, deciding they were going to be farmers like "real Americans," and with no background in farming, buying land in rural West Virginia and learning how to survive and fit into a community composed of people very different from themselves.

This made me start thinking, and I realized that as far back as I can remember, I've felt different from other people, and had a lot of difficulties as a result of this difference and my inability to fit in with peers, relatives, or other people generally. This was all compounded by my own shyness and tendency to isolate myself, and by the frequent moves that my family made while I was growing up....

The way in which this connects with my work on diversity is that my main strategy for dealing with my difference from others, as far back as I can remember, was *not* to try to be more *like* them (similarity-based), but to try to be *helpful* to them (contiguity-based). This is a bit oversimplified, because I also saw myself as somewhat of a "social chameleon," adapting to whatever situation I was in, but this adaptation was much more an *interactional* adaptation than one of becoming fundamentally similar to other people.

It now seems incomprehensible to me that I never saw the connections between this background and my academic work....

[The remainder of the memo discusses the specific connections between my experience and the theory of diversity and community that I had been developing, which sees both similarity (shared characteristics) and contiguity (interaction) as possible sources of solidarity and community.]

Example 3.2   How One Researcher Used Her Personal Experience to Refocus Her Research Problem

I had spent countless hours in the library, reading the literature on women's practice of breast self-examination (BSE). The articles consisted of some research studies, some

(Continued)

(Continued)

editorials in major medical journals, and some essays. The research base was very weak, mainly surveys asking some group of women whether they did BSE, and if not, why not. The groups often were not large or representative. The questions and format varied tremendously from study to study. That most women did not do it was clear, having been found repeatedly. Why they did not do it was not at all clear. I was developing a long list of possible reasons women did not do it. They seemed to fall into three categories: (1) Women were ignorant of how or why to do BSE; (2) women were too modest to touch themselves; and (3) women were too fearful of what they would find. The reasons all seemed quite plausible, but somehow were not satisfactory. The question kept repeating itself, "Why *don't* women do BSE?" Then I asked the question of myself, "Why don't I do BSE?" I knew none of the reasons explained my behavior. Then I changed the question: "What would get me to do it?" It occurred to me that, if a friend called each month and asked if I had done it, I would do it, either in anticipation of her call or immediately afterward. Changing the question to a positive one completely changed my way of thinking about the problem: "What would *encourage* women to do BSE?" The new question opened a range of possibilities by putting BSE in the context of behavior modification, which offered a variety of testable techniques for changing behavior. (Grady & Wallston, 1988, p. 41)

PRIOR THEORY AND RESEARCH

The second major source of modules for your conceptual framework is prior theory and research—not simply published work, but other people's theories and research in general. I will begin with theory, because it is for most people the more problematic and confusing of the two, and then deal with using prior research for other purposes than as a source of theory.

I'm using the term "theory" to refer to something that is considerably broader than its usual meaning in discussions of research methods (see Maxwell & Mittapalli, 2008a, for a more detailed discussion). By "theory," I mean simply a set of concepts and ideas and the proposed relationships among these, a structure that is intended to capture or model something about the world. As LeCompte and Preissle (1993) stated, "theorizing is simply the cognitive process of discovering or manipulating abstract categories and the relationships among these categories" (p. 239). My only modification of this is to include not simply abstract categories, but concrete and specific concepts as well.

This use encompasses everything from so-called grand theory, such as behaviorism, psychoanalysis, or rational choice theory, to specific, everyday explanations of a particular event or state, such as "Dora (my older daughter) doesn't want to go to school today because she's angry at her teacher for correcting her yesterday." That is, I'm not using the term "theory" to denote a particular *level* of complexity, abstraction, or generality of explanatory propositions, but to refer to the *entire range* of such propositions. All such explanations have fundamental features in common, and for my purposes, the similarities are more important than the differences.[3]

Thus, theory is not an arcane and mysterious entity that at some point in your training you learn to understand and master. As Groucho Marx used to say on the 1950s TV game show *You Bet Your Life*, "It's an ordinary household word, something you use every day." The simplest form of theory consists of two concepts joined by a proposed relationship. Such a theory can be as general as "Positive reinforcement leads to continuation of the reinforced behavior," or as specific as "An asteroid impact caused the extinction of the dinosaurs." The important point is what *makes* this a theory: the linking of two concepts by a proposed relationship.

A major function of theory is to provide a model or map of *why* the world is the way it is (Strauss, 1995). It is a simplification of the world, but a simplification aimed at clarifying and explaining some aspect of how it works. Theory is a statement about what is going on with the phenomena that you want to understand. It is not simply a framework, although it can provide that, but a *story* about what you think is happening and why. A useful theory is one that tells an enlightening story about some phenomenon, one that gives you new insights and broadens your understanding of that phenomenon. (See the discussion of causal processes in Chapter 2.)

Glaser and Strauss's (1967) term "grounded theory," which has had an important influence on qualitative research, does not refer to any particular *level* of theory, but to theory that is inductively developed during a study (or series of studies) and in constant interaction with the data from that study. This theory is "grounded" in the actual data collected, in contrast to theory that is developed conceptually and then simply tested against empirical data. In qualitative research, both existing theory and grounded theory are legitimate and valuable.

The Uses of Existing Theory

Using existing theory in qualitative research has both advantages and risks. The advantages of existing theory can be illustrated by two metaphors.

Theory is a coat closet. (I got this metaphor from Jane Margolis, personal communication, who once described Marxism as a coat closet: "You can hang anything in it.") A useful high-level theory gives you a framework for making sense of what you see. Particular pieces of data, which otherwise might seem unconnected or irrelevant to one another or to your research questions, can be related by fitting them into the theory. The concepts of the existing theory are the "coat hooks" in the closet; they provide places to "hang" data, showing their relationship to other data. However, no theory will accommodate all data equally well; a theory that neatly organizes some data will leave other data disheveled and lying on the floor, with no place to put them.

Theory is a spotlight. A useful theory *illuminates* what you see. It draws your attention to particular events or phenomena, and sheds light on relationships that might otherwise go unnoticed or misunderstood. Bernd Heinrich (1984), discussing his investigation of the feeding habits of caterpillars, described his reaction to seeing a partially eaten leaf on the ground that had obviously been subsequently clipped from the tree by a caterpillar. He stated,

> The clipped leaf stood out as if flagged in red, because it didn't fit my expectations or theories about how I thought things ought to be. My immediate feeling was one of wonder. But the wonder was actually a composite of different theories that crowded my mind and vied with each other for validation or rejection. . . . Had I no theories at all, the partially eaten leaf on the ground would not have been noticed. (pp. 133–134)

This is what William James meant when he (reportedly) said that you can't pick up rocks in a field without a theory (Agar, 1980, p. 23). To pick up rocks (rather than something else), you need a theory that tells you what a rock is and how it differs from other things.

By the same token, however, a theory that brightly illuminates one area will leave other areas in darkness; no theory can illuminate everything.

Example 3.3 Using Existing Theory

Eliot Freidson's (1975) book *Doctoring Together: A Study of Professional Social Control* is an account of his research in a medical group practice, trying to understand how the physicians and administrators he studied identified and dealt with violations of professional norms. In conceptualizing what was going on in this practice, he used three broad theories of the social organization and control of work. He referred to these as the entrepreneurial, or physician-merchant, model, deriving from the work of Adam Smith; the bureaucratic, or physician-official, model, deriving to a substantial extent from Max Weber; and the professional, or physician-craftsman, model, which has been less clearly conceptualized and identified than the others. He showed how all three theories provide insight into the day-to-day work of the group he studied, and he drew far-ranging implications for public policy from his results.

Freidson (1975) also used existing theory in a more focused (and unexpected) way to illuminate the results of his research. He argued that the social norms held by the physicians he studied allowed considerable differences of opinion about both the technical standards of work performance and the best ways to deal with patients. These norms "limited the critical evaluation of colleagues' work and discouraged the expression of criticism" (p. 241). However, the norms also strongly opposed any outside control of the physicians' practice, defining physicians as the only ones capable of judging medical work. "The professional was treated as an individual free to follow his own judgment without constraint, so long as his behavior was short of blatant or gross deficiencies in performance and inconvenience to colleagues" (p. 241). Freidson continued,

> This is a very special kind of community that, structurally and normatively, parallels that described by Jesse R. Pitts as the "delinquent community" of French schoolchildren in particular and French collectivities in general during the first half of the twentieth century. . . . Its norms and practice were such as to both draw all members together defensively against the outside world . . . and, internally, to allow each his freedom to act as he willed. (pp. 243–244)

He presented striking similarities between the medical practice he studied and the French peer group structure identified by Pitts. He coined the phrase, "professional delinquent community" to refer to professional groups such as the one he described, and used Pitts's theory to illuminate the process by which this sort of community develops and persists.

A study that makes excellent use of existing theory is described in Example 3.3.

However, Becker (2007) warned that the existing literature, and the assumptions embedded in it, can deform the way you frame your research, causing you to overlook important ways of conceptualizing your study or key implications of your results. The literature has the advantage of what he calls "ideological hegemony," so that it is difficult to see any phenomenon in ways that are different from those that are prevalent in the literature. Trying to fit your insights into this established framework can deform your argument, weakening its logic and making it harder for you to see what a new way of framing the phenomenon might contribute. He explained how his research on marijuana use was deformed by existing theory:

> When I began studying marijuana use in 1951, the ideologically dominant question, the only one worth looking at, was "Why do people do a weird thing like that?" and the ideologically preferred way of answering it was to find a psychological trait or social attribute which differentiated people who did from people who didn't . . . [M]y eagerness to show that this literature (dominated by psychologists and criminologists) was wrong led me to ignore what my research was really about. I had blundered onto, and then proceeded to ignore, a much larger and more interesting question: how do people learn to define their own internal experiences? (Becker, 2007, pp. 147–148)

I had the same experience with my dissertation research on kinship in an Inuit community in northern Canada. At the time that I conducted the research, the literature on kinship in anthropology was dominated by a debate between two theories of the meaning of kinship, one holding that in all societies kinship was fundamentally a matter of biological relationship, the other arguing that biology was only one possible meaning of kinship terms, another being social relatedness. I framed my dissertation (Maxwell, 1986) in terms of these two theories, arguing that my evidence mainly supported the second of these theories, though with significant modifications. It was only years later that I realized that my research could be framed in a more fundamental and interesting way—What is the nature of relationship and solidarity in small, traditional communities? Are these based on, and conceptualized in terms of, similarity (in this case, biological similarity or shared genetic substance) or social interaction? (See Example 3.1.) My research could have been much more productive if I had grasped this theoretical way of framing the study at the outset.

Becker (2007) argued that there is no way to be sure when the dominant approach is wrong or misleading or when your alternative is superior. What you can do is to try to identify the ideological components of the established approach, and to see what happens when you abandon these assumptions. He claimed that "a serious scholar ought routinely to inspect competing ways of talking about the same subject matter," (p. 149) and cautioned, "use the literature, don't let it use you" (p. 149). An awareness of alternative sources of concepts and theories about the phenomena you are studying—including sources other than the literature—is an important counterweight to the ideological hegemony of existing theory and research.

The importance of being able to identify both the insights that a theory can provide and the limitations, distortions, and blind spots in this theory has been well captured by the writing teacher Peter Elbow (1973, 2006), in what he called the "believing game" and the "doubting game." In the believing game, you accept the theory and look for ways it can deepen your understanding of the things you study; in the doubting game, you challenge the theory, looking for its flaws. Students' (and other researchers') use of theory is often distorted by the perceived authority of the literature; they rarely challenge the theories they employ, and often present their results as completely supporting these theories (Dressman, 2008, p. 92). Dressman (2008) argued that such uncritical use of theory threatens not only the credibility of the findings of these studies, but the ability of the research to contribute to our understanding.

An important, and often neglected, source of theory is the theories held by the participants in your study. Contrary to the debunking attitude toward participants' views found in some earlier sociological writing (Berger, 1981, described by Becker, 2007, pp. 65–66), and the almost total neglect of such theories in quantitative research, these theories are important for two reasons. First, these theories are real phenomena; they inform the participants' actions, and any attempt to interpret or explain the participants' actions without taking account of their actual beliefs, values and theories is probably fruitless (Blumer, 1969; Menzel, 1978). Second, participants have far more experience with the things you are studying than you do, and may have important insights into what is going on that you can miss if you don't take their theories seriously.

Both of these points are illustrated by an incident that Glesne (2011) described from her research in Mexico, on improving an indigenous community's relationship with its environment. In response to her question about young people's attitudes toward the environment, one participant replied, "We don't really talk of the environment here, but rather of *harmony*" (p. 215). He described this harmony as a connection among all things; each field, tree, rock, or river had a *dueno* or guardian, to whom people make offerings before cutting a tree or removing a rock. Glesne stated,

> His sentence . . . shattered my assumed categories. Even though I had heard people talk about nature spirits before, even though I had read about the importance of *harmony* in Oaxaca . . . I had kept assigning what I was reading and hearing and experiencing to my Western categories of people, animals, environment, religion/spirituality, etc. . . . I know that I do not yet fully understand the concept of *harmony* the way many in Oaxaca do, but I know better some of my own myths of perception. (p. 215)

To be genuinely qualitative research, a study must take account of the theories and perspectives of those studied, rather than relying entirely on established theoretical views or the researcher's perspective. This doesn't mean that participants' perspectives are necessarily beyond criticism, or that other perspectives are illegitimate (Menzel, 1978). It *does* mean that participants' theories need to be taken seriously.

The imposition of external, dominant theories can be a serious ethical problem as well as a scientific or a practical one (Lincoln, 1990); it can marginalize or dismiss the understandings of participants in the research, and conceal or facilitate oppression or exploitation of the group studied. (In some cases, the dominant theory is itself ethically problematic, as in the case of theories that unjustifiably blame the victim.) I discuss some of these issues in Chapter 5, under research relationships.

There are thus two main ways in which qualitative researchers often fail to make good use of existing theory: by not using it enough, and by using it too uncritically and exclusively. The first fails to explicitly apply *any* prior analytic abstractions or theoretical framework to the study, thus missing the insights that existing theory can provide. Every research design needs *some* theory of the phenomena you are studying, even if it is only a commonsense one, to guide the other design decisions you make. The second type of failure has the opposite problem: It *imposes* theory on the study, shoehorning questions, methods, and data into preconceived categories and preventing the researcher from seeing events and relationships that don't fit the theory.

The tension between these two problems in applying theory (underuse and uncritical overuse) is an inescapable part of research, not something that can be solved by some technique or insight. A key strategy for dealing with this is embodied in the scientific method, as well as in interpretive approaches such as hermeneutics: Develop or borrow theories and continually *test* them, looking for discrepant data and alternative ways (including the research participants' ways) of making sense of the data. (I discuss this further in Chapter 6, as a central issue in validity.) Bernd Heinrich (1984) described searching for crows' nests, in which you look through the trees for a dark spot against the sky, and then try to see a glimmer of light through it (real crows' nests are opaque): "It was like science: first you look for something, and then when you think you have it you do your best to prove yourself wrong" (p. 28).

Concept Maps

For some students, the development and use of theory is the most daunting part of a qualitative study. At this point, therefore, I want to introduce a tool for developing and clarifying theory, known as *concept mapping*. This was originally developed by Joseph Novak (Novak & Gowin, 1984), first as a way to understand how students learned science, and then as a tool for teaching science. A similar strategy is one that Miles and Huberman (1994, pp. 18–22) called a *conceptual framework*. Anselm Strauss (1987, p. 170) provided a third variation, which he called an *integrative diagram*. These approaches have so much in common that I will present them as a single strategy, ignoring for the moment some important differences in the way they are used.

A concept map of a theory is a visual display of that theory—a picture of what the theory says is *going on* with the phenomenon you're studying. These maps do not depict the study itself, nor are they a specific part of either a research design or a proposal. However, concept maps *can* be used to visually present the design or operation of a study—my model of research design (Figure 1.1) is just such a map. Rather, concept mapping is a *tool* for developing and presenting the conceptual framework for your design. And like a theory, a concept map consists of two things: concepts and the relationships among these. These are usually represented, respectively, as labeled circles or boxes and as arrows or lines connecting these. Figures 3.1 through 3.6 provide a variety of examples of concept maps; additional examples can be found in Miles and Huberman (1994), Ravitch and Riggan (2011), and Strauss (1987, pp. 170–183).There are several reasons for creating concept maps:

1. To pull together, and make visible, what your implicit theory is, or to clarify an existing theory. This can allow you to see the implications of the theory, its limitations, and its relevance for your study.

2. To *develop* theory. Like memos, concept maps are a way of "thinking on paper"; they can help you see unexpected connections, or to identify holes or contradictions in your theory and figure out ways to resolve these.

Concept maps usually require considerable reworking to get them to the point where they are most helpful to you; don't expect to generate your final map on the first try. The concept map for my model of qualitative research design (Figure 1.1) went through many iterations before settling into its current form. In addition, no map can capture everything important about the phenomena you're studying; every map is a simplified and incomplete model of a more complex reality.

One useful way of developing a concept map is on a blackboard or whiteboard, where you can erase unsuccessful attempts or pieces that don't seem to work well, and play with possible arrangements and connections. (The disadvantage of this is that it doesn't automatically create a paper trail of your attempts; such a trail can help you understand how your theory has changed and avoid repeating the same mistakes.) There are also many computer programs that can be used to create concept maps; I used one

Figure 3.1   A Study of Newfoundland Principals' Craft Knowledge

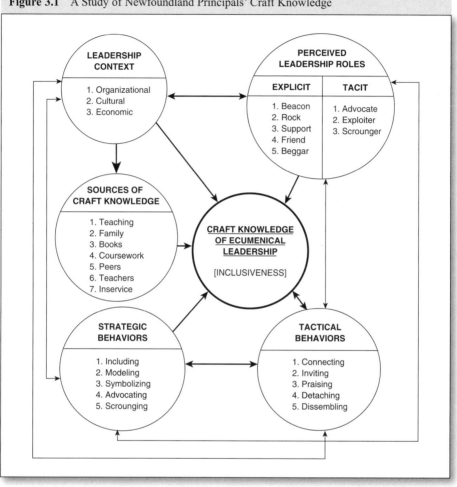

SOURCE: From *Swamp Leadership: The Wisdom of the Craft*, by B. Croskery, 1995, unpublished doctoral dissertation, Harvard Graduate School of Education.

of the most popular ones, Inspiration, to create many of the diagrams for this book. Strauss (1987, pp. 171–182) provided a valuable transcript of his consultation with one student, Leigh Star, in helping her develop a conceptual framework and concept map for her research. Exercise 3.1 suggests some ways of getting started on creating concept maps of your conceptual framework.

Figure 3.2   Factors Affecting the Decision to Keep a Dependent Adult Child at Home

The following factors appear to influence the decisions to keep at home an adult family member who is dependent because of disabilities, rather than "placing" or "institutionalizing" the adult child.

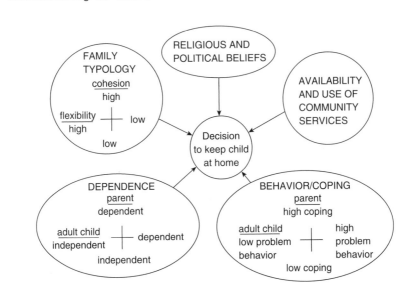

FAMILY TYPOLOGY is a model of intrafamily interactions and permeability of family boundaries developed by David Kantor and expanded by Larry Constantine. Although I have not collected data on family typologies, intuition and existing data favor the prediction that families in the upper-right quadrant (closed family systems) and lower-right quadrant (synchronous family systems) are more likely to keep the dependent adult child at home, whereas families in the upper-left quadrant (open families) and lower-left quadrant (random families) are more likely to place the adult child.

  In the Dependence grid, preliminary data indicate that the upper-left quadrant (high parental dependence, low child dependence) tends to correlate with a decision to keep the adult child at home, whereas the lower-right quadrant (parental independence, high care needs in a child) tends to correlate with placing the adult child.

  Similarly, in the behavior/coping grid, the upper-left quadrant (minimal behavior problems, high parental coping) tends to correlate with keeping the adult child at home, whereas the lower-right quadrant (serious behavior problems, low parental coping) tends to correlate with a decision to place the adult child.

SOURCE: Adapted from *The Families of Dependent Handicapped Adults: A Working Paper*, by B. Guilbault, 1989, unpublished manuscript.

Figure 3.3   Causes of Changes in Blackfeet Kin Terminology

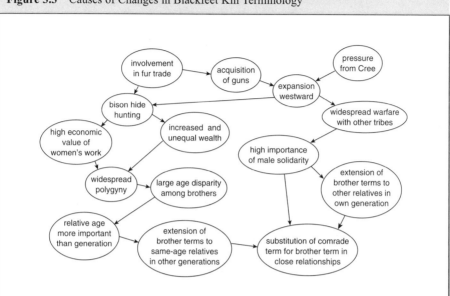

This map displays some of the events and influences leading to the wide-spread use of brother terms in Blackfeet society by the late 1800s. More than any other Plains tribe, the Blackfeet were involved in the fur trade. This led to increased wealth (including guns), a greater value of women's work in preparing bison hides for trade, a highly unequal distribution of wealth that favored men who had many horses for bison hunting, and a massive increase in polygyny, as wealthy men acquired large numbers of wives to process hides. The acquisition of guns and horses allowed the Blackfeet to move westward into the Plains, driving out the tribes that had previously lived there. The increase in warfare and bison hunting created a greater need for male solidarity and led to the widespread use of brother terms between men of the same generation to enhance this solidarity. However, the increased polygyny led to a wider range of ages within a man's generation and to the extension of brother terms to men of other generations who were of about the speaker's age. This proliferation of the use of brother terms eventually diluted their solidarity value, generating a new term, "comrade," which was often used in close relationships between men.

SOURCE: Adapted from *The Development of Plains Kinship Systems*, by J. A. Maxwell, 1971, unpublished master's thesis, University of Chicago, and "The Evolution of Plains Indian Kin Terminologies: A Non-Reflectionist Account," by J. A. Maxwell, 1978, *Plains Anthropologist*, *23*, 13–29.

Figure 3.4   Excerpt From an Event-State Network: Perry-Parkdale School

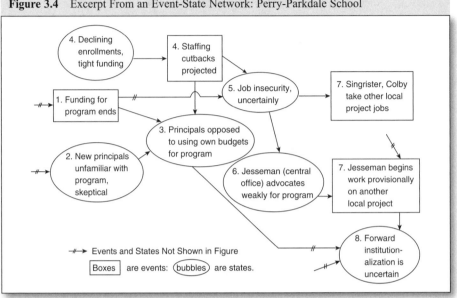

SOURCE: From *Qualitative Data Analysis: An Expanded Sourcebook* (2nd ed.), by M. B. Miles and A. M. Huberman, 1994, Thousand Oaks, CA: Sage.

Figure 3.5   Excerpt From a Causal Network: Perry-Parkdale School

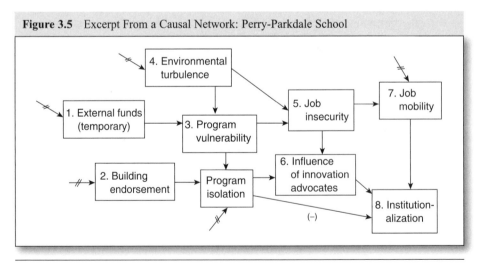

SOURCE: From *Qualitative Data Analysis: An Expanded Sourcebook* (2nd ed.), by M. B. Miles and A. M. Huberman, 1994, Thousand Oaks, CA: Sage.

Figure 3.6 is a more elaborate concept map developed by Kate Zinsser for a team study of children's development of socioemotional competence, and Example 3.1 is a detailed memo on this map; my comments to Kate are in brackets.

Figure 3.6 Concept Map for a Study of Children's Development of Socioemotional Competence

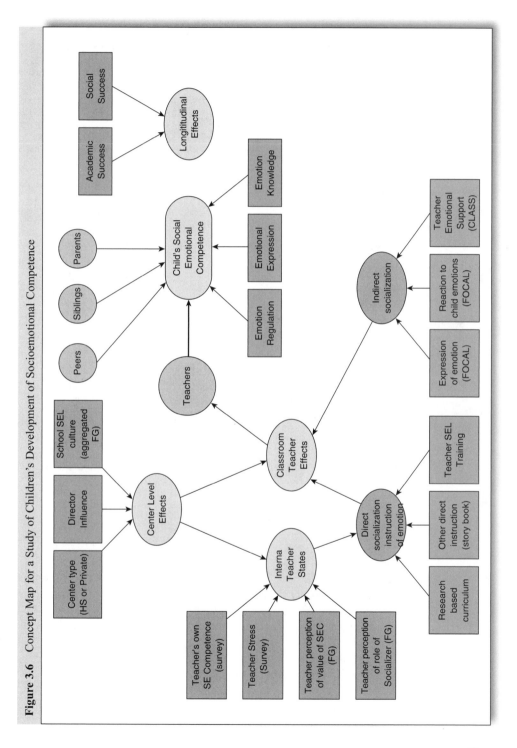

Example 3.1   Memo on the Concept Map in Figure 3.6

With the number of three- and four-year-olds in preschool steadily increasing, it is critical that we thoroughly explore how their interactions with adults outside of the home can additionally influence their development. Social emotional competence (SEC) has been linked to later achievement both academically and socially, but the process of becoming competent is not a matter of just attending to lessons on sharing and being nice. Teachers operate in a complex context, and their interactions with students, either directly planned or more informal, are influenced by their past experiences, personal beliefs and skills, and center level requirements and culture. The TASSEL project will be using a wide range of methods to grapple with all of these sources of influence to understand what teachers are doing to help children become socially and emotionally competent.

The attached concept map depicts our most recent foray into the social emotional world of three- and four-year-olds. Starting on the right-hand side, children's social emotional competence is understood to impact concurrent and longitudinal academic and social success. Children who are more competent are viewed by the teachers as more engaged learners, are more well liked by their peers, and are better adjusted to the formal classroom environment. But what constitutes a socially and emotionally competent child? We define competence as the integration of three skills that children are building and learning throughout early childhood: emotion regulation, emotion knowledge, and emotion expression. [One of the common limitations of concept maps is that the arrows can represent a number of different things, which usually aren't distinguished in the map. For example, emotion regulation etc. are *components of* SEC, rather than influences on this, but this isn't clear from the map. Graphically representing these *as* components could raise some interesting questions—for example, do teachers predominantly influence one of these more than others?]

Social emotional competence develops through transactional relationships with other social players in a child's world: parents, peers, sibling, and teachers. Previous work by Dr. Susanne Denham has examined the influences of parents and peers on social emotional development; this project focuses on the role of teachers. For teachers, this socialization process (represented by the bold arrow from teacher to SEC) is more than the teacher showing the child emotion flashcards or teaching him not to bite. The teacher-child processes that contribute to a child's social emotional competence can be broken into two categories: direct/instructional socialization and indirect/informal socialization.

Direct socialization may include any social emotional learning (SEL) curriculum that the teacher is implementing in the classroom (e.g., Al's Pals or PATHS), any previous training she received on increasing children's social emotional learning (SEL) [but this would depend on whether she *uses* this; would it make more sense to see this as an influence *on* curriculum?], and any use of everyday instructional moments to emphasize emotional constructs, such as identifying emotions felt by characters in a storybook. A majority of this direct socialization process we can measure using surveys of the teachers [I'm not sure about "a majority," particularly for everyday instructional moments (is the teacher always aware of these?)] and center directors, or by enumerating the number of emotion words a teacher uses when describing pictures in a wordless storybook.

Indirect socialization of emotions encompasses teacher behaviors in the classroom outside of purposeful/planned emotion instruction. This can include what emotions she expresses in the classroom (happiness, sadness, anger, frustration, pride, etc.) and how she reacts to children's displays of emotions (dismissing, acknowledging, ignoring, etc.). We assess these behaviors through an observational coding technique called the FOCAL. Additionally, indirect socialization can include a teacher's overall provision of emotional support in the classroom: How available is she for student interaction? How aware is she of student needs and potential causes of frustration or conflict? Emotional support is also coded using a naturalistic behavioral observation of the teachers called the CLASS.

Paramount to understanding the direct and indirect processes of socialization is understanding the context in which they're occurring. We've broken the teacher socialization context into two areas: center level effects and internal teacher states. Center level effects encompass aspects of the school environment that may be influencing how a teacher directly or indirectly socializes children's SEC. The type of center (Head Start, private, Montessori, etc.) may impose corporate or federal constrains on the way teachers interact with students, the curriculum that is taught in classrooms, and so on. Similarly, the director may have some control over classroom processes, schedules, and curriculum choices. The center and director level influences will be assessed using surveys and by examining programmatic standards and manuals. Last, the center itself may have a collective culture surrounding the importance of children's SEL that may influence both internal teacher perceptions and classroom processes. The SEL culture in a school will be examined via focus group responses examined at the center level.

Finally, a teacher's experiences with emotions may be influencing her interactions with students in her class. Probably the most direct internal contributor will be a teacher's social emotional competence. Less competent teachers may struggle to regulate negative emotions in the classroom (which may be observed with the FOCAL) or have difficulty separating stress (personal or school related) from her interactions with students. Additionally, teachers' perceptions of the value of SEC and her beliefs about who is responsible for teaching children about emotions may also influence her reactions to students' emotions (as observed with the FOCAL) and her ability to implement any required curriculum or use her training with high fidelity. Teachers'

(Continued)

(Continued)

perceptions and beliefs will be captured using focus groups, one-on-one follow-up interviews, and surveys. [These two categories of socialization context seem to ignore a potentially important contextual influence—the teacher's *relationships* with the students, or with a particular student. I'm not convinced that this can be reduced to "internal states," because it depends on the student as well as the teacher.]

Exercise 3.1   Creating a Concept Map for Your Study

How do you develop a concept map? First, you need to have a set of concepts to work with. These can come from existing theory, from your experience, or from the people you are studying—their *own* concepts of what's going on. The main thing to keep in mind is that at this point you are trying to represent the theory *you already have* about the phenomena you are studying, not primarily to invent a new theory.

If you don't already have a clear conceptual framework for this, there are several strategies you can use to develop your map.

1. Think about the key words you use in talking about this topic; these probably represent important concepts in your theory. You can pull some of these concepts directly from things you've already written about your research.

2. Take something you've already written and try to map the theory that is implicit (or explicit) in this. (This is often the best approach for people who don't think visually and prefer to work with prose.)

3. Take one key concept, idea, or term and brainstorm all of the things that might be related to this, then go back and select those that seem most directly relevant to your study.

4. Ask someone to interview you about your topic, probing for what you think is going on and why; then listen to the tape and write down the main terms you use in talking about it. Don't ignore concepts based on your experience rather than the literature; these can be central to your conceptual framework.

Strauss (1987, pp. 182–183) and Miles and Huberman (1994, p. 22) provided additional advice on how to develop concept maps for your study.

Once you've generated some concepts to work with, ask yourself how these are related. What connections do you see among them? Leigh Star (quoted in Strauss, 1987, p. 179) suggested beginning with one category or concept and drawing "tendrils" to others. What do you think are the important connections between the concepts you're using? The key pieces of a concept map aren't the circles, but the arrows;

these represent proposed *relationships* between the concepts or events. Ask yourself the following questions: What do I mean by this particular arrow? What does it *stand for?* Think of *concrete* examples of what you're dealing with, rather than working only with abstractions. Don't lock yourself into the first set of categories you select, or the first arrangement you try. Brainstorm different ways of putting the concepts together; move the categories around to see what works best. Ask questions about the diagram, draw possible connections, and think about whether they make sense.

Finally, write a *narrative or memo* of what this concept map says about the phenomena you are studying. Try to capture in words the ideas that are embodied in the diagram. Figures 3.2 and 3.3 present concept maps with accompanying narratives; Miles and Huberman (1994, pp. 135–136, 159–161) and Strauss (1987, pp. 203–209) provided additional examples. This is an important part of the exercise, and can suggest ways to develop your theory. For example, it can point out when something in your map is simply a placeholder for the actual concept or relationship that you need; Becker (2007) described such placeholders as "meaning nothing in themselves, [but] they mark a place that needs a real idea" (p. 83; he also gave a good example of this on pp. 52–53).

Avoid getting stuck in what Miles and Huberman (1994, p. 22) called a "no-risk" map, in which all the concepts are global and abstract and there are two-directional arrows everywhere. This sort of diagram can be useful as a brainstorming exercise at the beginning, providing you with a conceptual checklist of things that may be important in your research, but at some point, you need to *focus* the theory. It can be useful at some point to narrow your map to two concepts and the relationship between them, as an exercise in focusing on what's most central to your theory. Make *commitments* to what you think is most important and relevant in your theory.

An initial framework often works best with large categories that hold a lot of things that you haven't yet sorted out. However, you should try to differentiate these categories, making explicit your ideas about the relationships among the items in them. One way to start this is by analyzing each one into subcategories, identifying the different *kinds* of things that go into each. (Figure 3.1 does this for the peripheral categories that connect to the core category.) Another way is to *dimensionalize* the categories (Strauss & Corbin, 1990), trying to separate out their different properties. (Figure 3.2 does this for several of the categories.)

How do you know whether something is a category or a relationship? This is not an easy question to answer; I do this rather intuitively. In fact, many things can be seen as either; there is no one right concept map for the phenomena you're studying, and different maps incorporate different understandings of what's going on. You should try *alternative* maps for the theory you are developing, rather than sticking rigidly with one formulation. There are also different *kinds* of concept maps, with different purposes; these include the following:

   a. An abstract framework mapping the relationship among concepts

   b. A flowchart-like account of events and how you think these are connected

   c. A causal network of variables or influences

   d. A treelike diagram of the meanings of words (e.g., Miles & Huberman, 1994, p. 133)

   e. A Venn diagram, representing concepts as overlapping circles (e.g., Miles & Huberman, 1994, p. 249)

You can use more than one of these in a given study; the bottom line is their *usefulness* to you in advancing your understanding of what's going on. Most of Miles and Huberman's (1994) examples are best suited to studies of social processes; they aren't necessarily the most useful models for a study of meanings and their relationship to one another. Remember that a concept map is not an end in itself; it is a *tool* for developing theory and making that theory more explicit. Also, keep in mind that a concept map is not something that you do once and are finished with; you should go back and rework your concept maps as your understanding of the phenomena you are studying develops. Don't try to make your map too elegant; this may be the visual equivalent of what Becker (2007) called "classy writing" (p. 28), in which you are trying to impress people rather than develop and communicate your actual ideas.

Different authors use concept maps in different ways. Novak and Gowin (1984) took a very inclusive approach—their concepts and relationships could be almost anything, and they labeled their connections in order to keep these clear. Miles and Huberman (1994), on the other hand, were much more focused—their connections generally referred to causal relationships or influences. My advice is to aim for something in between. You can start with a fairly inclusive map, but you should work to focus it and to make it a map of a real *theory* of what's going on.

A key distinction, but one that you may not want to think about until *after* you've developed an initial concept map, is the difference between *variance* maps and *process* maps. (See Chapter 2 on the distinction between variance theory and process theory.) One way to tell the difference is that a variance map usually deals with abstract, general concepts that can take different values (in other words, *variables*), and is essentially timeless; it depicts a general causal or correlational relationship between some factors or properties of things and others. A process map, on the other hand, tells a story; there is a beginning and an end, and the concepts are often specific events or situations, rather than variables.[4] Many students create a variance map in their first attempt at concept mapping, because this is their idea of what theory "ought to" look like, even if their research questions are "how" questions that cry out for a process theory. Figures 3.2 and 3.5 are variance maps, while Figures 3.3 and 3.4 are process maps.

Other Uses of Existing Research

A review of prior research can serve many other purposes besides providing you with existing theory (cf. Strauss, 1987, pp. 48–56). Locke, Silverman, and Spirduso (2009) provide a clear and detailed explanation of how to read research publications for a variety of useful tools and resources, which they describe as "finding valuables in research reports" (p. 3). These valuables include new terminology, including keywords to use in searches; references to other publications and researchers; ways of framing research questions, describing the research, or presenting theory, results, or conclusions; and identification of validity issues and ways of dealing with these. Students often overlook such information in their literature reviews, not seeing its value for their research. You need to learn to read for all of these types of information, and to use these in designing your research.

I would emphasize four specific things, in addition to theory, that prior research can contribute to your research design. First, it can help you to develop a *justification* for your study—to show how your work will address an important need or unanswered question. Martha Regan-Smith (1991) used prior research on medical school teaching in this way in her proposal (see Appendix A), showing why the topic she planned to study was important, and demonstrating that previous studies had not answered the specific questions she posed. Such a justification connects your plans to your goals for doing the study (Chapter 2), and I discuss this in more detail in Chapter 7, as part of creating an argument for your research proposal.

Second, prior research can inform your decisions about *methods,* suggesting alternative approaches or identifying potential methodological problems or solutions. Don't skip the methods sections of papers; see if what the authors did makes sense, if there were problems with their study that bring their results into question, and if you can use any of their strategies or methods for your study. If you need more information on what they did, contact the authors; they will usually be glad to help you.

Third, prior research can be a source of *data* that can be used to test or modify your theories. You can see if existing theory, pilot research, or your experiential understanding are supported or challenged by previous results. Doing this will often require thinking through the *implications* of your theory or understanding to see if these are consistent with others' findings. This is one example of a *thought experiment*, which I discuss later in this chapter.

Finally, prior research can help you *generate* theory. Bernd Heinrich (1984, pp. 55–68), while conducting his thesis research on thermoregulation in sphinx moths, discovered that his experimental finding that these moths maintain a constant body temperature while flying was directly contradicted by others' research. He described his response as follows:

> As a first step in my decision to proceed, I spent a few months in the library reading about insect physiology in general and everything about sphinx moths in particular. Something in the known physiology and morphology might provide a clue. It would be necessary to collect more and more details on the problem until I could visualize it as closely as if it were a rock sitting in the palm of my hand. I wanted to find out *how* the moths were thermoregulating. . . .
>
> I came across an obscure French paper of 1919 by Franz Brocher on the anatomy of the blood circulatory system in sphinx moths. The odd thing about these moths is that the aorta makes a loop through their thoracic muscles. In many or most other insects, it passes *underneath* these muscles. (Heinrich, 1984, pp. 63–64)

This paper gave Heinrich the critical clue to how these moths were regulating their body temperature: They were shunting blood through the thoracic muscles (which move the moths' wings) to cool these muscles, which would otherwise overheat, and then losing the excess heat from the abdomen, in the same way that a car's water pump and radiator cool the engine. This theory was confirmed by subsequent experiments.

It is possible, of course, to become *too* immersed in the literature; as C. Wright Mills (1959) warned, "You may drown in it. . . . Perhaps the point is to know when you ought to read, and when you ought not to" (p. 214). One of Mills's main ways of dealing with this problem was, in reading, to always be thinking of empirical studies that could test the ideas he gained from the literature, both as preparation for actual research and as an exercise of the imagination (p. 205). These two strategies connect to the final two sources for your conceptual framework: pilot studies and thought experiments.

PILOT AND EXPLORATORY STUDIES

Pilot studies serve some of the same functions as prior research, but they can be focused more precisely on your concerns and theories. You can design pilot studies specifically to test your ideas or methods and explore their implications, or to inductively develop *grounded* theory. What Light, Singer, and Willett (1990) said about an illustrative quantitative study is equally true for qualitative research: "Many features of their design could not be determined without prior exploratory research" (p. 212). And they argued that

> No design is ever so complete that it cannot be improved by a prior, small-scale exploratory study. Pilot studies are almost always worth the time and effort. Carry out a pilot study if *any* facet of your design needs clarification. (p. 213)

Example 3.4 describes how Carol Kaffenberger (1991), whose decision to study adolescent cancer survivors and their siblings was presented in Example 2.1, used a pilot study to help design her dissertation research.

Example 3.4   How a Student Used a Pilot Study to Help Design Her Dissertation Research

Following her decision to change her dissertation topic, and a review of the literature on her new topic, Carol Kaffenberger decided to conduct a pilot study to help her plan her dissertation research. She chose to use her family for this pilot study, for several reasons. First, she wanted to practice her interviews, and believed that her family would provide good feedback and suggestions about her methods and what it was like to be a participant in such a study. Second, she wanted to get a better understanding of the meaning of the cancer experience for her family (one of the personal goals of her research), and to test her assumptions about this experience. Third, for personal reasons, she wanted her children to have firsthand knowledge of the work she was about to begin. Finally, her family was a convenient choice, and wouldn't require her to find and gain approval from other families.

Carol learned several valuable things from this pilot study. First, she found that she needed to revise her interview guide, adding questions about issues that she hadn't realized were important, such as family relationships before the diagnosis, the support siblings received during diagnosis and treatment, and how they thought the experience would affect their future. She also discovered additional useful questions, such as asking participants to describe specific events that illustrated what they had been saying. Second, she gained a deeper understanding of her children's experiences, modifying her conceptual framework. Both previous research and her prior beliefs had led her to underestimate the long-term consequences of the cancer experience for her family. She learned that she needed to step back and listen to participants' experiences in new ways. Finally, she found that her children's responses were sometimes guarded and predictable, due to the consequences of what they said for family relationships, and tended to minimize negative feelings or blame. Although the pilot study was valuable, it could not fully answer the questions she had (Kaffenberger, 1999).

One important use that pilot studies have in qualitative research is to develop an understanding of the concepts and theories held by the people you are studying—a potential source of theory described earlier. You can't usually gain information about these without doing pilot research or until you've actually begun your study—one reason that your conceptual framework must often change in response to what you are learning. This is not simply a source of additional terms or concepts to use in your theory, ones that are drawn from the language of participants; the latter is a type of concept that Strauss (1987, pp. 33–34) called "in-vivo codes." More important, it provides you with an understanding of the *meaning* that these things, actions, and events have for the people who are involved in them, and the perspectives that inform their actions. These meanings and perspectives are not theoretical abstractions; they are real, as real as people's behavior, though not directly visible (Maxwell, 2011b). People's ideas, meanings, and values are essential parts of the situations and activities you study, and if you don't understand these, your theories about what's going on will often be incomplete or mistaken (Maxwell, 2004a; Menzel, 1978). In a qualitative study, these meanings and perspectives should constitute a key component of your theory; as discussed in Chapter 2, they are one of the things your theory is *about,* not simply a source of theoretical insights and building blocks for the latter. In Example 3.2, the norms and values held by the physicians studied by Freidson (1975) were a major part of what was going on in the medical practice, and were fundamental to his theory. Such meanings and perspectives are also key components of all of the previous examples of concept maps (Figures 3.1 through 3.6). Even in Figure 3.5, in which the concepts are mostly stated in behavior or contextual terms, "job insecurity" refers to *perceived* insecurity; if participants were unaware that their jobs might be eliminated, their behavior wouldn't be affected.

THOUGHT EXPERIMENTS

Thought experiments have a long and respected tradition in the physical sciences; much of Einstein's work was based on thought experiments, and Galileo's classic disproof of Aristotle's view that objects fall at a speed relative to their mass, supposedly shown by dropping two balls of different weights from the top of the Leaning Tower of Pisa, was actually a simple thought experiment (Galilei, 1628/2008; see "Galileo's Leaning Tower of Pisa Experiment," n.d.), completely convincing without any need for empirical demonstration. Thought experiments are also common in biology; for example, Bernd Heinrich (1999, pp. 252–254) provides a detailed thought experiment on how the reported "guiding" behavior of ravens, leading Eskimo hunters to their prey, could have evolved. Thought experiments are regularly used in social sciences such as economics, but have received little attention as an explicit technique in discussions of research design, particularly qualitative research design.

The best guide to thought experiments in the social sciences that I know of is that of Lave and March (1975), who used the phrase "speculative model building" for this concept. Don't be intimidated by the word "model"; models are no more esoteric than theory, and Lave and March defined *model* as "a simplified picture of a part of the real world" (p. 3). They described their book as "a practical guide to speculation," and provided a detailed introduction to the development and use of speculative models of some process that could have produced an observed result. Although the orientation of their later chapters is mainly quantitative, the first three chapters are very readable and extremely useful for qualitative researchers. Lave and March stated,

> We will treat models of human behavior as a form of art, and their development as a kind of studio exercise. Like all art, model building requires a combination of discipline and playfulness. It is an art that is learnable. It has explicit techniques, and practice leads to improvement. (p. 4)

Thought experiments challenge you to come up with plausible explanations for your and others' observations, and to think about how to support or disprove these. They draw on both theory and experience to answer "what if" questions, and to explore the logical implications of your models, assumptions, and expectations of the things you plan to study. They can both generate new theoretical models and insights, and test your current theory for problems; in fact, all theory building involves thought experiments to some extent. They encourage creativity and a sense of discovery, and can help you to make explicit the experiential knowledge that you already possess. Ursula LeGuin, a master of science-fiction thought experiments (e.g., 2003), stated, "The purpose of a thought-experiment, as the term was used by Schroedinger and other physicists, is not to predict the future . . . but to describe reality, the present world." (LeGuin, 2000, p. xi).

Example 3.5 is an illustration of this kind of speculative thinking, and Exercise 3.2 (based on one of Lave and March's, 1975, examples) provides a simple problem on which to practice your speculative skills. According to Lave and March (1975), "the best way to learn about model building is to do it" (p. 10).

Example 3.5   Using a Thought Experiment to Develop a Theory of the Persistence of Illiteracy

One of my students, Dixie Hallaj, doing research on illiteracy in the Middle East, used the concept of "cycle of illiteracy" in a memo explaining the persistence of illiteracy in parts of this area. This concept has a certain immediate plausibility—illiterate parents are much more likely to have illiterate children than are literate parents. However, my first reaction to the memo was to perform a thought experiment—to try to think of a *process* by which illiteracy in one generation would create illiteracy in the next generation. Lack of reading materials in the home would have some impact, as might parental values regarding literacy. However, none of these seemed powerful enough to reproduce illiteracy at a time when most children have access to schooling. On the other hand, I *could* easily imagine (and support with data that this student had presented) a cycle of *poverty,* in which poor (and often illiterate) families would be under great pressure to keep their children out of school to work in the home or in farming, depriving the children of their main opportunity to learn to read and write. As a result, these children's lack of schooling would make it difficult for them to get jobs that would enable them to escape from poverty, thus recreating the conditions that led to their illiteracy. This theory suggests that reducing poverty would have a major impact on illiteracy. It also implies that research on the causes of illiteracy needs to address the role of economic factors. Dixie used this thought experiment to develop a more complex model, which she called a "spiral of illiteracy," that incorporated poverty and other factors, as well as the increasing literacy demands of society (Hallaj, 2006).

Exercise 3.2   Creating a Model of the Development of Friendship Patterns

Suppose we were interested in patterns of friendship among college students. Why are some people friends and not others? We might begin by asking all of the residents of single rooms along a particular dormitory corridor to give us a list of their friends. These lists of friends are our initial data, the results we wish to understand.

If we stare at the lists for a while, we eventually notice a pattern in them. Friends tend to live close to one another; they tend to have adjacent dormitory rooms. What process could have produced this pattern of friendship?

STOP AND THINK. Take a minute to think of a possible process that might produce this observed result.

One *possible* process that might have led to this result is that students can choose their dormitory rooms, and that groups of friends tend to choose adjacent rooms. This process is a speculation about the world. *If* the real world were like our model world, the observed facts should match the model's prediction. Thus, we have found a model, a process, that accounts for our results.

We do not stop here, however. We next ask what other implications this model has. For one, it implies that students in each dormitory friendship group must have known one another previously; thus, they must have attended the university the previous year; thus, there will be fewer friendship clusters among freshmen.

A survey of both a freshman dorm and a junior-senior dorm shows that there are as many friendship clusters among freshmen as among juniors and seniors. This would not be predicted by our model, unless the students knew one another in high school. However, examining the backgrounds of the freshmen shows that almost all of them come from different high schools.

So our model does not do a very good job of explaining what we observed. Some process other than mutual selection by prior friends must be involved. So we try to imagine another process that could have led to these results. Our new speculation is that most college students come from similar backgrounds, and thus have enough in common that they could become friends. Pairs of students who live near each other will have more opportunities for interaction, and are more likely to discover these common interests and values, thus becoming friends. This new speculation explains the presence of friendship clusters in freshman dorms as well as in junior-senior dorms.

STOP AND THINK. What other implications does this model have that would allow you to test it? *How* would you test it?

One implication is that since the chance of contact increases over time, the friendship clusters should become larger as the school year progresses. You could test this by surveying students at several different times during the year. If you did so and discovered that the prediction was correct, the model would seem more impressive. (Can you think of other testable implications?)

—Adapted from Lave and March
(1975, pp. 10–12)

One issue that Lave and March's example does *not* deal with is the possibility of alternative models that *also* predict most of the same things as the model you have developed. This is one of the most challenging aspects of model building, and the source of a common flaw in theoretical modeling—accepting a model that successfully predicts a substantial number of things, without seriously attempting to come up with alternative models that would make the same (or better) predictions. For example, Lave and March make an assumption, a widespread one in modern Western societies, that friendship is necessarily based on common characteristics—shared interests and values. An alternative model would be one that abandons this assumption, and postulates that friendship can be created by interaction itself, and not necessarily by common characteristics (see Example 3.1 and Maxwell, 2011b, Chapter 4).

STOP AND THINK. What tests could distinguish between these two models?

One possible test would be to investigate the beliefs, interests, and values of freshman dormitory students at both the beginning and the end of the year, to see if pairs of friends consistently had more in common at the beginning of the year than did pairs of students in the same dorm who did *not* become friends. (Determining this similarity at the beginning of the year addresses a possible alternative explanation for greater similarity of beliefs and interests within friendship pairs—that this similarity is a *result* of their friendship, rather than a cause.) If you find that pairs of friends did *not* consistently have more in common than pairs of nonfriends, then Lave and March's model seems less plausible (at least without modification), because it predicts that friends will have more in common than nonfriends. My alternative model *does* predict this result, and therefore, would deserve further consideration and testing. Eventually, you might develop a more complex model that incorporates both processes.

All of the tests described previously (and the standard approach to model testing in general) are based on variance theory—measuring selected variables to see if they fit the model's predictions. However, there is a much more direct way to test the model—*investigate the actual process*, rather than just its predicted consequences (Menzel, 1978, pp. 163–168). For example, you might do participant observation of student interactions at the beginning of the year, looking at how friendships originate, or interview students about how they became friends with other students. This realist, process-oriented approach to model testing is much better suited to qualitative research than is simply predicting outcomes and collecting data to see if these are confirmed (Maxwell, 2004a, 2004c, 2011b).

Experience, prior theory and research, pilot studies, and thought experiments are the four major possible sources of the conceptual framework for your study. Putting together a conceptual framework from these sources is a unique process for each study, and specific guidelines for how to do this are not of much use; you should look at examples of others' conceptual frameworks to see how they have done this (e.g., Ravitch & Riggan, 2011). The main thing to keep in mind is the need for integration of these components with one another, and with your goals and research questions. The connections between your conceptual framework and your research questions will be taken up in the next chapter.

NOTES

1. This understanding of a conceptual framework as simply a visual model of the main concepts of your theory often creates difficulties in making explicit your real conceptual framework for your study—your actual understanding of the things you plan to study. As explained in my discussion of concept maps, such a simplified visual display can be useful for representing your ideas, but it necessarily leaves out a key ingredient: the nature of the connections that you see between these concepts—the arrows in your map.

2. For a more detailed explanation of this point, see Locke, Spirduso, and Silverman (2007, pp. 68–70) and Maxwell (2006).

3. For a detailed account of the ways in which researchers can use theory in formulating their goals, research questions, and methods, see Dressman (2008) and LeCompte and Preissle (1993, pp. 115–157).

4. Miles and Huberman (1994) tended to refer to variance maps as "causal networks," and to process maps as "event-state networks" (pp. 101–171). This incorrectly equates causal analysis with variance analysis; process analysis can also be causal, as discussed in Chapter 2 (see also Maxwell, 2004a, 2011b).

4

Research Questions

What Do You Want to Understand?

Your research questions—what you specifically want to understand by doing your study—are at the heart of your research design. They are the component that most directly links to all of the other components of the design. More than any other aspect of your design, your research questions will have an influence on, and should be responsive to, every other part of your study.

In many works on research design, research questions are presented as the *starting point* and primary determinant of the design. Such approaches don't adequately capture the interactive and inductive nature of qualitative research. Certainly, *if* you already have well-grounded, feasible research questions that are *worth* answering (and this implies goals and knowledge that justify these questions), the rest of your design (especially your methods and conceptual framework) should initially be constructed to address these questions. In qualitative research, however, you usually can't come up with such questions without making use of the other components of your design. Locking onto your research questions before having a pretty good sense of what your theoretical and methodological commitments and options are, and the implications of these for your questions, creates the danger of what quantitative researchers call a Type III error—answering the wrong question.

For this reason, qualitative researchers often don't develop their final research questions until they have done a significant amount of data collection and analysis. (See Example 4.1 and Weiss, 1994, pp. 52–53.) This doesn't mean that qualitative researchers begin a study with *no* questions, simply going into their research with an open mind and seeing what is there to be investigated. As discussed in the previous two chapters, every researcher begins with certain goals and a substantial base of experience and theoretical knowledge, and these inevitably highlight certain problems or issues and generate questions about these. These early, provisional questions frame the study in important ways, guide decisions about methods, and influence (and are influenced by) the conceptual framework, preliminary results, and potential validity concerns. My point is that well-constructed, focused questions are generally the result of an interactive design process, rather than being the starting point for developing a design.

Example 4.1   The Inductive Development of Research Questions

Suman Bhattacharjea's (1994) dissertation dealt with the ways in which the female administrators in an educational district office in Pakistan defined, implemented, and controlled their professional tasks and working environment in a gender-segregated and male-dominated society. She began her fieldwork with a single broad question: What do staff in this office do every day, and who does what? Her position as a consultant to a computer implementation project required her to spend much of her time interacting with the women in this office; the fact that she was female, spoke virtually the same language, and (being from India) was familiar with some aspects of their situation led to acceptance and trust. When she submitted her dissertation proposal, a year after she began the research, she had focused her study on two specific questions:

1. What is the nature of the expectations that affect female administrators' actions?

2. What strategies do female administrators adopt to deal with these constraints in the context of a gender-segregated and male-dominated environment?

On the basis of the research she had already done, she was able to formulate three propositions (or hypotheses) as tentative answers to these questions:

1. Female administrators' actions reflect their desire to *maintain harmony* between their roles as women in a gender-segregated society and their roles as officials within a bureaucracy.

2. The major strategy female administrators use in this regard is to try to create a family-like environment at work, interacting with their colleagues in ways that parallel their interactions in a domestic setting and thus blurring the distinction between "public" and "private."

3. The implications of this strategy for female administrators' actions depend on the *context* of their interaction—in particular, where this context lies on the public/private continuum. Women use different strategies when interacting with other women (most private or family-like), with male colleagues within the office, and with other men (least private or family-like).

In this chapter, I will discuss the purposes that research questions can accomplish in a research design, consider the kinds of questions that a qualitative study can best investigate, and give some suggestions on how you can develop appropriate and productive research questions.

THE FUNCTIONS OF RESEARCH QUESTIONS

In a research proposal or published paper, the function of your research questions is to explain specifically what your study is intended to learn or understand. In your research *design*, the research questions serve two other vital functions as well: to help you to focus the study (the questions' relationships to your goals and conceptual framework) and to give you guidance for how to conduct it (their relationship to methods and validity) (cf. Miles & Huberman, 1994, pp. 22–25).

A design in which the research questions are too general or too diffuse creates difficulties both in conducting the study—in knowing what sites or participants to choose, what data to collect, and how to analyze these data—and in clearly connecting your results to your goals and conceptual framework. If your questions remain on the "What's going on here?" level, you have no clear guide in deciding what data to collect, in selecting or generating relevant theory for your study, or in anticipating and dealing with significant validity issues. More precisely framed research questions, in contrast, can point you to specific areas of theory that you can use as modules in developing an understanding of what's going on, and can suggest ways to do the study.

On the other hand, it is possible for your questions to be *too* focused; they may create tunnel vision, leaving out things that are important to the goals (both intellectual and practical) of the study or your understanding of what is going on and why. Research questions that are precisely framed too early in the study may lead you to overlook relevant areas of theory or prior experience, or cause you to not pay enough attention to data that reveal important and unanticipated phenomena and relationships.

A third potential problem is that you may be smuggling unexamined assumptions into the research questions themselves, imposing a conceptual framework that doesn't fit the reality you're studying. A research question such as "How do teachers deal with the experience of isolation from their colleagues in their classrooms?" assumes that teachers do experience such isolation. Such an assumption needs to be carefully examined and justified, and a question of this form may be better placed as a subquestion to broader questions about the nature of classroom teachers' experience of their work and their relations with colleagues.

Fourth, there is the possibility, an unfortunate but not unknown one with students beginning to write dissertation proposals, that the stated research questions bear little relationship to the students' actual goals and beliefs about what's going on. Instead, they are constructed to satisfy what the students think research questions should look like, or what they think committee members will want to see in the proposal. Such questions may be inconsistent with other parts of the design. (See the discussion of Potemkin villages in Chapter 7.) In qualitative research, such questions are often the result of adopting quantitative research conventions for framing questions, conventions that are often inappropriate for a qualitative study.

For all of these reasons, there is a real danger in not carefully formulating your research questions in connection with the other components of your design. Your research questions need to take account of why you want to do the study (your goals), your connections to a (or several) research paradigm(s), and what is already known about the things you want to study and your tentative theories about these phenomena (your conceptual framework). You don't want to pose questions for which the answer is already available, that don't clearly connect to what you think is actually going on, or that, even if you answer them, won't advance your goals.

Similarly, your research questions need to be answerable by the kind of study you could actually conduct. You don't want to pose questions that no feasible study could answer, either because the data that might answer them could not be obtained or because the conclusions you might draw would be subject to serious validity threats. These issues will be covered in more detail in the next two chapters.

To develop appropriate research questions for your study, you need to understand clearly what a research question is, and the different kinds of research questions that you might construct. I will first discuss the nature of research questions in general, and then introduce some specific distinctions among research questions that are important for qualitative studies.

RESEARCH QUESTIONS AND OTHER KINDS OF QUESTIONS

A common problem in developing research questions is confusion between your research questions and the goals of your study, and within the latter, between intellectual goals—what you want to understand by doing the study—and practical goals—what you want to accomplish. According to LeCompte and Preissle (1993), "distinguishing between the purpose and the research question is the first problem" (p. 37) in coming up with workable research questions. As discussed in Chapter 2, practical concerns often can't be directly addressed by your research questions. These practical goals should inform your research questions, but usually shouldn't be directly incorporated into these questions. Instead, you should frame your research questions so they point you to the information and understanding that will help you accomplish your practical goals or develop the practical implications of what you learn.

For example, a research question such as "How can support services for minority students entering college be improved?" incorporates implicit value assumptions about what would constitute "improvement," and can't be directly answered by the data you collect. (This is different from a research question asking, "How do staff and administrators in this program *believe that* support services for minority students entering college can be improved?" which is a very answerable question for a qualitative study, and one that has direct implications for improving the program.) The former question is often best kept as a goal of the study (to improve support services for minority students entering college). To develop relevant research questions for this goal, you need to ask yourself, "What data could I collect, and what conclusions might I draw from these, that would help me to accomplish this goal?" Your intellectual goals for the study can function as a link between your practical goals and your research questions: What do you need to understand in order to improve these services? The coherence between your practical goals, intellectual goals, and research questions is often something that takes considerable thought and multiple iterations of these.

A second distinction, one that is critical for interview studies, is that between *research* questions and *interview* questions. Your research questions identify the things that you want to understand; your interview questions generate the data that you need to understand these things. These are rarely the same; the distinction is discussed in more detail in Chapter 5.

Research Hypotheses in Qualitative Designs

Research questions are not the same as research hypotheses. Research questions state what you want to learn. Research hypotheses, in contrast, are a statement of your tentative answers to these questions, what you think is going on; these answers are normally based on your theories about, or experiences with, the things you are studying. (See example 4.1.)

The use of explicit research hypotheses is often seen as incompatible with qualitative research. My view, in contrast, is that there is no inherent problem with formulating qualitative research hypotheses; the difficulty has been partly a matter of terminology and partly a matter of the inappropriate application of quantitative standards to qualitative research hypotheses.

Many qualitative researchers explicitly state their ideas about what is going on as part of the process of theorizing and data analysis. These may be called "propositions" rather than hypotheses (Miles & Huberman, 1994, p. 75), but they serve the same function. The distinctive characteristic of hypotheses in qualitative research is that they are typically formulated *after* the researcher has begun the study; they are "grounded" (Glaser & Strauss, 1967) in the data and are developed and tested in interaction with them, rather than being prior ideas that are simply tested against the data.

This runs counter to the view, widespread in quantitative research, that unless a hypothesis is framed in advance of data collection, it can't be legitimately tested by the data. This requirement is essential for the statistical test of a hypothesis; if the hypothesis is framed after seeing the data, the assumptions of the statistical test are violated. Colloquially, this is referred to as a "fishing expedition"—searching through the data to find what seem to be significant relationships. However, qualitative researchers rarely engage in statistical significance testing, so that this argument is largely irrelevant to qualitative research. In addition, statistical significance testing has been widely criticized by many prominent statisticians and researchers; see Endnote 2 in Chapter 2. "Fishing" for possible answers to your questions is perfectly appropriate in qualitative research, as long as these answers are then tested against additional evidence and possible validity threats (see Chapter 6).

One risk in explicitly formulating hypotheses is that, like prior theory, they can act as blinders, preventing you from seeing what's going on. You should regularly reexamine these hypotheses, asking yourself what alternative ways there are of making sense of your data; thought experiments (Chapter 3) are a good way to do this.

I next want to discuss three specific distinctions among kinds of research questions, ones that are important to consider in developing the questions for your study. These distinctions are between general and particular questions, between instrumentalist and realist questions, and between variance and process questions.

GENERAL QUESTIONS AND PARTICULAR QUESTIONS

There is a widespread, but often implicit, assumption, especially in quantitative research, that research questions should be framed in general terms, and then "operationalized" by means of specific sampling and data collection decisions. For example, there is a tendency to state a research question about racial and ethnic differences in a school as "How do students deal with racial and ethnic difference in multiracial schools?" and to then answer this by studying a particular school as a sample from this population of schools, rather than to state the question at the outset as "How do students at North High School deal with racial and ethnic difference?" I will refer to these two types of questions as general and particular questions, respectively.

The assumption that research questions should be stated in general terms may derive, in part, from logical positivism, in which causal explanation was seen as inherently involving general laws, and the goal of science was to discover such laws. However, this assumption has been challenged by some qualitative researchers (e.g., Miles & Huberman, 1994; Schwandt, 1997, p. 14) and realist philosophers (see Maxwell, 2004a), who argue for researchers' ability to observe causation in single cases. It also does not fit a great deal of research in the social sciences and in fields such as education, where particular questions can be appropriate and legitimate. It is especially misleading in applied research, where the focus is usually on understanding and improving some particular program, situation, or practice.

These two types of questions are linked to the difference between a sampling approach and a case-study approach to research. In a sample study, the researcher states a general question about a broad population, and then selects a particular sample from this population to answer the question. In a case study, in contrast, the researcher often selects the case and then states the questions in terms of the particular case selected. A sample study justifies the sampling strategy as a way of attaining representativeness of the specific data collected for the population sampled. A case study, on the other hand, justifies the selection of a particular case in terms of the goals of the study and existing theory and research (this is often called "purposeful selection," and is discussed in Chapter 5), and needs a different kind of argument to support the generalizability of its conclusions (see Chapter 6).

Both approaches are legitimate in qualitative research. Interview studies, in particular, sometimes employ a "sampling" logic, selecting interviewees to generalize to some population of interest. In addition, the larger the study, the more feasible and appropriate a sampling approach becomes; large multisite studies in which generalizability is important (such as those described in Miles & Huberman, 1994) must pay considerable attention to issues of sampling and representativeness.

However, qualitative studies often employ small samples of uncertain representativeness, and this usually means that the study can provide only suggestive answers to any question framed in general terms, such as "How do kindergarten teachers assess the readiness of children for first grade?" A plausible answer to this general question would normally require some sort of probability sampling from the population of all kindergarten teachers, and a larger sample than most qualitative studies can manage. Furthermore, the phrase "kindergarten teachers" is itself in need of further specification. Does it refer only to American teachers? Only to public school teachers? Only to certified teachers? These concerns, and analogous ones that could be raised about any research questions framed in general terms, presuppose a sample framework for the study, and may push the study in a quantitative direction.

On the other hand, a qualitative study *can* confidently answer such a question posed in particular terms, such as "How do the kindergarten teachers *in this school* assess the readiness of children for first grade?" This way of stating the question, although it does not entirely avoid issues of sampling, frames the study much more in "case" terms. The teachers are treated not as a *sample* from some much larger population of teachers to whom the study is intended to generalize, but as a *case* of a group of teachers who are studied in a particular context (the specific school and community). The *selection* of this particular case may involve considerations of representativeness (and certainly any attempt to generalize from the conclusions must take representativeness into account), as discussed in Chapter 5, but the primary concern of the study is not with generalization, but with developing an adequate description, interpretation, and explanation of this case.

In a qualitative study, framing your questions in terms specific to the setting or participants included in your research has several advantages. First, it helps to protect you from inappropriate generalization—assuming that other people or settings are similar to the ones you studied. Second, it can help you to recognize the diversity among the individuals, or within the settings, that you study—not assuming that you have to come up with conclusions or a theory that ignores or minimizes these differences (see Maxwell, 2011b, Chapter 4). Finally, it helps you to focus on the specific beliefs, actions, and events that you observe or ask about, and the actual contexts within which these are situated, rather than seeing these as simply manifestations of abstract, context-free categories. As Marshall and Rossman (1999) stated, a site-specific study is "defined by and intimately linked to that place" (p. 68).

INSTRUMENTALIST QUESTIONS AND REALIST QUESTIONS

As discussed in Chapter 2, social science was long dominated by the positivist view that only theoretical terms whose meaning could be precisely specified in terms of the research operations used to measure them (what came to be called "operational defini-tions") were legitimate in science. (The statement "Intelligence is whatever intelligence tests measure" is a classic example of this view.) Although this position (often called "instrumentalism") has been abandoned by almost all philosophers of science, it still influences the way many researchers think about research questions. Advisors and reviewers often recommend framing research questions in terms of what the respond-ents say or report, or in terms of what can be directly observed, rather than in terms of inferred beliefs, behavior, or causal influences.

For example, Gail Lenehan, for her dissertation, proposed to interview nurses who specialize in treating sexual assault victims, focusing on their cognitive, behavioral, and emotional reactions to this work. Although there is considerable anecdotal evi-dence that these nurses often experience reactions similar to those of their victims, no one had systematically studied this phenomenon. Her research questions included the following:

1. What, if any, are the effects on nurses of working with rape victims?

2. Are there cognitive, psychological, and behavioral responses to having experiences of rape shared with them as well as witnessing victims' suffering after the assault?

Her proposal was not accepted, and the committee, in explaining its decision, argued (among other concerns) that

> The study relies solely on self-report data, but your questions do not reflect this limitation. Each question needs to be reframed in terms that reflect this limitation. Some examples might be: "How do nurses perceive and report . . . the effects of working with rape vic-tims?" or "What specific cognitive, psychological (emotional?), and behavioral responses do nurses report?"

This disagreement illustrates the difference between instrumentalist and realist approaches (Norris, 1983) to research questions. Instrumentalists formulate their ques-tions in terms of observable or measurable data. They worry about the validity threats (such as self-report bias) that the researcher risks in making inferences to unobservable phenomena, and prefer to stick with what they can directly verify. Realists, in contrast, do not assume that research questions and conclusions about feelings, beliefs, inten-tions, prior behavior, effects, and so on, need to be reduced to, or reframed as, questions and conclusions about the actual data that one collects. Instead, they treat these unob-served phenomena as *real,* and their data as *evidence* about these, to be used critically to develop and test ideas about the existence and nature of the phenomena (Campbell, 1988; Cook & Campbell, 1979; Maxwell, 1992, 2011b).

This is not just philosophical hairsplitting; it has important implications for how you conduct your research, and each of the two approaches has its risks. The main risk of instrumentalist questions is that you will lose sight of what you're really interested in, and narrow your study in ways that exclude the actual phenomena you want to investi-gate, ending up with a rigorous but uninteresting conclusion. As in the joke about the man who had lost his keys at night and was looking for them under the streetlight (rather than where he dropped them) because the light was better there (Kaplan, 1964, p. 11), you may never find what you started out to look for. An instrumentalist approach to your research questions may also make it more difficult for you to address important goals of your study (such as developing programs to deal with the actual effects on nurses of talking to rape victims), and can inhibit your theorizing about phenomena that are not directly observable.

The main risk with realist questions, on the other hand, is that your increased reliance on inference may lead you to draw unwarranted conclusions, ignoring potential validity threats such as participants' deliberate or unintentional distortions of the actual effects on them, or your possible biases in inferring these. My preference is to use realist questions, and to address as systematically and rigorously as possible the validity threats that this approach involves. I have several reasons for this. First, the seriousness of these validity threats (such as self-report bias) depends on the topic, goals, and methods of the research, and needs to be assessed in the context of a particular study; these threats are often not as serious as instrumentalists imply. Second, there are usually effective ways to address such threats in a qualitative design; some of these are discussed in Chapters 5 and 6. Finally, I take a realist position that unobservable phenomena (e.g., black holes, quarks, and the extinction of the dinosaurs) can be just as real as observable ones, and just as legitimate as objects of scientific study.

Thus, in my view, the risk of trivializing your study by restricting your questions to what can be directly observed is usually more serious than the risk of drawing invalid conclusions. What the statistician John Tukey (1962) said about precision is also true of certainty: "Far better an approximate answer to the right question, which is often vague, than an exact answer to the wrong question, which can always be made precise" (p. 13; cited in Light & Pillemer, 1984, p. 105). My advice to students in Lenehan's position is to argue for the legitimacy of framing your questions in realist terms (which she successfully did). Even if you are required to restrict your *proposal* to instrumentalist questions, you should make sure that your actual *design* incorporates any realist concerns that you want your study to address.

One issue that is not entirely a matter of realism versus instrumentalism is whether research questions in interview studies should be framed in terms of the respondents' *perceptions* or *beliefs* about what happened, rather than what actually happened. This was an issue for Lenehan's study, described previously; one recommendation of the committee was to focus the questions on how nurses *perceive* the effects of working with rape victims, rather than on the actual effects. Both of these are, in principle, realist questions, because, from a realist perspective, perceptions and beliefs are real phenomena, and neither participants' perceptions nor actual effects can be inferred with certainty from interview data.

This decision should be based not simply on the seriousness of the risks and validity threats for each, but also on what you actually want to understand. In many qualitative studies, the real interest is in how participants make sense of what has happened (itself a real phenomenon), and how this perspective informs their actions, rather than in determining precisely what happened or what they did. Furthermore, in some circumstances you may be more interested in how participants organize and communicate their experiences (another real phenomenon) than in the "truth" of their statements (e.g., Linde, 1993). Jackson (1987, pp. 292–294), after finishing his study of death row inmates, was asked how he knew the men he interviewed were telling the truth, or even if they believed what they told him. He eventually decided that he was in fact most interested in how the men constructed a presentation of self, a narrative of their life. As he said,

> Whether the condemned men who speak to you on these pages *believe* their presentations is interesting, but not finally important; what is important is first that they feel the need to organize their verbal presentations of themselves so they are rational, and second that they know how to do it. (p. 293)

VARIANCE QUESTIONS AND PROCESS QUESTIONS

Finally, I want to return to the distinction between variance theory and process theory that I introduced in Chapter 2, and relate this to the framing of research questions. Variance questions focus on difference and correlation; they often begin with "does," "how much," "to what extent," and "is there a relationship." Process questions, in contrast, focus on *how* things happen, rather than *whether* there is a particular relationship or how much it is explained by other variables. The fundamental distinction here is between questions that focus on variables and differences and those that focus on processes; it closely parallels the distinction between positivist and realist approaches to causation.

For example, asking "Do second-career teachers remain in teaching longer than teachers for whom teaching is their first career, and if so, what factors account for this?" is a variance question, because it implies a search for a difference and for the particular variables that explain the difference. An example of a process question would be "How do second-career teachers decide whether to remain in teaching or to leave?" The focus in the latter question is not in explaining a difference (a dependent variable) in terms of some independent variables, but on understanding how these teachers think about and make decisions on remaining in teaching.

In a qualitative study, it can be risky for you to frame your research questions in a way that focuses on differences and their explanation. This may lead you to begin thinking in variance terms, to try to identify the variables that will account for observed or hypothesized differences, and to overlook the real strength of a qualitative approach, which is in understanding the processes by which things take place. Variance questions are normally best answered by quantitative approaches, which are powerful ways of determining *whether* a particular result was related to one or another variable, and *to what extent* these are related. However, qualitative research is often better at showing *how* this occurred. (See the discussion of causality in Chapter 2.) In my introductory qualitative methods course, I strongly discourage students from attempting to answer variance questions, because doing so will often interfere with their learning what is most essential to qualitative research. Variance questions can be legitimate in qualitative research, but they are often best grounded in the answers to prior process questions.

Qualitative researchers thus tend to focus on three kinds of questions that are much better suited to process theory than to variance theory: (1) questions about the *meaning* of events and activities to the people involved in these, (2) questions about the influence of the physical and social *context* on these events and activities, and (3) questions about the *processes* by which these events and activities and their outcomes occurred. (See the discussion of the goals of qualitative research in Chapter 2.) Because all of these types of questions involve situation-specific phenomena, they do not lend themselves to the kinds of comparison and control that variance theory requires. Instead, they generally involve an open-ended, inductive approach, in order to discover what these meanings and influences are and *how* they are involved in these events and activities— an inherently processual orientation.

One student, Bruce Wahl, wrote to me about having changed his research questions while he was analyzing the data for his dissertation, an evaluation of math projects for community college students that engaged different learning styles:

> I don't know if you remember, but two years ago when I was writing my proposal, you stressed that I should be writing my research questions beginning with words like "how" and "what" and "why" instead of the yes/no questions I was asking. For example, my first question was, "Do the projects help students to grasp mathematical concepts?" As I am writing up the interview results, I finally understand what you were saying. What I really wanted to know was "How do the projects help (or not help!) the students to grasp mathematical concepts?" It seems so clear now, it is a wonder that I didn't understand it back then. I have rewritten the five research questions for myself with that in mind and will include those new, and I hope, improved questions with the [dissertation] draft I deliver next week.

DEVELOPING RESEARCH QUESTIONS

Light, Singer, and Willett (1990) pointed out that formulating research questions is not a simple or straightforward task:

> Do not expect to sit down for an hour and produce an elaborate list of specific questions. Although you must take the time to do just that—sit down and write—your initial list will not be your final list. Expect to iterate. A good set of research questions will evolve, over time, after you have considered and reconsidered your broad research theme. (p. 19)

And they cautioned to "Be wary of the desire to push forward before going through this process" (p. 19).

What follows is an exercise for you to work through in developing your research questions. This exercise will not only generate research questions, but will also help you connect these questions to the other four components of your research design, in

Exercise

order to make these questions as relevant and practicable as possible. These connections are two-way streets; try to see not only what questions, or changes in questions, the other four components suggest, but also what changes in these other components your questions may imply.

Exercise 4.1   Developing Your Research Questions

Like most of the other exercises in this book, this one asks you to write a memo that addresses the following sets of issues for your research. This involves trying to connect your tentative research questions to the other four components of your design. At this point, your answers to Items 5 and 6 may need to be very tentative; that's fine. You can repeat this exercise as you get a better sense of what your study will look like.

1. Begin by setting aside whatever research questions you already have, and starting with your concept map (Chapter 3). What are the places in this map that you *don't* understand adequately, or where you need to test your ideas? Where are the holes in, or conflicts between, your experiential knowledge and existing theories, and what questions do these suggest? What could you learn in a research study that would help you to better understand what's going on with these phenomena? Try to write down all of the potential questions that you can generate from the map.

2. Next, take your original research questions and compare them to the map and the questions you generated from it. What would answering these questions tell you that you *don't* already know? What changes or additions to your questions does your map suggest? Conversely, are there places where your questions imply things that *should* be in your map, but aren't? What changes do you need to make to your map?

3. Now go through the same process with your researcher identity memo (Chapter 2). What could you learn in a research study that would help to accomplish these goals? What questions does this imply? Conversely, how do your original questions connect to your reasons for conducting the study? How will answering these *specific* questions help you achieve your goals? Which questions are most *interesting* to you, personally, practically, or intellectually?

4. Now *focus*. What questions are most *central* for your study? How do these questions form a coherent set that will guide your study? You can't study everything interesting about your topic; start making choices. Three or four main questions are usually a reasonable maximum for a qualitative study, although you can have additional subquestions for each of the main questions.

5. In addition, you need to connect your questions to the methods you might use. *Could* your questions be answered by these methods and the data that they

would provide? What methods would you *need* to use to collect data that would answer these questions? Conversely, what questions can a qualitative study of the kind you are planning productively address? At this point in your planning, this may primarily involve thought experiments about the way you will conduct the study, the kinds of data you will collect, and the analyses you will perform on these data. This part of the exercise is one you can usefully repeat when you have developed your methods and validity concerns in more detail; Exercise 5.2, in the next chapter, also addresses these issues.

6. Assess the potential answers to your questions in terms of their validity. What are the plausible validity threats and alternative explanations that you would have to rule out? How might you be wrong, and what implications does this have for the way you frame your questions?

Don't get stuck trying to precisely frame your research questions, or in specifying in detail how to measure things or gain access to data that would answer your questions. Try to develop some meaningful and important questions that would be *worth* answering. Feasibility is obviously an important issue in doing research, but focusing on it at the beginning can abort a potentially valuable study. My experience is that there are very few important questions that can't be potentially answered by some sort of research.

An extremely valuable additional step is to share your questions, and your reflections on these, with a small group of fellow students or colleagues. Ask them if they understand the questions and why these would be worth answering, what other questions or changes in the questions they would suggest, and what problems they see in trying to answer them. If possible, tape-record the discussion; afterward, listen to the tape and take notes.

Your research questions will often need to evolve over the course of your study. However, you may not be aware of subtle ways in which your thinking has changed, or how your data are suggesting that you should modify your research questions. To help my students with this, I developed a strategy that I call the "Jeopardy exercise," after the television game show of that name, in which contestants are given an answer and have to try to guess the question. The basic idea of this exercise is for you to take your tentative results or conclusions, or even a preliminary analysis of your data, and ask yourself, "If these are my answers, what questions are they answering?" This requires you to set aside your original questions and to look at your data and results with new eyes, trying to see what they are telling you.

You might ask, "Why should I bother to revise my research questions? Why shouldn't I just take my results and present these?" I think there are two reasons for explicitly realigning your research questions with what you've learned. First, your research questions do not simply (as in linear models of research design) help you plan your research methods and then go on vacation, with no further responsibilities. They need to be actively involved in the *actual* design of your study throughout the entire research process. Your revised research questions should help you further focus your analysis, suggest possible changes in your conceptual framework, and allow you to better anticipate potential validity threats. Second, your research questions will play an important role in *communicating* whatever you write about your research, helping your reader understand what questions your results answer and why these are important.

Example 4.2 shows how one student, Jennifer Buxton, used the Jeopardy exercise in her data analysis.

Example 4.2 Revising Your Research Questions

When Jennifer Buxton began analyzing her interviews with her former elementary school students about their perceptions of the changes in homework from elementary to middle school, her previous excitement about her study began to evaporate. She began by sorting her data into the organizational categories that she had initially developed, and writing notes and memos to herself about the ideas she was getting from the data. However, as she described in her final project report,

> I quickly became frustrated and confused using this approach because so much of the data was so intertwined and applicable to a number of my initial categories, while some of the data didn't fit anywhere. I knew that this meshing of ideas and meaning would eventually be valuable in connecting my data, but at that point, I was very anxious and worried about it not making sense. . . .
>
> Instead of ignoring the anxiety, I knew I needed to face it to figure out what was causing me to feel like that. As I reflected on what I was doing in my research process, the error of my ways was immediately clear. I figured out that I made the novice mistake, of which I was warned of in the readings and in class, of trying to fit the data to my preconceived ideas instead of listening to what it was trying to say.
>
> I remembered the advice about determining the questions that the data answers. I printed another copy of the transcriptions and played Jeopardy with the data. With my initial ideas awake in the back of my mind, I used this exercise to develop a list of the questions my data answered. I found in doing this I was able to more comfortably and logically able to chunk the data into categories. In the process, I felt my anxiety fading away.

5

Methods

What Will You Actually Do?

In this chapter, I discuss some of the key issues involved in planning what you will do in conducting your research—the who, where, when, and how of collecting and making sense of your data. These issues are not limited to qualitative data collection (typically, participant observation and interviewing), but also include establishing research relationships with those you study, selecting sites and participants, and analyzing the data that you collect. The focus is on how to *design* the use of specific approaches and methods in a qualitative study, not on how to actually do qualitative research; I am assuming that you already know (or are learning) the latter.

At the outset, I want to emphasize that there is no "cookbook" for qualitative methods. The appropriate answer to almost any general question about the use of these methods is "it depends." Decisions about research methods depend on the issues you are studying and the specific context of your research, as well as on other components of your design. The bottom line for any decision about methods is the actual result of using these methods in your study; what would be an excellent decision in one study could be a serious mistake in another. What I want to discuss here are some of the things that your methodological decisions depend *on*—the issues that you will need to think about in designing your research methods.

First, a point about data. The data in a qualitative study can include virtually anything that you see, hear, or that is otherwise communicated to you while conducting the study. As Barney Glaser (2001) said,

> All is data . . . what is going on in the research scene is the data, whatever the source, whether interview, observations, documents, in whatever combination. It is not only what is being told, how it is being told and the conditions of its being told, but also all the data surrounding what is being told. (p. 145)

There is no such thing as "inadmissible evidence" in trying to understand the issues or situations you are studying. (However, there may be evidence that you are ethically prohibited from *citing* in what you write, if it could violate confidentiality or privacy or be potentially damaging to particular individuals or groups.) Qualitative data are not restricted to the results of specified methods; as I described earlier, you *are* the research instrument in a qualitative study, and your eyes and ears are the tools you use to gather information and to make sense of what is going on. In planning your research methods, you should always include whatever informal data-gathering strategies are feasible, including hanging out, casual conversations, and incidental observations. This is particularly important in an interview study, where such information can provide important contextual information, a different perspective from the interviews, and a check on your interview data. As Dexter (1970) emphasized,

> No one should plan or finance an entire study in advance with the expectation of relying chiefly upon interviews for data unless the interviewers have enough relevant background to be sure that they can make sense out of interview conversations or unless there is a reasonable hope of being able to hang around or in some way observe so as to learn what it is meaningful and significant to ask. (p. 17)

Such less formally collected sorts of data should be systematically recorded in memos or a field journal. In addition, *all* data should be treated critically, and not simply accepted at face value. Any data may be interpreted in different ways, and you will need to assess the validity threats (discussed in Chapter 6) to the particular interpretations you make from them.

MORE AND LESS STRUCTURED APPROACHES

An important issue in designing a qualitative study is the extent to which you decide on your methods in advance, rather than developing or modifying these during the research. Some qualitative researchers believe that, because qualitative research is necessarily inductive, any substantial prior structuring of the methods leads to a lack of flexibility to respond to emergent insights, and can create methodological "tunnel vision" in making sense of your data. They often justify this decision on philosophical or ethical grounds as well practical ones; structured approaches are equated with quantitative research, positivism, or power inequalities between researcher and researched. The choice between more and less structured methods is rarely discussed in a way that clarifies the relative advantages and disadvantages of each (significant exceptions are Miles & Huberman, 1994; Robson, 2011; and Sayer, 1992).

Structured approaches can help ensure the comparability of data across individuals, times, settings, and researchers, and are particularly useful in answering questions that deal with *differences* between people or settings. Less structured approaches, in contrast, allow you to focus on the *particular* phenomena being studied, which may differ between individuals or settings and require individually tailored methods. Less structured methods trade generalizability and comparability for internal validity and contextual understanding, and are particularly useful in revealing the processes that led to specific outcomes, what Miles and Huberman (1994) called "local causality" (cf. Maxwell, 2004a, 2011b).

However, Miles and Huberman (1994) also cautioned that

Highly inductive, loosely designed studies make good sense when experienced researchers have plenty of time and are exploring exotic cultures, understudied phenomena, or very complex social phenomena. But if you're new to qualitative studies and are looking at a better understood phenomenon within a familiar culture or subculture, a loose, inductive design is a waste of time. Months of fieldwork and voluminous case studies may yield only a few banalities. (p. 17)

They also pointed out that prestructuring your methods reduces the amount of data that you have to deal with, simplifying the analytic work required (Miles & Huberman 1994, p. 16).

In general, I agree with Miles and Huberman's (1994) assessment, although I think their involvement with multiple-site research has led them to advocate more prestructuring than is appropriate for most single-site studies. However, like nearly everyone else, they treat prestructuring as a single dimension, and view it in terms of metaphors such as hard versus soft and tight versus loose. Such metaphors, in addition to their one-dimensional implications, have value connotations (although these are different for different people) that can interfere with your assessment of the trade-offs involved in specific design decisions for a particular study, and the best ways to combine different aspects of prestructuring within a single design. These metaphors can lead you to overlook or ignore the numerous ways in which studies can vary, not just in the *amount* of prestructuring, but also in *how* prestructuring is used.[1]

For example, Festinger, Riecker, and Schachter (1956), in a classic study of an end-of-the-world cult, employed an extremely open approach to data collection, relying primarily on descriptive field notes from covert participant observation in the cult. However, they used these data mainly for a confirmatory test of explicit hypotheses based on a prior theory, rather than to inductively develop new questions or theory (Maxwell & Loomis, 2002, pp. 260–263). In contrast, the approach often known as ethnoscience or cognitive anthropology (Spradley, 1979; Werner & Schoepfle, 1987) employs highly structured data collection techniques, but interprets these data in a largely inductive manner, with very few preestablished categories. Thus, the decision you face is not primarily *whether* or *to what extent* you prestructure your study, but *in what ways* you do this, and *why.*

Finally, it is worth keeping in mind that you can lay out a *tentative* plan for some aspects of your study in considerable detail, but leave open the possibility of substantially revising this if necessary. (See the discussion of field paleontology in Chapter 1, and the evolution of Maria Broderick's research design, presented in Example 1.1.) The extent to which you prestructure your anticipated research methods is a separate decision from how much flexibility you leave yourself to revise the plan during your study. Emergent insights may require not only new research questions, as discussed in Chapter 4, but also new participant selection decisions, unexpected relationships, different kinds of data, and different analytic strategies. As stated earlier, all research has an implicit, if not explicit, design. Avoiding decisions about your design may mean only that you aren't examining the design that is implicit in your thinking and actions, and are failing to recognize the consequences that these implicit decisions will have. Deliberate attention to these consequences can help you construct a design that will enable you to answer your questions, advance your goals, and possibly save you a lot of trouble.

I see qualitative methods—what you will actually do in conducting a qualitative study—as having four main components:

1. The research relationships that you establish with those you study
2. Selection: what settings or individuals you decide to observe or interview, and what other sources of information you decide to use
3. Data collection: how you gather the information you will use
4. Data analysis: what you do with this information to make sense of it

This is a somewhat broader definition of methods than is usual in discussions of research design. My justification for this definition is that all of these components are important aspects of how you gather and make sense of your data, and all of them influence the value and validity of your conclusions. It is therefore useful to think about these as *design* decisions—key issues that you should consider in planning your study, and that you should rethink as you are engaged in it. In the rest of this chapter, I will discuss what I see as the most important considerations that should affect your decisions about each of these components.

NEGOTIATING RESEARCH RELATIONSHIPS

The relationships that you create with participants in your study (and also with others, sometimes called "gatekeepers," who can facilitate or interfere with your study) are an essential part of your methods, and how you initiate and negotiate these relationships is a key *design* decision. Bosk (1979, p. ix) noted that fieldwork is a "body-contact" sport; with few exceptions, you need to actually interact with other people (including online interaction) to collect your data, and your research relationships create and structure this interaction. Conversely, your ongoing contact with participants, including data collection, continually restructures these relationships. These are both aspects of what Hammersley and Atkinson (2007, pp. 14–18) called "reflexivity"—the fact that the researcher is part of the social world he or she studies, and can't avoid either influencing this or being influenced by it.

In some books on qualitative methods, these relationships are conceptualized as "gaining access" to the setting (e.g., Bogdan & Biklen, 2003, pp. 75–80) or as "negotiating entry" (e.g., Marshall & Rossman, 1999, p. 82). While this is one important *goal* in negotiating a relationship, such phrases may lead you to think that this is something that, once achieved, requires no further attention. The process of negotiating a relationship is much more complex than these phrases suggest; not only does it typically require ongoing negotiation and renegotiation of your relationships with those you study, but it rarely involves any approximation to total access. Nor is total access usually necessary for a successful study; what you need are relationships that allow you to ethically gain the information that can answer your research questions.

Conceptualizing your relationships entirely in terms of rapport is also problematic, because it represents a relationship by a single continuous variable, rather than emphasizing the *nature* of that relationship. Seidman (1998, pp. 80–82; cf. McGinn, 2008) made the important point that it is possible to have too much rapport, as well as too little, but I would add that it is the *kind* of rapport, as well as the amount, that is critical. A participant can be very engaged intellectually in an interview, but not be revealing anything deeply personal, and for some studies, this kind of relationship may be ideal. Conversely, someone may be very open about personal matters to a stranger whom they never expect to see again, but not be willing to critically reflect on this material.

Thus, the relationship you have with any participant in your study is a complex and changing entity. In qualitative studies, the researcher is the instrument of the research, and the research relationships are the means by which the research gets done. These relationships have an effect not only on the participants in your study, but also on you, as both researcher and human being, as well as on other parts of the research design. (See the discussion of Alan Peshkin's research relationships in Example 2.2.) In particular, the research relationships you establish can facilitate or hinder other aspects of the research design, such as participant selection and data collection.

For example, in my dissertation research in an Inuit community, the outcome of my initial negotiations with the community was that I would live with different families on a monthly basis. This gave me access to detailed information about a wider range of families than is often available to anthropologists, who typically establish close ties with a small number of individuals or families. However, the ways in which this arrangement was negotiated made it more difficult for me to develop working relationships with those families with whom I did not live (Maxwell, 1986). Rabinow (1977) has provided an insightful account of the way in which his changing relationships with his Moroccan informants affected his research plans, and Bosk (1979) and Abu-Lughod (1986) described how their relationships with the people they studied both facilitated and constrained their research. Many other accounts by qualitative researchers provide similar insights; rather than attempting to sum these up in a few, only partially generalizable guidelines, I urge you to look at these and other examples, so that your decisions can be informed by a range of researchers' experiences.

I want to emphasize that these are *design* decisions, not simply practical issues that are separate from design. You will need to reflect on the particular decisions (conscious or unconscious) that you make about your relationships, as well as on the relationship issues that you will face in doing the study, and the effects these can have on your research. How to make these decisions gets deeper into issues of qualitative methods than this book can go, but the principle stated by Weiss (1994) for interview studies is valid for qualitative research in general:

> What is essential in interviewing is to maintain a working research partnership. You can get away with phrasing questions awkwardly and with a variety of other errors that will make you wince when you listen to the tape later. What you can't get away with is failure to work with the respondent as a partner in the production of useful material. (p. 119)

In addition to these considerations, there are philosophical, ethical, and political issues that should inform the kinds of relationships that you want to establish. In recent years, the dominance of the traditional research relationship has been challenged by alternative modes of research that involve quite different sorts of relationships between the researcher and the researched, and in some cases break down this distinction entirely. For example, Tolman and Brydon-Miller (2001) advocated interpretive and participatory action methods in qualitative research, methods that are "relational in that they acknowledge and actively involve the relationships between researchers and participants, as well as their respective subjectivities" (p. 5). They believed that qualitative research should be participatory in the sense of working collaboratively with research participants to generate knowledge that is useful to the participants as well as to the researcher, contributing to personal and social transformation (pp. 3–4). Similarly, Lawrence-Lightfoot and Hoffman Davis (1997) criticized the tendency, even in qualitative research, to treat relationships as a tool or strategy for gaining access to data, rather than as a connection (p. 135). They argued that "relationships that are complex, fluid, symmetric, and reciprocal—that are shaped by both researchers and actors—reflect a more responsible ethical stance *and* are likely to yield deeper data and better social science" (pp. 137–138), and they emphasized the continual creation and renegotiation of trust, intimacy, and reciprocity.

Burman (2001) cautioned, however, that the dominant humanitarian/democratic agenda of qualitative research, including such goals as equality and participation, are easily co-opted into the perpetuation of existing power relationships, and she asserted, "The progressive . . . character of research is always ultimately a matter of politics, not technique" (pp. 270–271). My advocacy of incorporating research relationships into your research design is not an advocacy of any *particular* type of relationship. Although I mostly agree with Burman (2001), Tolman and Brydon-Miller (2001), and Lawrence-Lightfoot and Hoffman Davis (1997), the types of relationships (and goals) that are ethically and politically appropriate depend on the particular context (including the participants' views), and should always be subjected to the sort of critique raised by Burman. (For more in-depth discussion of these issues, see Cannella & Lincoln, 2011; Christians 2011; Glesne, 2011; McGinn, 2008.)

Whatever your methodological and political views, remember that what is a "research project" for you is always, to some degree, an intrusion into the lives of the participants in your study. A primary ethical obligation, therefore, is to try to understand how the participants will perceive your actions and respond to these. A first step in this is to put yourself in their position, and ask how you would feel if someone did to you what you are thinking of doing. However, you shouldn't assume that how *you* understand this is the same as what your participants understand. In my dissertation fieldwork in an Inuit community, many of my initial difficulties in developing productive relationships were due to my almost complete ignorance of how the inhabitants of this community defined the situation and my presence, and why they responded the way they did to my attempts to negotiate mutually acceptable arrangements for my research. It was only when I began to grasp these definitions and the reasons for their actions that I was able to improve my relationships with them (Maxwell, 1986; 2011b, pp. 166–167). Thus, you will need to *learn* what your participants' perceptions and understanding are of you and your research in order to develop useful and ethically appropriate relationships with them.

In addition, what you learn about your participants' perspectives through negotiating these relationships can be valuable to you in gaining an understanding of the things you are studying. Becker (2007) noted that

> When anthropologists and sociologists do field research . . . they typically have problems establishing and maintaining those relationships with people that will let them observe what they want to . . . But experienced fieldworkers know that the difficulties provide valuable clues to the social organization they want to understand. How people respond to a stranger who wants to study them tells something about how they live and are organized. If the poor people in a city neighborhood you want to study are suspicious and won't talk to you, that is a real problem. You may eventually discover that they are standoffish because they think you might be an investigator trying to catch violators of the welfare regulations. The trouble, personally painful, will have taught you something worth knowing. (p. 64)

I say more about this in Chapter 6, in discussing intervention as a validity strategy.

Gaining these understandings is most critical when you are dealing with a culture different from your own, or a group of people with whose standards you are not familiar. However, it is still important even in a situation that you think you completely understand. Several of my students have had very uncomfortable and unproductive interviews with people whom they knew well, and with whom (despite my expressed concerns) they didn't anticipate any problems. They had failed to realize that these participants perceived the interview very differently from how the student saw it. These perceptions involved, among other issues, fear of the possible consequences of what they said (particularly if the interview is recorded), power differences between the student and the interviewee, a lack of understanding of the purpose of the study and what the student would do with the interview data, and even the setting of the interview itself. You need to anticipate, as best you can, potential concerns that the participant may have, and plan how to address these, both in your prior explanation and negotiation of the research, and in the interview itself, if these issues emerge.

Finally, you need to be aware of the purposes and assumptions that *you* bring to the relationship, which you may not initially be aware of. Are you concerned about presenting yourself as a competent researcher? Do you have a desire to demonstrate the correctness of your own views? Do you hold unexamined stereotypes about the participants? Such purposes and assumptions can have negative consequences for your research; the researcher identity memo (Exercise 2.1) can be used to help you become aware of, and to deal with, these.

I don't want to exaggerate the likelihood of such problems; in many situations, people will be happy to help you by agreeing to be interviewed, and they may even enjoy the interview and find it valuable to them. However, you will need to be alert for potential problems, and be careful to clearly explain the purpose of your study, what you are asking them to do, and what will be done with the data. Doing this can help you avoid some difficulties that result from misunderstandings of these, but it is not a panacea, and doesn't by itself address issues of difference in status and power between you and the participant.[2]

Finally, think about what you can give to participants in return for the time and inconvenience of being involved in your research. What can you do to help people feel that this has been a worthwhile experience and that they aren't just being used? This can range from helping out in the setting you're studying, to providing some gift or service, to simply being an empathic listener. In my dissertation fieldwork, my relationships were improved significantly by my banjo playing, by giving guitar lessons to some of the teenagers in the community, and by teaching a class on English for community members, as well as by gifts to people with whom I worked. What's appropriate to offer depends on the setting and individual and on what you are asking that person to do, but *some* acknowledgment of your appreciation is always appropriate. As one of my students, Caroline Linse, reminded me, "The interview isn't over until the thank-you note is delivered."

Example 5.1   Negotiating Relationships in a Practitioner Research Study

Bobby Starnes, a doctoral student with extensive experience as a teacher and administrator and a longtime political commitment to collaborative decision making, came to the Harvard Graduate School of Education to see how what she had learned about teaching and learning with children could inform her work with adults. When she was seeking a dissertation study that would allow her to apply and test her ideas, she was hired as director of a daycare center, serving a low-income population, which had a history of ineffective, top-down management. Her dissertation research was a study of what happened when she attempted to implement a system of shared decision making in this setting—how the system evolved, and how it affected staff morale, competence, and performance.

Bobby's study required her to have a very different relationship to her study participants than that found in most research; she was both their boss and a researcher trying to understand their perspective on the organizational changes she instituted. In addition, her political views led her to design a study in which she was engaged in real-world action to improve people's lives, not ivory-tower research. This combination posed both substantial risks of bias and distortion of the data, and unique opportunities for understanding the process of organizational change. It was thus absolutely essential for her study that her participants be open about their perceptions and feelings, and that they trust her not to use the data she collected in ways that would be harmful to them.

Bobby was able to accomplish this by establishing an organizational climate in which staff were not afraid to voice their opinions and disagree with her, and in which they were convinced that she would not violate confidences or take action against them as a result of what she learned. (Obviously, this was not an easy task, and required all of her skill and experience to carry out; for a detailed description of how she did this, see Starnes, 1990.) Without this relationship, the conclusions of her study would not have been trustworthy. However, she did not assume that the relationship that she had with her staff would automatically eliminate problems of distortion and concealment. She gathered some data by anonymous questionnaires, and had another researcher conduct half of the final interviews.

Because the impact of these issues is particular to each individual study, the best strategy for dealing with them is to think about them in the context of your research. The following exercise should help you to do this.

Exercise 5.1   Reflecting on Your Research Relationships

This exercise involves writing a memo reflecting on your relationships (actual or planned) with participants and other important people you plan to involve in your research, how you will present yourself and your research, and what arrangements you expect to negotiate for doing the research and reporting your results. The following questions are ones you should keep in mind as you work on this memo:

1. What kinds of relationships have you established, or do you plan to establish, with the people in your study or setting? How did these relationships develop, or how do you plan to initiate and negotiate them? *Why* have you planned to do this? How do you think these relationships could (or already have) facilitate or impede your study? What alternative kinds of relationships could you create, and what advantages and disadvantages would these have?

2. How do you think you will be seen by the people you interact with in your research? In what ways could this be influenced by status and power differences between you and these people? How will this affect your relationships with these people? What could you do to better understand and (if necessary) try to modify this perception?

3. What explicit agreements do you plan to negotiate with the participants in your study about how the research will be conducted and how you will report the results? What *implicit* understandings about these issues do you think these

people (and you) will have? How will both the implicit and the explicit terms of the study affect your relationships and your research? Do any of these need to be discussed or changed?

4. What ethical issues or problems do these considerations raise? How do you plan to deal with these?

As with the memo on research questions (Exercise 4.1), this can be a valuable memo to discuss with colleagues or fellow students.

SITE AND PARTICIPANT SELECTION

Decisions about where to conduct your research and whom to include in it (what is traditionally called *sampling*) are an essential part of your research methods. Even a single case study involves a choice of this case rather than others, as well as requiring such decisions *within* the case itself. Miles and Huberman (1984) asked, "Knowing, then, that one cannot study everyone everywhere doing everything, even within a single case, how does one limit the parameters of a study?" (p. 36). They argued that

> Just *thinking* in sampling-frame terms is healthy methodological medicine. If you are talking with one kind of informant, you need to consider *why* this kind of informant is important, and, from there, which *other* people should be interviewed. This is a good, bias-controlling exercise.
>
> Remember that you are not only sampling *people,* but also *settings, events, and processes.* It is important to line up these parameters with the research questions as well, and to consider whether your choices are doing a representative, time-efficient job of answering them. The settings, events, or processes that come rapidly to mind at the start of the study may not be the most pertinent or data-rich ones. A systematic review can sharpen early and later choices. (p. 41)

LeCompte and Preissle (1993, pp. 56–85), Miles and Huberman (1994, pp. 27–34), and Morgan (2008b) provide valuable discussions of the whole issue of sampling decisions, and I will not repeat all of their advice here. Instead, I want to talk about the *purposes* of different selection strategies, and some of the considerations that are relevant to such decisions.

First, I feel that the term "sampling" is problematic for qualitative research, because it connotes a purpose of "representing" the population sampled, the usual goal of sampling in quantitative research. Quantitative methods texts typically recognize only two main types of sampling: probability sampling (such as random sampling) and convenience sampling (e.g., Light et al., 1990, pp. 56–57). In probability sampling, each member of the population has a known, nonzero probability of being chosen, allowing statistical generalization from the sample to the population of interest. Light et al.

stated, "Probability samples are a paragon of high-quality research" (p. 56), a view that is widespread. As a result, any nonprobability sampling strategy is seen as convenience sampling, and is strongly discouraged.

This view ignores the fact that, in qualitative research, the typical way of selecting settings and individuals is neither probability sampling nor convenience sampling. It falls into a third category, which I call *purposeful selection* (Light et al., 1990, p. 53); *purposive sampling* (Palys, 2008) is another common term. In this strategy, particular settings, persons, or activities are selected deliberately to provide information that is particularly relevant to your questions and goals, and that can't be gotten as well from other choices. For example, Weiss (1994) argued that many qualitative interview studies do not use samples at all, but *panels*—"people who are uniquely able to be informative because they are expert in an area or were privileged witnesses to an event" (p. 17); this is one form of purposeful selection. Selecting those times, settings, and individuals that can provide you with the information that you need to answer your research questions is the most important consideration in qualitative selection decisions.

Patton (1990, pp. 169–186) and Miles and Huberman (1994, pp. 27–29) described a large number of types of sampling that can be employed in qualitative research, almost all of which are forms of purposeful selection. Patton mentioned convenience sampling only to warn against its use, claiming,

> While convenience and cost are real considerations, they should be the last factors to be taken into account after strategically deliberating on how to get the most information of the greatest utility from the limited number of cases to be sampled. . . . *Convenience sampling is neither purposeful nor strategic.* (p. 181, emphasis in original)

However, Weiss (1994, pp. 24–29) argued that there are situations in which convenience sampling is the only feasible way to proceed—for example, in attempting to learn about a group that is difficult to gain access to, or a category of people who are relatively rare in the population and for whom no data on membership exist, such as "house husbands." He listed several strategies for maximizing the value of such convenience samples.

In qualitative studies with large numbers of participants (e.g., Huberman, 1989/1993) in which generalizability is an important goal, random sampling is a valid and often appropriate procedure. However, simple random sampling is a very poor way to draw a small sample, due to the high likelihood of substantial chance variation in such samples; Morgan (2008a) provided a sobering quantitative table of the variability in results from different size random samples. Most of the advantages of random sampling depend on having a reasonably large sample size to make such variations unlikely. Light et al. (1990), in discussing *site* selection, stated, "With only a limited number of sites, consider *purposeful selection,* rather than relying on the idiosyncrasies of chance" (p. 53); the same logic applies to selecting interview participants and observation settings.

There are a few circumstances in which random sampling can be useful in a small-scale qualitative study. Bobby Starnes (1990), in her study of shared decision making in a daycare center (Example 5.1), used stratified random sampling of center staff when she had more volunteers than she could interview, mainly to avoid the perception of favoritism in selecting interviewees. However, in one case, she altered the random selection to include a point of view that she believed would not otherwise have been represented (p. 33).

There are at least five possible goals for purposeful selection; Creswell (2002, pp. 194–196) listed others, but I see these five as most important. The first is achieving representativeness or typicality of the settings, individuals, or activities selected. Because, as noted previously, random sampling is likely to achieve this only with a large sample size, deliberately selecting cases, individuals, or situations that are known to be typical provides far more confidence that the conclusions adequately represent the average members of the population than does a sample of the same size that incorporates substantial random or accidental variation.

The second goal that purposeful selection can achieve is the opposite of the first—to adequately capture the heterogeneity in the population. The purpose here is to ensure that the conclusions adequately represent the entire *range* of variation, rather than only the typical members or some "average" subset of this range; Guba and Lincoln (1989, p. 178) referred to this as "maximum variation" sampling. This is best done by defining the dimensions of variation in the population that are most relevant to your study and systematically selecting individuals or settings that represent the most important possible variations on these dimensions.[3] The trade-off between this approach and selecting a more homogeneous sample is that you have fewer data about any *particular* kind of case, setting, or individual within the study, and will not be able to say as much about typical instances.

The third possible goal is to deliberately select individuals or cases that are critical for testing the theories that you began the study with, or that you have subsequently developed.[4] Extreme cases often provide a crucial test of these theories, and can illuminate what is going on in a way that representative cases cannot. For example, Wievorka (1992) described a study in which the researcher, in order to test the view that the working class was not being assimilated into middle-class society, selected a case that would be highly unfavorable to this position: workers who were extremely affluent. The finding that these workers still retained a clear working-class identity provided more convincing support for his conclusions than a study of "typical" workers would. Example 3.3 also illustrates such a selection goal. The group practice that Freidson (1975) studied was atypical; it was staffed by physicians who were better trained and whose views were more progressive than usual, and was structured precisely to deal with the issues he was addressing—an ideal test case for his theory that social controls for dealing with such issues would be unworkable.

A fourth goal in purposeful selection can be to establish particular comparisons to illuminate the reasons for differences between settings or individuals. While such comparisons are less common in qualitative than in quantitative research, comparative designs are often used in multicase qualitative studies, as well as in mixed-method research (Maxwell & Loomis, 2002). However, explicit comparisons are usually not very productive in a small-scale qualitative study, because the small number of cases in any group limits your ability to draw firm conclusions about the differences between the groups. In addition, an emphasis on comparisons can skew your study toward the analysis of differences (variance theory), as described in Chapter 4, and lead you to neglect the main strength of qualitative research, which is its ability to elucidate *local* processes, meanings, and contextual influences in particular settings or cases.

Finally, a fifth goal can be to select groups or participants with whom you can establish the most productive relationships, ones that will best enable you to answer your research questions. This is often seen as convenience sampling, but it is, in fact, a form of purposeful selection, one that is widely used but rarely discussed explicitly. It is purposeful because it is intended to provide the best data for your study, although the potential unrepresentativeness of the participants needs to be addressed. This is an issue that should inform, as well as be informed by, your research questions. For example, in studying teachers' (or other practitioners') knowledge and practices, you are far more likely to develop good relationships with exemplary teachers, who not only are unlikely to be defensive about discussing their teaching but may be eager to share what they do, than with less proficient teachers, who may justifiably be concerned about revealing their inadequacies. This can be one reason (although not the only possible one) for focusing your study on successful individuals and practices rather than unsuccessful ones, unless you can plan a strategy for developing productive relationships with the latter sorts of participants. (See Martha Regan-Smith's proposal for a study of exemplary medical school teachers, in Appendix A.)

In many situations, selection decisions require considerable knowledge of the setting of the study. In Jane Margolis's (1990) study of classroom discourse norms in a college department, she could interview only a small percentage of the students, and needed to develop some criteria for selecting participants. Her committee (of which I was a member) recommended that she interview sophomores and seniors, believing that this would provide the optimal diversity of views. When she consulted with members of the department, however, they told her that sophomores were too new to the department to fully understand the norms of discourse, while seniors were too deeply involved in their theses and in planning for graduation to be good informants. Juniors turned out to be the only appropriate choice.

Selection decisions should also take into account the feasibility of access and data collection, your research relationships with study participants, validity concerns, and ethics. For example, in Martha Regan-Smith's (1991) study of how medical school teachers help students learn basic science (see the Appendix), her choice of four award-winning teachers was based not only on the fact that these teachers were the most likely to exhibit the phenomena she was interested in (purposeful selection), but also because (as a fellow award winner) she had close and collegial relationships with them that would facilitate the study. In addition, as exemplary teachers, they would be more likely to be candid about their teaching, and the research would be less likely to create ethical problems arising from her discovery of potentially damaging information about them.

One particular selection problem in qualitative studies has been called "key informant bias" (Pelto & Pelto, 1975, p. 7). Qualitative researchers sometimes rely on a small number of informants for a major part of their data, and even when these informants are purposefully selected and the data themselves seem valid, there is no guarantee that these informants' views are typical. In addition, Poggie (1972) presented evidence that key informants themselves assume greater uniformity than actually exists. There is increasing recognition that cultural groups incorporate substantial diversity and that homogeneity cannot be assumed (Hannerz, 1992; Maxwell, 2011b). Thus, you need to do systematic sampling to be able to claim that key informants' statements are representative of the group as a whole (Heider, 1972; Sankoff, 1971).

DECISIONS ABOUT DATA COLLECTION

Most qualitative methods texts devote considerable space to the strengths and limitations of different qualitative data collection methods (see particularly Bogdan & Biklen, 2003; Patton, 2001), and I don't want to repeat these discussions here. Instead, I want to address two key conceptual issues in selecting and using different data collection methods: the relationship between research questions and data collection methods and the triangulation of different methods. (The relative advantages of more and less structured methods, discussed previously, are also important considerations in planning data collection methods.)

The Relationship Between Research
Questions and Data Collection Methods

The point that I want to emphasize here is that the methods you use to collect your data (including your interview questions) don't necessarily follow by logical deduction from the research questions; the two are distinct and separate parts of your design. This can be a source of confusion, because researchers often talk about "operationalizing" their research questions, or of "translating" the research questions into interview questions. Such language is a vestige of logical positivist views of the relationship between theory and data, views that have been almost completely abandoned by philosophers (Phillips, 1987). There is no way to mechanically convert research questions into methods; your methods are the *means* to answering your research questions, not a logical transformation of the latter. Their selection depends not only on your research questions, but also on the actual research situation and on what will work most effectively in that situation to give you the data you need. (The same argument holds for the relationship between methods and validity, an issue that I deal with in Chapter 6.)

A striking example of this, concerning interview questions, was provided by Kirk and Miller (1986, pp. 25–26), who conducted research in Peru on the use of coca leaves. Their open-ended questions about coca use, drawn fairly directly from their research questions, elicited a uniform, limited set of beliefs and practices that simply confirmed the things they had already read about coca. Frustrated and getting desperate, they began asking less logical questions, such as "When do you give coca to animals?" or "How did you discover that you didn't like coca?" Taken off guard, their informants began to open up and talk about their personal experience with coca, which was far more extensive than the previous data would have indicated.

This is an extreme case, but it holds in principle for any study. Your research questions formulate what you want to understand; your *interview* questions are what you ask people to gain that understanding. The development of good interview questions (and observational strategies) requires creativity and insight, rather than a mechanical conversion of the research questions into an interview guide or observation schedule, and depends fundamentally on your understanding of the context of the research (including your participants' definitions of this) and how the interview questions and observational strategies will actually work in practice.

This doesn't mean that you should conceal your research questions from participants, or treat them simply as subjects to be manipulated to produce the data you need, as discussed previously in the section titled Negotiating Research Relationships. Carol Gilligan (personal communication) emphasized the value of asking your interviewees *real* questions, ones to which you are genuinely interested in the answer, rather than contrived questions designed to elicit particular sorts of data. Doing this creates a more symmetrical and collaborative relationship in which participants are able to bring their knowledge to bear on the questions in ways that you might never have anticipated.

There are two important implications that the lack of a direct logical connection between research questions and interview questions has for your research. First, you need to anticipate, as best you can, how people will understand these questions, and how they are likely to respond. Try to put yourself in your interviewee's place and imagine how you would react to these questions (this is another use of thought experiments), and get feedback from others on how they think the questions (and the interview guide as a whole) will work. Second, if at all possible, you should *pilot-test* your interview guide with people as much like your planned interviewees as possible, to determine if the questions work as intended and what revisions you may need to make (see Example 3.4).

In addition, there are some cultures, settings, and relationships in which it is simply not appropriate or productive to conduct interviews, or even to ask questions, as a way of gaining information. Charles Briggs (1986) described how, in his research on traditional religious wood carving in a Spanish-speaking community in northern New Mexico, the cultural norms of the community made the interviews he had planned to conduct completely inappropriate, and rendered these largely useless when he persisted with them. This situation forced him to discover the culturally appropriate way to learn about this topic, which was by apprenticeship. Similarly, Mike Agar, conducting research on heroin use, found that, on the streets, you don't ask questions. First, doing so raises suspicions that you will pass information on to the police or use it to cheat or rob the person you asked. Second, asking questions shows that you're not "hip," and therefore don't belong there (Hammersley & Atkinson, 1995, p. 128). Hammersley and Atkinson (1995) provided other examples of how traditional interviews may be inappropriate or unproductive (pp. 127–130), and Charles Briggs (1986) argued that interviewing imposes particular Anglo-American discourse norms on one's participants, which can damage the relationship or reduce the amount of useful information you get.

This lack of a deductive relationship between questions and methods also holds, more obviously, for observation and other data collection methods. As with interviews, you need to anticipate what information you will actually be able to collect, in the setting studied, using particular observational or other methods, and, if possible, you should pretest these methods to determine if they will actually provide this information. Your data collection strategies will probably go through a period of focusing and revision, even in a carefully designed study, to enable them to better provide the data that you need to answer your research questions and to address any plausible validity threats to these answers.

Using Multiple Data Collection Methods

Collecting information using multiple methods is common in qualitative research, but there has been limited discussion of this as a *design* issue (one exception is Flick, 2007). Using multiple methods has been much more systematically addressed in what is generally termed *mixed-methods research*—the joint use of qualitative and quantitative methods in a single study (Greene, 2007; Tashakkori & Teddlie, 2003, 2010). This literature has identified a number of purposes for combining methods; here, I will focus on three of these purposes.

The first purpose, and the earliest to receive systematic treatment in the research methods literature, is *triangulation* (Fielding & Fielding, 1986). This involves using different methods as a check on one another, seeing if methods with different strengths and limitations all support a single conclusion. This strategy reduces the risk that your conclusions will reflect only the biases of a specific method, and allows you to gain a more secure understanding of the issues you are investigating. (I discuss the use of triangulation generally, as a way to deal with validity threats, in Chapter 6.)

Bobby Starnes's (1990) study (Example 5.1) provides a good illustration of the use of triangulation. She used four sources of data (the direct-care staff, her administrative team, her notes and journals, and the center records) and several different methods of collecting these data. For example, the data from the staff were collected through journals, formal and informal interviews, participation in center activities, and anonymous questionnaires. These multiple sources and methods gave her conclusions far more credibility than if she had been limited to one source or method.

A second purpose for using multiple methods is to gain information about different *aspects* of the phenomena that you are studying, or about different phenomena. This purpose includes what Greene (2007, pp. 101–104) called *complementarity* and *expansion*. In this approach, different methods are used to broaden the range of aspects or phenomena that you address, rather than simply to strengthen particular conclusions about some phenomenon. For example, observation is often used to describe settings, behavior, and events, while interviewing is used to understand the perspectives and goals of actors.

However, while the *immediate* result of observation is description, this is equally true of interviewing; the latter gives you a description of what the participant *said,* not a direct understanding of his or her perspective. Generating an interpretation of someone's perspective is inherently a matter of inference from descriptions of that person's behavior (including verbal behavior), whether the data are derived from observations, interviews, or some other source such as written documents (Maxwell, 1992). Although interviewing is often an efficient and valid way of understanding someone's perspective, observation can enable you to draw inferences about this perspective that you couldn't obtain by relying exclusively on interview data. This is particularly important for getting at tacit understandings and "theory-in-use," as well as aspects of the participants' perspective that they are reluctant to directly state in interviews. For example, watching how a teacher responds to boys' and girls' questions in a science class may provide a much better understanding of the teacher's actual views about gender and science than what the teacher says in an interview.

Conversely, although observation provides a direct and powerful way of learning about people's behavior and the context in which this occurs, interviewing can also be a valuable way of gaining a description of actions and events—often the *only* way, for events that took place in the past or for situations to which you can't gain observational access. As Weiss (1994) stated, "Interviewing gives us access to the observations of others. Through interviewing we can learn about places we have not been and could not go and about settings in which we have not lived" (p. 1). Interviews can also provide additional information that was missed in observation, and can be used to check the accuracy of the observations.

For interviewing to be useful for this purpose, you need to ask about *specific* events and actions, rather than posing questions that elicit only generalizations or abstract opinions (Weiss, 1994, pp. 72–76). Asking people to describe a particular event or sequence of events taps into what has been termed "episodic memory," an important and distinct neurocognitive memory system (Dere, Easton, Nadel & Huston, 2008; Tulving, 2002). In this memory system, information is organized by sequencing in time and connection in space, rather than abstractly in terms of semantic relationships. (I discuss this in more detail in the section on data analysis.) Tulving (2002) argued that this memory system makes possible mental "time travel," uniquely enabling someone to retrieve their previous experiences, and Flick (2000) has applied this distinction to qualitative interviewing, developing a specific procedure for accessing episodic memory that he called *episodic interviewing.*[5]

Weiss (1994), although he made no reference to episodic memory, provided guidance for interviewing that is strikingly consistent with this concept. He stated that asking a question in present tense (e.g., "What happens while you're waiting to be called [in a court case]?") elicits a *generalized* account, and that when respondents provide such an account, "their description expresses a kind of theory about what is most typical or most nearly essential" (pp. 72–73) in such situations, rather than a concrete description of a single event. This may be useful information, but it isn't the same as eliciting what actually happened at a specific time and place. The latter is better obtained by using past tense ("What *happened* while you *were* waiting to be called?") to refer to a particular occasion, or by questions such as "Can you walk me through that incident?"

Weiss (1994) also argued, however, that generalized accounts permit respondents to minimize information about which they feel diffident, and to avoid potentially embarrassing details, things that are more difficult to do in recounting an actual experience. For this reason, you should be reasonably sure that your relationship with the participant will support your asking for a description of a particular event, and have thought about how to respond if the participant seems uncomfortable.

In this situation, the joint use of generalized, present-tense and specific, past-tense questions, as with the joint use of observations and interviews, can address the *same* issues and research questions, but from different perspectives. This use of multiple methods overlaps with Greene's (2007) category of complementarity, but the goal is to gain a greater *depth* of understanding rather than simply greater breadth or confirmation of the results of a single method. It is central to what Greene called a *dialectic* stance for combining methods. This strategy generates a dialogue among the results of different methods, an engagement with differences in findings that forces you to reexamine your understanding of what is going on (pp. 79–82). Greene argued that the use of triangulation to simply confirm a conclusion has been overemphasized and overrated in mixed method research, and that the use of different methods is most valuable for providing *divergent* perspectives, and thus creating a more complex understanding of the phenomena studied (pp. 79–83).

DECISIONS ABOUT DATA ANALYSIS

Analysis is often conceptually separated from design, especially by writers who see design as what happens *before* the data are actually collected. Here, I treat analysis as a part of design (Coffey & Atkinson, 1996, p. 6), and as something that must itself be designed. Any qualitative study requires decisions about how the analysis will be done, and these decisions should inform, and be informed by, the rest of the design. The discussion of data analysis is often the weakest part of a qualitative proposal; in extreme cases, it consists entirely of generalities and "boilerplate" language taken from methods texts, and gives little sense of how the analysis will actually be done, let alone why these strategies were chosen.

One of the most common problems in qualitative studies is letting your unanalyzed field notes and transcripts pile up, making the task of final analysis much more difficult and discouraging. There is a mountaineer's adage that the experienced climber begins lunch immediately after finishing breakfast, and continues eating lunch as long as he or she is awake, stopping briefly to eat supper (Manning, 1960, p. 54). In the same way, the experienced qualitative researcher begins data analysis immediately after finishing the first interview or observation, and continues to analyze the data as long as he or she is working on the research, stopping briefly to write reports and papers. Bernd Heinrich's (1984) rationale for immediately analyzing his biological data applies equally to the social sciences:

> On a research project I usually try to graph my data on the same day I collect them. From day to day the points on the graph tell me about my progress. It's like a fox pursuing a hare. The graph is the hare's track, and I must stay close to that hare. I have to be able to react and change course frequently. (p. 71)

As Coffey and Atkinson (1996) stated, "We should never collect data without substantial analysis going on simultaneously" (p. 2). Again, this is a *design* decision, and how it will be done should be systematically planned (and explained in your proposal).

Strategies for Qualitative Data Analysis

For novices, data analysis may be the most mysterious aspect of qualitative research. As with data collection methods, the following discussion is not intended to fully explain how to *do* qualitative data analysis; some good sources for this are Bogdan and Biklen (2003, Chapter 5), Coffey and Atkinson (1996), Emerson, Fretz, and Shaw (1995), Miles and Huberman (1994), Strauss (1987; Corbin & Strauss, 2007), and Weiss (1994, Chapter 6). Instead, I want to provide an overview of the different strategies and conceptual tools that can be used for qualitative analysis, and then discuss some specific issues in making decisions about analytic methods. The following presentation is based on the much more detailed account in Maxwell and Miller (2008), reprinted with a few modifications in Maxwell (2011b).

The initial step in qualitative analysis is *reading* the interview transcripts, observational notes, or documents that are to be analyzed (Emerson et al., 1995, pp. 142–143). Listening to interview tapes prior to transcription is also an opportunity for analysis, as is the actual process of transcribing interviews or of rewriting and reorganizing your rough observation notes. During this listening and reading, you should write notes and memos on what you see or hear in your data, and develop tentative ideas about categories and relationships.

At this point, you have a number of analytic options. These fall into three main groups: (1) memos, (2) categorizing strategies (such as coding and thematic analysis), and (3) connecting strategies (such as narrative analysis). Unfortunately, most qualitative texts and published articles deal explicitly *only* with coding, treating this as the fundamental activity in analysis and giving the impression that coding *is* qualitative analysis. In fact, many researchers informally use other strategies as well; they just don't usually describe these as part of their analysis. I want to emphasize that reading and thinking about your interview transcripts and observation notes, writing memos, developing coding categories and applying these to your data, analyzing narrative structure and contextual relationships, and creating matrices and other displays are *all* important forms of data analyses. As discussed earlier for methods in general, there is no "cookbook or single correct way for doing qualitative analysis; your use of these strategies needs to be planned (and modified when necessary) in such a way as to fit the data you have, to answer your research questions, and to address any potentially serious validity threats to your conclusions.

As discussed earlier, memos can perform other functions not related to data analysis, such as reflection on your goals, methods, theory, or your prior experiences and your relationships with participants. However, they are also an essential technique for qualitative analysis (Groenewald, 2008; Miles & Huberman, 1994, pp. 72–75; Strauss, 1987). You should regularly write memos while you are doing data analysis; memos not only capture your analytic thinking about your data, but also *facilitate* such thinking, stimulating analytic insights.

The distinction between categorizing and connecting strategies is basic to understanding qualitative data analysis. Although this distinction is widely recognized in practice, it has rarely been theoretically analyzed. A particularly clear statement of the difference is by L. Smith (1979):

> I usually start . . . at the beginning of the notes. I read along and seem to engage in two kinds of processes—comparing and contrasting, and looking for antecedents and consequences. . . .
>
> The essence of concept formation [the first process] is . . . "How are they alike, and how are they different?" The similar things are grouped and given a label that highlights their similarity. . . . In time, these similarities and differences come to represent clusters of concepts, which then organize themselves into more abstract categories and eventually into hierarchical taxonomies.
>
> Concurrently, a related but different process is occurring. . . . The conscious search for the consequences of social items . . . seemed to flesh out a complex systemic view and a concern for process, the flow of events over time. In addition it seemed to argue for a more holistic, systemic, interdependent network of events at the concrete level and concepts and propositions at an abstract level. . . . At a practical level, while in the field, the thinking, searching, and note recording reflected not only a consciousness of similarities and differences but also an attempt to look for unexpected relationships, antecedents, and consequences within the flow of items. (p. 338)

I see this distinction as involving two different modes of relationship: similarity and contiguity (Maxwell & Miller, 2008). Similarity relations involve resemblances or common features; their identification is based on comparison, which can be independent of time and place. In qualitative data analysis, similarities and differences are generally used to define categories and to group and compare data by category. I refer to analytical strategies that focus on relationships of similarity as *categorizing* strategies. Coding is a typical categorizing strategy in qualitative research.

Contiguity-based relations, in contrast, involve juxtaposition in time and space, the influence of one thing on another, or relations among parts of a text; their identification involves seeing actual *connections* between things, rather than similarities and differences. In qualitative data analysis, contiguity relationships are identified among data in an actual context (such as an interview transcript or observational field notes). Contiguity relationships may also be identified among abstract concepts and categories, as a subsequent step to a categorizing analysis of the data. I refer to strategies that focus on relationships of contiguity as *connecting* strategies; in earlier work (e.g., Maxwell, 1996), I had called these "contextualizing" strategies. Some narrative approaches to interview analysis are examples of primarily connecting strategies, as are microethnographic approaches (Erickson, 1992) to observational data. Neither of these strategies can be assimilated to the other; they are based in different forms of relationship in your data, although it is possible to combine the two strategies.

The main categorizing strategy in qualitative research is coding. This is quite different from coding in quantitative research, which consists of applying a preestablished set of categories to the data according to explicit, unambiguous rules, with the primary goal being to generate frequency counts of the items in each category. In qualitative research, the goal of coding is not primarily to count things, but to "fracture" (Strauss, 1987, p. 29) the data and rearrange them into categories that facilitate comparison between things in the same category and that aid in the development of theoretical concepts. Another form of categorizing analysis involves organizing the data into broader themes and issues.

Categorizing analysis begins with the identification of units or segments of data that seem important or meaningful in some way; Seidman (1998, p. 100) described this as "marking what is of interest in the text." This identification can be based on your prior ideas of what is important, or on an inductive attempt to capture *new* insights. The latter strategy is often called "open coding" (Corbin & Strauss, 2007, pp. 195–204); this involves reading the data and *developing* your coding categories, based on what data (including the participants' terms and categories) seem most important. Coding labels these data segments and groups them by category; they are then examined and compared, both within and between categories. Coding categories "are a means of sorting the descriptive data you have collected . . . so that the material bearing on a given topic can be physically separated from other data" (Bogdan & Biklen, 2003, p. 161).

An important set of distinctions in planning your categorizing analysis is among what I call "organizational," "substantive," and "theoretical" categories. Although these types of categories are not completely separate in practice, and intermediate forms are common, I think that the conceptual distinction is valuable.

Organizational categories are broad areas or issues that you want to investigate, or that serve as useful ways of ordering your data. These are often established (either explicitly, or implicitly in your thinking about your study) prior to your interviews or observations. McMillan and Schumacher (2001) referred to these as "topics" rather than categories, stating, "A topic is the descriptive name for the subject matter of the segment. You are not, at this time, asking 'What is said?' which identifies the meaning of the segment" (p. 469). In a study of elementary school principals' practices of retaining children in a grade, examples of such categories are "retention," "policy," "goals," "alternatives," "and "consequences" (p. 470). Organizational categories function primarily as bins for sorting the data for further analysis. They may be useful as chapter or section headings in presenting your results, but they don't directly help you make sense of what's going on (cf. Coffey & Atkinson, 1996, pp. 34–35), because they don't explicitly identify what the person actually said or did, only the category that what they said or did is relevant to.

This latter task requires substantive and/or theoretical categories, ones that explicitly identify the *content* of the person's statement or action—what they actually did or meant. These latter categories can often be seen as subcategories of the organizational ones, but they are generally *not* subcategories that, in advance, you could have known would be significant, unless you are already fairly familiar with the kind of participants or setting you're studying or are using a well-developed theory. They implicitly make some sort of *claim* about the topic being studied—that is, they could be *wrong,* rather than simply being conceptual boxes for holding data.

Substantive categories are primarily *descriptive,* in a broad sense that includes description of participants' concepts and beliefs; they stay close to the data categorized, and don't inherently imply a more abstract theory. In the study of grade retention mentioned previously, examples of substantive categories would be "retention as failure," "retention as a last resort," "self-confidence as a goal," "parent's willingness to try alternatives," and "not being in control (of the decision)" (drawn from McMillan & Schumacher, 2001, p. 472). Categories taken from participants' own words and concepts (what are generally called "emic" categories, ones that represent the participants' own meanings and understanding; see Fetterman, 2008) are usually substantive, but many substantive categories are not emic, being based on the *researcher's* understanding of what's going on. Substantive categories are often inductively generated through a close "open coding" of the data. They can be used in *developing* a more general theory of what's going on, but they don't *depend on* this theory.

Theoretical categories, in contrast, place the coded data into a more general or abstract framework. These categories may be derived either from prior theory or from an inductively developed theory (in which case the concepts and the theory are usually developed concurrently). They typically represent the *researcher's* concepts (what are called "etic" categories), rather than denoting participants' concepts. For example, the categories "nativist," "remediationist," and "interactionist," used to classify teachers' beliefs about grade retention in terms of prior analytic dimensions (Smith & Shepard, 1988), would be theoretical.

The distinction between organizational categories and substantive or theoretical categories is important because beginning qualitative researchers often use mostly organizational categories to formally analyze their data, and don't systematically create and apply substantive or theoretical categories in developing their conclusions. The more data you have, the more important it is to create the latter types of categories; with any significant amount of data, you can't hold all of the data relevant to particular substantive or theoretical points in your mind, and need a formal organization and retrieval system that explicitly identifies the latter points. In addition, creating substantive categories is particularly important for capturing ideas (including participants' ideas) that don't fit into existing organizational or theoretical categories; such substantive ideas may get lost, or never developed, unless they can be captured in such categories.

A tool for displaying and further developing the results of a categorizing analysis of your data is a matrix that is structured in terms of your main research questions, categories, or themes and the data that address or support these. An example of such a matrix (which I call a "themes × data" matrix) is Figure 5.1, a matrix developed by Sarah Daily for her study of how teachers understand young children's metacognitive abilities, listing the main themes she had developed and the quotes from each participant that addressed these themes.

Figure 5.1 A Data Analysis Matrix for Teachers' Views of Children's Metacognitive Abilities

		Categorical Coding Matrix 7/20/09		
1. *These teacher's beliefs about learning and the tone they set for the classroom play an important role in fostering children's independence*				
	Grace	Elaine		Abby
Classroom norms can empower children.	I like Responsive Classroom . . . . because it transfers into the problem solving and expression of thought on the academic side . . . . it really demands that children use specific language and that they listen to each other and respond to each other to show that they are listening and that can transfer to how you solve a problem in math, not only how you solve the problem on the playground.	I'm such a believer in responsive classroom....which is all about how you start the year and set the tone, what makes our classroom ours, what are we going to do. You are supposed to start with a blank slate and then they together decide what we are going to put on the walls because this is their classroom and [the students] make everything.		You've heard me talk about choice a lot and how I believe young students can really handle that kind of responsibility and that they can really have control over the classroom.
Beliefs guide practices.	I try to teach children . . . .to problem solve that on their own.	. . .its important that you [the student] knows what works for you.		My goal is to get them as independent as possible.
Teachers believe in fostering student independence.	I try to give kids lots of chances to try [a challenging learning task] on their own and then the children who are persistent enough to figure out the rule or the pattern I encourage them to talk about how they tried that,	I realized that the chart helped him understand that he has control, it helped him to think, well what can I do. *************************************** Back then [as a first grade teacher] teachers would come to me after my kids had moved to their classroom and tell		My first year of teaching I ended up doing so much.Like kids would say, we're out of tissues, the pencil sharpener is jammed, or my pencil broke and I spent my whole day problem solving things, like I need the tape, where are the scissors. And I

(Continued)

Figure 5.1 (Continued)

	Categorical Coding Matrix 7/20/09		
	what examples did they use, trial and error, what patterns did they notice, what did they think about, what connections did they make to their former knowledge	me stories about how my kids were problem solvers, they [the students] would be like, "no no, I'm a problem solver" and they [the teachers] would be like, "where did they get this language?"	thought you know what this is ridiculous, you kids are fully capable of going to get the scissors or going to get the tape they just need to know where it is . . .we talked about ripping out pages lots of different ways and we talked about how do you fix it what do you do and we talk about its okay to be upset if your paper rips or your crayons break but you need to figure out what to do.
	Grace	Elaine	Abby
2. These teachers see young children use metacognition in a reading or math task, problem solving, and in resolving conflicts with their peers.			
Young children can demonstrate metacognitive abilities	I have a behavior modification plan in place for a little girl who has a lot of focus issues and emotional issues.. she's very effective at knowing how to evaluate her behavior. So that kind of activity works for her. I don't think every child needs that. But a chart, a visual record can be really powerful to show kids how	[H]e got [his words] all right, but he had waffled between the word "it" and the word "at" and he went and he got a piece of paper and says to me, "Hold on one second," and I was all worried like "Oh know he's going to hit somebody," but he went and he got a piece of paper and wrote "it" and "at" on either side of the paper and folded it up like one of our flashcards and said, "I have to	[T]hinking about thinking is a high level skill so if you are just struggling to get all your letters down correctly you might not be able to verbalize how you might change your story. So it's not that they are not participating in metacognition, but the task that I am requiring them to do is more cognitively challenging so they don't have time for the

they are doing. So that kind of activity works for her. I don't think every child needs that. But a chart, a visual record can be really powerful to show how they are doing.	study this because I didn't really know this." So even though he had gotten them all right he was like, "No, I need to study." And the rest of the day, I mean, that just blew me over, and I took him to the principals office to be like, "Look how smart David is," and the rest of the day he would take out his sheet and show me, "it" "at" and he'd write it, he said, "Writing it helps me" and I hadn't even been, there had been none of my telling him what to do, he had really picked this up on his own.	metacognitive part. Cause they are thinking, how do I make an "a" or they are thinking about their picture, or they are just trying to put a coherent story together and remember what the beginning was about so the middle can be about the same thing.
Metacognition can be displayed when children use learning strategies.	A professional development training I went through this year talks about organizing reading into four different categories and then teaching a couple strategies under each category and then having those displayed . . . the sign that's on the wall is based on what the kids called [the reading strategy] . . . Another example is predictions. . . . I try to help them develop some ownership over which strategy they were practicing	My school does focus a lot on strategies, teaching them strategies, which seems to me to be basically metacognition.

You see that [metacognition] a lot with strategies, reading is very strategy based. When you come to a word you don't know, what do you do?

There are many other ways to use matrices for data analysis (see Miles & Huberman, 1994), and you can tailor your column and row categories to fit your specific needs. These matrices can be very useful, but they aren't a substitute for the work of developing your coding categories and using these to sort your data. Instead, the matrices are *based on* this prior analysis; they visually display the results of this analysis, enabling you to see where some participants don't exemplify a particular theme (empty cells), to further develop your analysis, and to modify your conclusions.

Categorizing as an analytic strategy has one significant limitation: It replaces the original set of contextual relationships within an interview transcript or observational field notes with a different, categorical structure. This can create analytic blinders, leading you to ignore the actual relationship of things within a specific context. Paul Atkinson (1992) described how his initial categorizing analysis of his notes on the teaching of general medicine affected his subsequent analysis of his surgery notes:

> [O]n rereading the surgery notes, I initially found it difficult to *escape* those categories I had initially established [for medicine]. Understandably, they furnished a powerful conceptual grid. Moreover, they exercised a more powerful physical constraint. The notes as I confronted them had been fragmented into the constituent themes. (pp. 458–459)

On returning to his original notebooks, Atkinson found,

> I am now much less inclined to fragment the notes into relatively small segments. Instead, I am just as interested in reading episodes and passages at greater length, with a correspondingly different attitude toward the act of reading and hence of analysis. Rather than constructing my account like a patchwork quilt, I feel more like working with the whole cloth. . . . To be more precise, what now concerns me is the nature of these products as *texts.* (p. 460)

What I call connecting strategies are intended to address this deficiency. Connecting strategies operate quite differently from categorizing ones such as coding. Instead of fracturing the initial text into discrete segments and resorting it into categories, connecting analysis attempts to understand the data (usually, but not necessarily, an interview transcript or other textual material) *in context,* using various methods to identify the relationships among the different elements of the text (Atkinson, 1992; Coffey & Atkinson, 1996; Mishler, 1986). It is thus often seen as holistic in that it is concerned with the relationships among the different parts of the transcript or field notes, rather than fragmenting these and sorting the data into categories.

Examples of approaches that involve connecting strategies include some types of case studies (e.g., Stake, 1995), profiles and vignettes (Seidman, 1998), some types of discourse analysis (Gee, 2005; Gee, Michaels, & O'Connor, 1992) and narrative analysis (Coffey & Atkinson, 1996; Josselson, Lieblich, & McAdams, 2007; Riessman, 1993), the "listening guide" strategy of reading for "voice" (Brown, 1988; Gilligan,

Spencer, Weinberg, & Bertsch, 2003), and ethnographic microanalysis of interaction (Erickson, 1992). What all of these strategies have in common is that they do not focus primarily on *similarities* that can be used to sort data into categories independently of context, but instead look for relationships that *connect* statements and events within a context into a coherent whole. (There are more examples of connecting strategies in Maxwell & Miller, 2008.)

The identification of connections among different categories and themes can also be seen as a connecting step in analysis (Dey, 1993), but it is a broader one that works with the results of a prior categorizing analysis. This connecting step is necessary for building theory, a primary goal of analysis. However, it cannot recover the contextual ties that were lost in the original categorizing analysis. A purely connecting analysis, on the other hand, is limited to understanding particular individuals or situations, and cannot develop a more general theory of what's going on without developing some sort of categorization of these individuals or situations. The two strategies need each other to provide a well-rounded account (Maxwell & Miller, 2008; see example 5.2).

Example 5.2   Integrating Categorizing and Connecting Analyses

Barbara Miller, in a course on qualitative research, conducted a research project on a study of adolescent friendships, interviewing adolescents about their relationships with friends and what these friendships meant to them. She described the analysis of her data as follows:

> Working with interviews with adolescents about their friendships, it seemed important to look closely at the features of the friendships, to understand in specific terms what they mean for the adolescents involved. In short, this seemed to call for a categorizing analysis, a close investigation of the components that seem to make up a relationship, for the purpose of investigating similarities across the friendships of different adolescents.
>
> I, therefore, began my analysis by formulating coding categories, coding the data, and constructing matrices [see Figure 5.1 for an example of such a matrix]. I coded the data for such elements as closeness, talk among friends, and dependence. These codes, for each interview, were then collected in matrices so that I could look across interviews for each concept. This helped me to focus on specific features of the data, informed by my research agenda as well as by the comments made by the adolescents themselves. With the completion of the matrices, though, two pressing issues emerged.

(Continued)

(Continued)

The first was that there was extensive overlap of data between the cells of the matrices. For example, many adolescents explained that part of being close to their friends involved talking with them. The matrix for closeness did not, however, capture the complexity of that talk, which involved information from other cells. These matrices seemed too simplistic for the complex, interconnected data I felt I had.

The second issue was that an essential aspect of the data was missing; namely, the narrative nature of the adolescents' accounts of their friendships. In their interviews, the adolescents did not offer isolated bits of information about their friends. Instead, what I heard were the stories of their relationships with their friends. As adolescents talked about their friends and explained why their friendships were important, they described their shared past and created a context from which to understand their relationship. This narrative quality of the data, and its implications for understanding their relationships, were lost in the process of coding and of creating the matrices.

To deal with the limitations of the matrices, and to capture the narrative quality of the data, I moved to what became the second phase of the analysis: the construction of narrative summaries. These summaries are narrative in that they seek to preserve the context and story of the relationship, yet they are summaries since they are my analytic abridgements of the narratives heard. These narrative summaries made use of extensive quotes from the data, but often involved a reorganization of the data to achieve what I, as the reader, perceived to be a concise account of the friendship narrative.

These narrative summaries were effective in holding on to the context as well as the story of the friendship. They did not, however, directly help me understand more clearly the meaning of that friendship experience for these adolescents. For that, I needed to look more closely at their relationships in light of my understanding of the larger context of that friendship. The next phase of my analysis, therefore, was to integrate the results of my categorizing and contextualizing strategies. This led to more depth within the concepts represented in the matrices; the category of closeness between friends, for example, was contextualized. By holding the narrative summaries against the matrices, I could track the meaning of closeness across different friendships for a particular adolescent or between adolescents, or trace its significance throughout a particular friendship.

Data analysis had become, for me, an iterative process of moving from categorizing to contextualizing strategies and back again. My understanding of the narrative context of the friendships informed my interpretation of the particular concepts and categories I had identified as important in these adolescents' friendships. At the same time, the particular concepts I focused on in the categorizing analysis allowed me to look at the narratives in new ways, and to see contextual relationships that were more complex than the temporal ordering of events within the narratives. My understanding of the meaning and experience of friendship for these adolescents was not stripped of the context, which the adolescents provided, nor was it locked into and limited to individual friendship stories. Coding and matrices were combined with narrative summaries to achieve an understanding of the interviews that neither could have provided alone.

The difference between categorizing and connecting strategies has important conse-quences for your overall design. A research question that asks about the way events in a specific context are connected cannot be answered by an exclusively categorizing analytic strategy (see Example 5.3). Conversely, a question about similarities and dif-ferences across settings or individuals cannot be answered by an exclusively connect-ing strategy. Your analysis strategies have to be compatible with the questions you are asking.

Example 5.3   A Mismatch Between Questions and Analysis

Mike Agar (1991) was once asked by a foundation to review a report on an interview study that it had commissioned, investigating how historians worked. The researchers had used the computer program The Ethnograph to segment and code the interviews by topic and collect together all the segments on the same topic; the report discussed each of these topics, and provided examples of how the historians talked about these. However, the foundation felt that the report hadn't really answered its questions, which had to do with how individual historians thought about their work—their theo-ries about how the different topics were connected and the relationships they saw between their thinking, actions, and results.

Answering the latter question would have required an analysis that elucidated these connections in each historian's interview. However, the categorizing analysis on which the report was based fragmented these connections, destroying the contextual unity of each historian's views and allowing only a collective presentation of shared concerns. Agar argued that the fault was not with The Ethnograph, which is extremely useful for answering questions that require categorization, but with its misapplica-tion. As he commented, "The Ethnograph represents a *part of* an ethnographic research process. When the part is taken for the whole, you get a pathological meto-nym that can lead you straight to the right answer to the wrong question" (p. 181).

Computers and Qualitative Data Analysis

Software designed specifically for qualitative data analysis (often labeled CAQDAS, an acronym for computer-assisted qualitative data analysis software) is now widely used, and is almost obligatory for large-scale projects, because of these programs' facil-ity in storing and retrieving large amounts of data and in coding and sorting these data. The more sophisticated programs can also link memos to particular codes or segments of text, and allow you to create concept maps of the categories you have generated, contributing to your development of theory. Since such software is continuing to develop, almost anything I could say about specific programs would quickly be out of date; NVivo currently has the largest market share, but there are many competitors, and the Internet and Amazon.com are your best sources for what is currently available and for books on how to use such programs.

The main strength of such software is in categorizing analysis, and many current books on using computers for qualitative data analysis focus almost entirely on coding. The only book on this topic that I know of that addresses connecting strategies in any detail is Pat Bazeley's (2007) *Qualitative Data Analysis With NVivo*, and even this has little to say, beyond a few suggestions, about how NVivo might be useful in such strategies. Thus, as Example 5.3 illustrates, such programs can subtly push your analysis toward categorizing strategies, ignoring narrative and other connecting approaches. This is an example of what Kaplan (1964, p. 28) called "The Law of the Instrument"; if you give a small boy a hammer, everything looks like a nail. As Pfaffenberger (1988) said,

> A technology is like a colonial power—it tells you that it is working in your best interests and, all the while it is functioning insidiously to dim your critical perception of the world around you. You will remain its victim so long as you fail to conceptualize adequately what it's up to. (p. 20)

LINKING METHODS AND QUESTIONS

To design a workable and productive study, and to communicate this design to others, you need to create a *coherent* design, one in which the different methods fit together compatibly, and in which they are integrated with the other components of your design. The most critical connection is with your research questions, but, as discussed previously, this is primarily an *empirical* connection, not a logical one. If your methods won't provide you with the data you need to answer your questions, you need to change either your questions or your methods.

A useful tool in assessing this coherence and compatibility is a matrix in which you list your research questions and identify how each of the components of your methods will help you answer these questions. I discussed such matrices in Chapter 1, and provided one example (Example 1.5) that incorporated a larger number of design components, including goals and validity issues. In this chapter, I have added another example of such a matrix (Figure 5.2), which Mittie Quinn developed for her study of school psychologists' views of how "culture" was addressed in the special education evaluation process, and a memo (Example 5.4) in which she explained some of her thinking about this matrix. Following this, I have provided an exercise for you to develop a matrix for your own study (Exercise 5.2). Such matrices display the *logic* of your methods decisions, and can be valuable as part of a research proposal; Elizabeth Riddle's proposal (Appendix B) includes such a matrix.

Figure 5.2 A Matrix for a Study of School Psychologists' Views of How Culture Is Addressed in the Special Education Evaluation Process

Research Questions What do I need to know?	Why do I need to know this?	Sampling decisions Where will I find this data?	Data collection methods– What kind of data will answer these questions?	Whom do I contact for access?	Data analysis
How do expert school psychologists employed by ___ County Public Schools perceive that the influence of culture is "excluded" in the special education evaluation process?	These individuals play a primary role in special education decision making. It is therefore important to understand their perceptions of these influences and processes.	School Psychologists	Interviews Field Notes Memos	Supervisor, Psychologists	audio taping transcription coding re-reading/ other readers
How do expert school psychologists employed by ___ County Public Schools evaluate the influence of culture on a child's school behavior?	To better understand how culture is assessed and understood by these key professionals.	School Psychologists Records review Sample reports	Interviews, Case examples, Observation of committee meetings	Supervisor, School Psychologists	coding immediate field notes memos
What aspects of culture do expert school psychologists consider in diagnosing a child's school difficulties?	To understand the meaning of culture for these key professionals and how this may impact on a child's eligibility.	School Psychologists, Records Review, Case history	Interviews, Reports	Supervisor, School Psychologists, Director of Student Services	ongoing analysis categories narrative analysis
What model of "culture" do school psychologists perceive is represented by the special education legislation (PL 94-142)?	To understand how the language of the legislation is perceived to affect the special education process.		Interviews with "experts"		

Example 5.4   A Memo Explaining Figure 5.2

1. Research Questions

My questions have evolved slightly based on feedback received from Joe. In particular, the third question (influence of culture on the diagnosis) has been changed to introduce the concept of the different aspects of culture. I am really interested in knowing what these experts know about "culture." I would ultimately hope to be able to place their perspectives into a definition of culture that will or won't align with some of the current theoretical perspectives (Cultural reproduction, cultural difference, cultural production, etc.). Thus, I have modified question three to address that interest and goal.

Second, I have added a final question about their perceptions of the legislation. I want to know if their perceptions differ from the demands of the legislation as they perceive that. I will argue that my perception of the language of the legislation is that it represents the "cultural difference" approach to culture. As a result, processes and structures that are based upon this legislation *cannot* accommodate current views of culture in anthropology. Consequently, I will argue, that school psychologists, and thus schools, are locked into an outdated mode of working with students of nondominant cultural background.

2 & 3.   Sampling & Rationale

I have determined that I will interview school psychologists from _____ county. This county is representative of many in the United States that have experienced a rapid change in demographics over the course of the last decade. Like many, it has been forced to change its processes and structures to accommodate those changes. This research will attempt to understand one aspect of that process and structure. I have chosen school psychologists because of my expertise in this field and my familiarity with their role, but also because of their acknowledged influential role in the decision making process of special education (Mehan, 1986; Dana, 1991).

I will interview expert school psychologists because I am attempting to develop a best case scenario. This will be useful for practitioners, training, future, as well as practicing school psychologists and for developing new processes that are more responsive to the unique needs and characteristics of students from nondominant cultures. I will seek nominations from colleagues that I respect for their work in this field. Colleagues from whom I will seek nominations will also be individuals who are sensitive to this issue, as demonstrated by their leadership in past training workshops that deal with this topic.

I have made these decisions in full recognition of the potential threats to validity that my familiarity with this system might introduce. It is my opinion that the benefits outweigh the disadvantages. My familiarity with the system will provide easier rapport building and hopefully a richness of data that might not otherwise be possible. Furthermore, my expertise provides me with a better framework for understanding what questions might elicit the information that I am seeking. My familiarity with the language and jargon of this profession will be invaluable in teasing out innuendos of meaning that may be present by asking pertinent follow-up questions. I am cognizant of the fact that I will be biased in my interpretations. To address this, I will audiotape all interviews. I will listen to the tapes immediately have the interview and make notes and record memos immediately after. I will also enlist the assistance of a second reader to evaluate themes present in the data *(Joe: What is reasonable to expect from a second reader?)*

4 & 5. Methods & Rationale

I will collect my data primarily through interviews. The nature of my questions lends itself naturally to qualitative, interview data. This is not the type of information that can be readily gleaned from surveys or tests. Surveys may address the issue of what particular, published assessment tools are used for this process, but cannot begin to elicit the rich data available that cannot be quantified. Furthermore, I am interested in a process and as such, it is difficult to measure or to investigate through closed questioning that typifies quantitative methodology.

I am also interested in this methodology because it represents a new (for psychology) horizon. Many questions in psychology remain unanswered and cannot be answered only through quantitative, positivist methods. I understand from our readings that this is a poor argument for this methodology, but I believe that in the field of psychology this is particularly true. I have been involved in several quantitative research projects and while these obviously have their place, I would suggest that they presume the "black box" conceptualization of the human brain. Cognitive psychology is at a point that recognizes the inadequacies of this model. The subject and the subject's ideas can be an important source of data. It is this source that my research will attempt to tap.

Exercise 5.2   Questions and Methods Matrix

This exercise has two purposes. The first is for you to link your research questions and your research methods—to display the logical connections between your research questions and your selection, data collection, and data analysis decisions. The second purpose is to gain experience in using matrices as a tool; matrices are useful not only for research design, but also for ongoing monitoring of selection and data collection (see Miles & Huberman, 1994, p. 94) and for data analysis.

Doing this exercise can't be a mechanical process; it requires thinking about *how* your methods can provide answers to your research questions. One way to do this is

(Continued)

(Continued)

to start with your questions and ask what data you would need, how you could get these data, and how you could analyze them to answer these questions. You can also work in the other direction: Ask yourself *why* you want to collect and analyze the data in the way you propose—what will you learn from this? Then examine these connections between your research questions and your methods, and work on displaying these connections in a matrix. (This is an application of the Jeopardy exercise described in Chapter 4.) Doing this may require you to revise your questions, your planned methods, or both. Keep in mind that this exercise is intended to help you *make* your methods decisions, not simply as a final formulation or display of these (although this is one possible use of the completed matrix).
The exercise has two parts:

1. Construct the matrix itself. Your matrix should include columns for research questions, selection decisions, data collection methods, and kinds of analyses, but you can add any other columns you think would be useful in explaining the logic of your design.
2. Write a brief narrative *justification* for the choices you make in the matrix. One way to do this is as a separate memo, organized by research question, of the rationale for your choices in each row; another way (although more limited in length) is to include this as a column in the matrix itself (as in Figure 1.5).

NOTES

1. This is simply another application of the variance versus process distinction discussed earlier. Rather than focusing on the *degree* of prestructuring and its consequences (treating prestructuring as a variable that can affect other variables), I am concerned with the *ways* that prestructuring is employed in actual studies and *how* it affects other aspects of the design.

2. These differences can involve studying people with *greater* power and status than you, although the ethical implications of this for your study are less serious than when you are studying people with less power. A classic discussion of the former situation is Dexter (1970), *Elite and Specialized Interviewing.*

3. This process resembles that used for stratified random sampling; the main difference is that the final selection is purposeful rather than random.

4. Strauss (1987; Corbin & Strauss, 2007) developed a strategy that he called "theoretical sampling," which can be seen as a variation on purposeful selection. Theoretical sampling is driven by the theory that is inductively developed *during* the research (rather than by prior theory); it selects for examination those particular settings, individuals, events, or processes that are most relevant to the emerging theory.

5. Flick (2007) refers to this joint use of episodic and semantic interviewing as a form of triangulation, using this term broadly for the use of multiple methods in general. I think it is more useful to see it as gaining greater depth, as a use of Greene's (2007) dialectic approach, rather than simply as providing verification or complementary, but separate, understandings.

6

Validity

How Might You Be Wrong?

In the movie *E.T. the Extra-Terrestrial,* there is a scene near the end of the film where the hero and his friends are trying to rescue E.T. and help him return to his spaceship. One of the boys asks, "Can't he just beam up?" The hero gives him a disgusted look and replies, "This is reality, Fred."

Validity, like getting to E.T.'s spaceship, is the final component of your design. And as with E.T.'s dilemma, there is no way to "beam up" to valid conclusions. This is reality. The validity of your results is not guaranteed by following some standard, accepted procedure. As Brinberg and McGrath (1985) put it, "Validity is not a commodity that can be purchased with techniques" (p. 13). Instead, it depends on the relationship of your conclusions to reality, and no methods can completely assure that you have captured this.

The view that methods *could* guarantee validity was characteristic of early forms of positivism, which held that scientific knowledge could ultimately be reduced to a logical system that was securely grounded in irrefutable sense data. This position has been abandoned by philosophers, although it still informs many research methods texts (Phillips & Burbules, 2000, pp. 5–10). Many prominent researchers, both quantitative (e.g., Shadish et al., 2002, p. 34) and qualitative (e.g., Mishler, 1990) have argued that validity is a property of inferences rather than methods, and is never something that can be proved or taken for granted on the basis of the methods used. Validity is also relative: It has to be assessed in relationship to the purposes and circumstances of the research, rather than being a context-independent property of methods or conclusions. Finally, validity threats are made implausible by *evidence*, not methods; methods are only a way of getting evidence that can help you rule out these threats (Irwin, 2008).

The realist claim that validity can't be reduced to methods is one of the two main reasons that, in the model presented here, I have made validity a distinct component of qualitative design, separate from methods. The second reason is pragmatic: Validity is generally acknowledged to be a key *issue* in research design, and I think it's important that it be explicitly addressed. Przeworski and Salomon (1988) identified, as one of the three questions that proposal readers seek answers to "How will we know that the conclusions are valid?" And Bosk (1979) stated, "All fieldwork done by a single field-worker invites the question, Why should we believe it?" (p. 193). A lack of attention to validity threats is a common reason for the rejection of research proposals. Making validity an explicit component of design can help you to address this issue.

THE CONCEPT OF VALIDITY

The concept of validity has been controversial in qualitative research. Many qualitative scholars abandoned the concept entirely, because they saw it as too closely tied to quantitative assumptions that were inappropriate for qualitative research. In particular, some prominent qualitative researchers (e.g., Guba & Lincoln, 1989; Lincoln & Guba, 1985; cf. Denzin & Lincoln, 2005a) argued that any concept of validity that referred to a "real world" was incompatible with a constructivist approach, which denied that there was a reality outside of the constructions of different individuals and societies, and thus that there was any objective standard for judging such constructions. They proposed a number of other concepts that they saw as more appropriate for qualitative research, such as trustworthiness, authenticity, and quality. However, other researchers continued to use the term, though often with substantial rethinking of its meaning (e.g., Lather, 1993; Richardson, 1997); Lincoln, Lynham, and Guba (2011) summarize some of these positions.

This debate is continually evolving, and is too complex to discuss in detail here. In this book, I use validity in what I think is a fairly straightforward, commonsense way, to refer to the correctness or credibility of a description, conclusion, explanation, interpretation, or other sort of account. I think that this commonsense use of the term is consistent with the way it is generally used by qualitative researchers, and does not pose any serious philosophical problems.[1] This use of the term "validity" does not imply the existence of any "objective truth" to which an account can be compared. However, the idea of objective truth isn't essential to a theory of validity that does what most researchers want it to do, which is to give them some grounds for distinguishing accounts that are credible from those that are not. Nor are you required to attain some ultimate truth for your study to be useful and believable.

Geertz (1973) told the story of a British gentleman in colonial India who, upon learning that the world rested on the backs of four elephants, in turn stood on the back of a giant turtle, asked what the turtle stood on. Another turtle. And that turtle? "Ah, Sahib, after that it is turtles all the way down" (p. 29). Geertz's point is that there is no "bottom turtle" of ethnographic interpretation, that cultural analysis is essentially incomplete. While I accept Geertz's point, I would emphasize a different, critical realist lesson: You do not have to get to the bottom turtle to have a valid conclusion. You only have to get to a turtle you can stand on securely.

As Campbell (1988), Putnam (1990), and others have argued, we don't need an observer-independent gold standard to which we can compare our accounts to see if they are valid. All we require is the possibility of *testing* these accounts against the world, giving the phenomena that we are trying to understand the chance to prove us wrong. A key concept for validity is thus the *validity threat: a way you might be wrong*. These threats are often conceptualized as alternative explanations or interpretations, or what Huck and Sandler (1979) called "rival hypotheses." Such alternative interpretations are other possible ways of understanding your data—for example, that the people you interviewed are not presenting their actual views, or that you have ignored data that don't fit your interpretation, or that there is a different theoretical way of making sense of your data. Validity, as a component of your research design, consists of your conceptualization of these threats and the strategies you use to discover if they are plausible in your actual research situation, and to deal with them if they are plausible.

Quantitative and qualitative research typically deal with validity threats in quite different ways. Quantitative and experimental researchers generally attempt to design, in advance, controls that will deal with both anticipated and unanticipated threats to validity. These include control groups, statistical control of extraneous variables, randomized sampling and assignment, the framing of explicit hypotheses in advance of collecting the data, and the use of tests of statistical significance. These prior controls deal with most validity threats in an anonymous, generic fashion; as Campbell (1984) put it, "Randomization purports to control an infinite number of 'rival hypotheses' *without specifying what any of them are*" (p. 8).

Qualitative researchers, on the other hand, rarely have the benefit of previously planned comparisons, sampling strategies, or statistical manipulations that "control for" plausible threats, and must try to address most validity threats after the research has begun, using evidence collected during the research itself to make these "alternative hypotheses" implausible. This strategy of addressing particular validity threats *after* a tentative account has been developed, rather than by attempting to eliminate such threats through prior features of the research design, is, in fact, more fundamental to the scientific method than is the latter approach (Campbell, 1988; Platt, 1964; Shadish et al., 2002). However, this approach requires you to identify the *specific* threat in question and to develop ways to attempt to rule out that particular threat.

Your conception of validity threats and how they can be dealt with is a key issue in a qualitative research proposal, as well as in your design itself. Many proposal writers make the mistake of talking about validity only in general, theoretical terms, presenting abstract strategies such as bracketing, member checks, and triangulation that will supposedly protect their studies from invalidity. Such presentations are often "boilerplate"—language that has been borrowed from methods books or successful proposals, without any demonstration that the author has thought through how these strategies will actually be applied in the proposed study. These sections of a proposal often remind me of magical charms that are intended to drive away evil. As the anthropologist Bronislaw Malinowski (1954) argued, magic is used when technical skills are seen as inadequate to assure a desired outcome: "We do not find magic wherever the pursuit is certain, reliable, and well under the control of rational methods and technological processes. Further, we find magic where the element of danger is conspicuous" (p. 17). This accurately describes how many students view the task of writing their proposals.

In the rest of this chapter, I provide some concrete strategies for dealing with validity issues, ones that I hope will eliminate the need for magical invocation of abstract concepts. The main emphasis of a qualitative proposal should be on how you will rule out *specific* plausible alternatives and threats to your interpretations and explanations. Citations of authorities and standard approaches are less important than providing a clear argument that the approaches described will adequately deal with the particular threats in question, in the context of the study being proposed. Martha Regan-Smith's (1991) proposal (see Appendix A) provides a good example of this.

TWO SPECIFIC VALIDITY THREATS: BIAS AND REACTIVITY

I argued previously that qualitative researchers typically deal with validity threats as particular events or processes that could lead to invalid conclusions, rather than as generic "variables" that need to be controlled. It clearly is impossible for me to list all, or even the most important, validity threats to the conclusions of a qualitative study, as Cook and Campbell (1979) attempted to do for quasi-experimental studies. What I want to do instead is to discuss two broad types of threats to validity that are often raised in relation to qualitative studies: researcher bias, and the effect of the researcher on the individuals studied, often called reactivity.

Researcher Bias

Two important threats to the validity of qualitative conclusions are the selection of data that fit the researcher's existing theory, goals, or preconceptions, and the selection of data that "stand out" to the researcher (Miles & Huberman, 1994, p. 263; Shweder, 1980). Both of these involve the subjectivity of the researcher, a term that most qualitative researchers prefer to bias. As discussed in Chapters 2 and 3, it is impossible to deal with these issues by *eliminating* the researcher's theories, beliefs, and perceptual lens. Instead, qualitative research is primarily concerned with understanding how a *particular* researcher's values and expectations may have influenced the conduct and conclusions of the study (which may be either positive or negative) and avoiding the negative consequences of these. Explaining your possible biases and how you will deal with these is a key task of your research proposal. As one qualitative researcher, Fred Hess (personal communication), phrased it, validity in qualitative research is not the result of indifference, but of integrity.

Reactivity

The influence of the researcher on the setting or individuals studied, generally known as "reactivity," is a second problem that is often raised about qualitative studies. Trying to "control for" the effect of the researcher is appropriate to a quantitative, "variance theory" approach, in which the goal is to prevent *differences* between researchers from being an unwanted cause of variability in the outcome variables. However, eliminating the *actual* influence of the researcher is impossible (Hammersley & Atkinson, 1995), and the goal in a qualitative study is not to eliminate this influence, but to understand it and to use it productively.

For participant observation studies, reactivity is generally *not* as serious a validity threat as some people believe. Becker (1970, pp. 45–48) pointed out that, in natural settings, an observer is generally much less of an influence on participants' behavior than is the setting itself (though there are clearly exceptions to this, such as situations in which illegal behavior occurs). For interviews, in contrast, reactivity—more correctly, what Hammersley and Atkinson (1995) called "reflexivity," the fact that the researcher is part of the world he or she studies—is a powerful and inescapable influence; what the informant says is *always* influenced by the interviewer and the interview situation. While there are some things you can do to prevent the more undesirable consequences of this (such as avoiding leading questions), trying to minimize your influence is not a meaningful goal for qualitative research. As discussed previously for bias, what is important is to understand *how* you are influencing what the informant says, and how this affects the validity of the inferences you can draw from the interview.

VALIDITY TESTS: A CHECKLIST

Although methods and procedures do not guarantee validity, they are nonetheless essential to the process of ruling out validity threats and increasing the credibility of your conclusions. For this reason, I provide next a checklist of some of the most important strategies that can be used for this purpose. Miles and Huberman (1994, p. 262) included a more extensive list, having some overlap with mine, and other lists can be found in Becker (1970), Kidder (1981), Lincoln and Guba (1985), and Patton (1990). What follows is not a complete compilation of what these authors said—I urge you to consult their discussions—but simply what I see as most important (Maxwell, 2004c).

The overall point I want to make about these strategies is that they primarily operate not by *verifying* conclusions, but by *testing* the validity of your conclusions and the existence of potential threats to those conclusions (Campbell, 1988). The fundamental process in all of these tests is looking for evidence that could challenge your conclusions, or that bears on the plausibility of the potential threats.

Keep in mind that these strategies work only if you actually *use* them. Putting them in your proposal as though they were magical spells that could drive away the validity threats (and criticism of the proposal) won't do the job; you will need to demonstrate that you have thought through how you can effectively use them in your study. Not every strategy will work in a given study, and even trying to apply all the ones that are feasible might not be an efficient use of your time. As noted previously, you need to decide what *specific* validity threats are most serious and plausible, and what strategies are best able to deal with these.

1. Intensive, Long-Term Involvement

Becker and Geer (1957) claimed that long-term participant observation provides more complete data about specific situations and events than any other method. Not only does it provide more, and more different kinds, of data, but also enables you to check and confirm your observations and inferences. Repeated observations and interviews, as well as the sustained presence of the researcher in the setting studied, can help rule out spurious associations and premature theories. They also allow a much greater opportunity to develop and test alternative hypotheses during the course of the research. For example, Becker (1970, pp. 49–51) argued that his lengthy participant observation research with medical students not only allowed him to get beyond their public expressions of cynicism about a medical career and uncover an idealistic perspective, but also enabled him to understand the processes by which these different views were expressed in different social situations, and how students dealt with the conflicts between these perspectives.

2. Rich Data

Both long-term involvement and intensive interviews enable you to collect "rich" data, data that are detailed and varied enough that they provide a full and revealing picture of what is going on[2] (Becker, 1970, pp. 51–62). In interview studies, such data generally require verbatim transcripts of the interviews, not just notes on what you felt was significant. For observation, rich data are the product of detailed, descriptive note taking (or videotaping and transcribing) of the specific, concrete events that you observe (Emerson, et al., 1995). Becker (1970) argued that such data

> counter the twin dangers of respondent duplicity and observer bias by making it difficult for respondents to produce data that uniformly support a mistaken conclusion, just as they make it difficult for the observer to restrict his observations so that he sees only what supports his prejudices and expectations. (p. 53)

Martha Regan-Smith's (1991) study of medical school teaching (see Appendix A) relied on lengthy observation and detailed field notes recording the teachers' actions in classes and students' reactions to these. In addition, she conducted and transcribed numerous interviews with students, in which they explained in detail not only what it was that the exemplary teachers did that increased their learning, but also how and why these teaching methods were beneficial. This set of data provided a rich, detailed grounding for, and test of, her conclusions.

3. Respondent Validation

Respondent validation (Bryman, 1988, pp. 78–80; Lincoln & Guba, 1985, referred to this as *member checks*, a term that has become widely used for this strategy) is systematically soliciting feedback about your data and conclusions from the people you are studying. This is the single most important way of ruling out the possibility of misinterpreting the meaning of what participants say and do and the perspective they have on what is going on, as well as being an important way of identifying your biases and misunderstandings of what you observed. However, participants' feedback is no more inherently valid than their interview responses; both should be taken simply as *evidence* regarding the validity of your account (cf. Hammersley & Atkinson, 1995). For a more detailed discussion of this strategy, see Bloor (1983), Bryman (1988, pp. 78–80), Guba and Lincoln (1989), Miles and Huberman (1994, pp. 242–243), and Sandelowski (2008).

4. Intervention

Although some qualitative researchers have seen experimental manipulation as inconsistent with qualitative approaches (e.g., Lincoln & Guba, 1985), informal interventions are often used within traditional qualitative studies that lack a formal "treatment." For example, Goldenberg (1992), in a study of two students' reading progress and the effect that their teacher's expectations and behavior had on this progress, shared his interpretation of one student's failure to meet these expectations with the teacher. This resulted in a change in the teacher's behavior toward the student, and a subsequent improvement in the student's reading. The intervention with the teacher, and the resulting changes in her behavior and the student's progress, supported Goldenberg's claim that the teacher's behavior, rather than her expectations of the student, was the primary cause of the student's progress or lack thereof. In addition, Goldenberg provided an account of the *process* by which the change occurred, which corroborated the identification of the teacher's behavior as the cause of the improvement in a way that a simple correlation could never do.

Furthermore, in field research, the researcher's presence is *always* an intervention in some ways, as discussed in Chapter 5, and the effects of this presence can be used to develop or test ideas about the group or topic studied. For example, J. Briggs (1970), in her study of an Eskimo family, used a detailed analysis of how the family reacted to her often inappropriate behavior as an "adopted daughter" to develop her theories about the culture and dynamics of Eskimo social relations.

5. Searching for Discrepant Evidence and Negative Cases

Identifying and analyzing discrepant data and negative cases is a key part of the logic of validity testing in qualitative research. Instances that cannot be accounted for by a particular interpretation or explanation can point to important defects in that account. However, there are times when an apparently discrepant instance is not persuasive, as when the interpretation of the discrepant data is itself in doubt. Physics is full of examples of supposedly "disconfirming" experimental evidence that was later found to be flawed. The basic principle here is that you need to rigorously examine both the supporting and the discrepant data to assess whether it is more plausible to retain or modify the conclusion, being aware of all of the pressures to ignore data that do not fit your conclusions. Asking others for feedback on your conclusions is a valuable way to identify your biases and assumptions and to check for flaws in your logic or methods. In particularly difficult cases, the best you may be able to do is to report the discrepant evidence and allow readers to evaluate this and draw their own conclusions (Wolcott, 1990).

6. Triangulation

Triangulation—collecting information from a diverse range of individuals and settings, using a variety of methods—was discussed in Chapter 5. This strategy reduces the risk of chance associations and of systematic biases due to a specific method, and allows a better assessment of the generality of the explanations that one develops. The most extensive discussion of triangulation as a validity-testing strategy in qualitative research is by Fielding and Fielding (1986).

One of Fielding and Fielding's (1986) key points is that it is not true that triangulation automatically increases validity. First, the methods that are triangulated may have the *same* biases and sources of invalidity, and thus provide only a false sense of security. For example, interviews, questionnaires, and documents are all vulnerable to self-report bias. Fielding and Fielding therefore emphasized the need to recognize the fallibility of *any* particular method or data, and to triangulate in terms of *validity threats.* As argued previously, you should think about what particular sources of error or bias might exist, and look for specific ways to deal with this, rather than relying on your selection of methods to do this for you. In the final analysis, validity threats are made implausible by *evidence,* not methods.

7. Numbers

Many of the conclusions of qualitative studies have an implicit quantitative component. Any claim that a particular phenomenon is typical, rare, or prevalent in the setting or population studied, or that some behaviors or themes were more common than others, is an inherently quantitative claim, and requires some quantitative support. Becker (1970) coined the term "quasi-statistics" to refer to the use of simple numerical results that can be readily derived from the data. As he argued that

> One of the greatest faults in most observational case studies has been their failure to make explicit the quasi-statistical basis of their conclusions. (pp. 81–82)

Using numbers in this way does not make a study quantitative in the sense of shifting it to a variance theory approach, as described in Chapters 2, 3, and 5; it simply makes explicit, and more precise, the implicitly quantitative nature of such claims. For more on the use of numbers in qualitative research, see Maxwell (2010) and Seale (1999).

The appropriate use of numbers not only allows you to test and support claims that are inherently quantitative, but also enables you to assess the *amount* of evidence in your data that bears on a particular conclusion or threat, such as how many discrepant instances exist and from how many different sources they were obtained. This strategy is used effectively in a classic participant-observation study of medical students by Becker, Geer, Hughes, and Strauss (1961), which presented more than 50 tables and graphs of the amount and distribution of observational and interview data supporting their conclusions. In addition, numbers are important for identifying and communicating the *diversity* of actions and perspectives in the settings and populations you study (Maxwell, 2011b, Chapter 4).

8. Comparison

Explicit comparisons (such as between intervention and control groups) for assessing validity threats are most common in quantitative, variance theory research, but there are numerous uses of comparison in qualitative studies, particularly in multicase or multi-site studies. Miles and Huberman (1994, p. 254) provided a list of strategies for comparison, as well as advice on their use. Such comparisons (including comparisons of the same setting at different times) can address one of the main objections to using qualitative methods for understanding causality—their inability to explicitly address the "counterfactual" of what would have happened *without* the presence of the presumed cause (Shadish et al., 2002, p. 501).

In addition, single-setting qualitative studies, or interview studies of a relatively homogeneous group of interviewees, often incorporate less formal comparisons that contribute to the interpretability of the results. There may be a literature on typical settings or individuals of the kind studied that makes it easier to identify the relevant characteristics and processes in an exceptional case and to understand their significance. In other instances, the participants in the setting studied may themselves have experience with other settings or with the same setting at an earlier time, and the researcher may be able to draw on this experience to identify the crucial factors and the effect that these have.

For example, Martha Regan-Smith's (1991) study of how exceptional medical-school teachers help students to learn (see Appendix A) included only faculty who had won the "Best Teacher" award. From the point of view of quantitative design, this was an "uncontrolled" study, vulnerable to all of the validity threats identified by Campbell and Stanley (1963). However, both of the previously mentioned forms of implicit comparison were employed in the research. First, there is a great deal of published information about medical school teaching, and Regan-Smith was able to use both this background and her extensive knowledge of medical schools to identify what it was that the teachers she studied did in their classes that was distinctive. Second, the students she interviewed explicitly contrasted these teachers with others whose classes they felt were not as helpful. In addition to these comparisons, the validity of her research conclusions depended substantially on a process approach; the students explained in detail not only *what* it was that the exemplary teachers did that increased their learning, but also *how* and *why* these teaching methods were beneficial. Many of these explanations were corroborated by Regan-Smith's experiences as a participant-observer in these teachers' classes and by the teachers' explanations of why they taught the way they did.

Matrices, described in Chapters 1 and 5, can be valuable in planning how to effectively use such strategies. Figure 6.1 is a matrix focused on validity concerns, developed by Sarah Daily for the study of early childhood teachers' views of developing children's emotional competence described in Example 3.1; Example 6.1 is a memo that she wrote reflecting on the matrix.

(Text continues on page 135.)

Figure 6.1 Validity Matrix for a Study of Early Childhood Teachers' Views of Developing Children's Emotional Competence

1. What do I need to know?	2. Why do I need to know this	3. What kind of data will answer the questions	4. Analysis Plans	5. Validity Threats	6. Possible strategies for dealing with validity threats	7. Rationale for strategies
RQ 1: How do early childhood education (ECE) teachers view/describe their role in developing children's emotional competence (EC)?	We know little about teacher's perceptions of and roles in children's social emotional learning (SEL) despite	Semi-structured focus group responses	Video Taping, transcribing, content analysis, coding, comparing coding with other coders, re-reading, examining data at the individual, school/center level, risk level (head start vs. private) and whole sample	2) Reactivity-participating in a focus group with co-workers/peers on children's SEL may increase socially desirable responses and not accurately reflect their true opinions	2) Use of open ended script that minimizes indications of researcher bias. A single focus group moderator will be used to maintain some level of consistency in question delivery, timing, emphasis, and reactivity potential. Other research team members will provide the moderator with feedback after watching taped sessions.	2) Pilot Focus Group showed a variety of opinions expressed and some debate amongst participants indicating comfort expressing non-conforming views. Merton, Fiske & Kendall (1990) discuss the importance of leaving questions open to allow for

partnership? in conflict? or not at all) with parents	level to identify patterns, similarities, and differences.		3) Presence of co-workers may influence minority expressions of opinions about SEL value	Finally – if discrepancies seem to exist between a teacher's responses during the focus group and her true opinion (e.g., she changes her mind after group pressure), we will allow for follow up in person or phone interviews with participants to clarify. 3) We will conduct separate focus groups for lead teachers and assistant teachers to remove potential pressure from supervisors' opinions	discussion of topics the researcher may not deem important or not agree with. 3) The industrial / organizational psychology literature emphasizes the potential impact of supervisors on employee responsiveness and expression
RQ2: How do (or do?) ECE teachers perceive their	If we're assessing teachers SEC, we should also	Focus group responses, Self rated emotional	1) Video taping, transcribing, conventional	1) Testing effect – teachers who participate in focus groups	1) Comparison for order effect (surveys first vs. focus groups first)	1) Teacher will complete surveys electronically and we'll be able to

(Continued)

Figure 6.1 (Continued)

1. What do I need to know?	2. Why do I need to know this	3. What kind of data will answer the questions	4. Analysis Plans	5. Validity Threats	6. Possible strategies for dealing with validity threats	7. Rationale for strategies
own emotional competence as impacting children's SEL?	have some understanding of how they feel it may/may not impact their performance in the classroom	intelligence scale (SREIS), Teachers social emotional learning beliefs scale (TSBS), Coping with children's negative emotions sclae (CCNES-T), Teacher's Socialization Self Test (TESST-S)	content analysis, coding, comparing coding with other coders, re-reading, etc. 2) Cluster analysis to divide teachers into SEC groups for comparison	may be more aware of own emotions/ reactions when completing surveys or vice versa and may respond differently to one than if they had never completed the other. 2) Perception of value of teacher EC may be highly correlated with own EC	2) Triangulation between survey responses and focus group responses	split the group using the date/time stamp on the survey into those completing surveys first and those participating in focus groups first to test for differences. 2) Maxwell (2005); Teddlie & Tashakkori (2003); Morgan (1997)

| RQ3: How do teacher views of SEL and EC relate to their observed classroom socialization practices? | Teachers who provide more effective SEL environments may also be those who place more value in SEL and see themselves as pivotal to children's development of these skills | FOCAL observations of teacher's expressions of emotions and reactions to children's expressions | Examine focus group coding and transcripts in comparison with rates/ frequencies of teacher's expressions of emotions and their reactions to child emotions (FOCAL). | 1) Potential for lack of variability in responses in focus group | 1) As discussed above, the focus group protocol will support the expression of varying opinions as was seen in the pilot group | Merton, Fiske & Kendall (1990) |
| | | | | 2) Potential for lack of variability in expression of emotions and/ or reactions to children's emotions. | 2) Anecdotal observations and pilot testing of the observational measurement tool will be examined for variability. Additionally, the inclusion of multiple center types and multiple levels of teacher experience/responsibility are expected to yield sufficient variability. | 2) We are following the procedures outlined by Altmann (1974) and Bakeman & Gottman (1997) that have been used with previous adaptations of this coding scheme. |

(Continued)

Figure 6.1 (Continued)

1. What do I need to know?	2. Why do I need to know this	3. What kind of data will answer the questions	4. Analysis Plans	5. Validity Threats	6. Possible strategies for dealing with validity threats	7. Rationale for strategies
						Significant variability has been seen in parents previously and we expect some carry over to teachers.
RQ3: How do teacher views of SEL and EC relate to their observed classroom socialization practices? (continued)				3) Teacher and/or child reactivity to observers in classroom	3) We will conduct "getting to know you" visits in every classroom during which researchers will attempt to blend into the background before any data is collected; also teachers will be observed repeatedly over multiple visits each year of the study - this longer involvement should help reduce reactivity spurious/ premature conclusions.	3) This method of acclimatization has been used in some of our previous projects with good results. Maxwell (2005) discusses the benefits of "long involvement" (p. 110).

Example 6.1   Memo to Accompany Figure 6.1

In a discussion on education research, John Platt (1973) talked about how some fields of scientific research are able to rapidly advance knowledge and understanding because of the systematic application of a process these disciplines use to approach research questions. The first step in this process is to devise alternative hypotheses, that is, to think about all the ways a given conclusion could be wrong (p. 204). Taking the time to think through the possible ways in which the possible conclusions to my research questions could be wrong is an important process because it will increase my ability to develop strong inference from my research, and add to the robustness with which I can convince readers that I have thoroughly worked to understand my data from all angles. The identified validity threats have helped me work though a set of possible barriers to understanding and developing conclusions about the emergence of SRL and the processes that influence SRL development.

Identifying these threats has also helped me to see how important it is to integrate and address validity threats in all aspects of my research design, and not simply think of validity as an item to address on my research process to-do list. For example, in thinking through the first threat—lack of intensive, long-term engagement, it occurred to me that addressing this validity threat has implications for the sequence of my research procedures, the interview guide I develop, my research questions, and data collection methods. Had I simply moved forward with developing my research design without thinking through these implications, it might not be possible for me to execute post hoc strategies to address these threats.

To identify strategies to address the validity threats I've identified I found myself revisiting Maxwell's *Using Qualitative Methods for Causal Explanation* (2004) paper and *Qualitative Research Design* (2005). I found these two resources most helpful because throughout the semester I've come closer to developing a qualitative research design. These two resources helped me think about which strategies could be used in a mixed methods study but may also more readily lend themselves to a more qualitative study such as mine. As a result, the validity matrix largely reflects the strategies identified from these resources and may be considered strategies that fall into the *observation and analysis of process* strategies and *developing and assessing alternative explanations approaches* strategies.

I decided to do the validity matrix and memo because it has been the most difficult concept for me to both understand and apply to my own research. Until this assignment, I had not taken the time to document these threats in a comprehensive way. As I reflect on this exercise one thing that strikes me is that these identified threats may just be the tip of the iceberg! There are so many moving parts in this, or perhaps any research study, that the opportunity for doubts to be cast upon my methods or conclusions are abundant. Moving forward I can see now that I still have

(Continued)

(Continued)

work to do to continue to build this matrix. I am reminded of Greene's discussion of Teddlie and Tashakkorri's *design quality* and *interpretive rigor*. That is, as I think about the validity of my study moving forward, this assignment has helped remind me not to think about validity as isolated variables that need to be controlled for, but rather how carefully working through the design of my study and the quality with which I interpret and present my results will continue to help strengthen the validity of my conclusions.

Exercise 6.1   Identifying and Dealing With Validity Threats

This exercise involves writing a memo similar to that in Example 6.1, which can either stand by itself or be based on (or enable you to develop) a matrix such as Figure 6.1. There are two main issues that you should address in this memo:

1. What are the most serious validity threats (alternative explanations) that you need to be concerned with in your study? In other words, what are the main ways in which you might be mistaken about what's going on? Be as specific as you can, rather than just giving general categories. Also, think about *why* you believe these might be serious threats.

2. What could you do in your research design (including data collection and data analysis) to assess the likelihood of these threats and deal with them if they are serious? Start by brainstorming possible strategies, and then consider which of these strategies are *practical* for your study, as well as theoretically relevant.

   Remember that some validity threats are unavoidable; you will need to acknowledge these in your proposal or in the conclusions to your study, but no one expects you to have airtight answers to *every* possible threat. The key issue is how plausible and how serious these unavoidable threats are.

GENERALIZATION IN QUALITATIVE RESEARCH

I have deliberately left generalization until the end, because I consider it a separate issue from validity proper. Generalization, in research, refers to extending research results, conclusions, or other accounts that are based on a study of particular individuals, settings, times, or institutions to other individuals, settings, times, or institutions than those directly studied (Polit & Beck, 2010). Qualitative researchers usually study a single setting or a small number of individuals or sites, using theoretical or purposeful rather than probabil-ity sampling, and rarely make explicit claims about the generalizability of their accounts.

However, an important distinction is that between *internal* and *external* generaliz-ability (Maxwell, 1992). Internal generalizability refers to the generalizability of a conclusion *within* the case, setting, or group studied, to persons, events, times, and set-tings that were not directly observed, interviewed, or otherwise represented in the data collected. External generalizability, in contrast, refers to its generalizability *beyond* that case, setting, or group, to other persons, times, and settings. This is not an absolute or clearcut distinction, because it depends on how the researcher defines the case, setting, or group studied, something that may change during the course of the research. However, I think it can be a useful distinction to consider in planning your methods and addressing potential limitations to your conclusions.

Internal generalizability is clearly a key issue for qualitative case studies; the validity of the conclusions of a case study depend on their internal generalizability to the case as a whole. If you are studying the patterns of interaction between the teacher and stu-dents in a single classroom, your account of that classroom as a whole is seriously jeopardized if you have selectively focused on particular students or kinds of interac-tions and ignored others. Sampling issues are particularly relevant to internal generaliz-ability, because it is impossible to observe everything even in one small setting, and a lack of internal generalizability can seriously impair the validity of a study's conclu-sions. A key issue for internal generalizability is to adequately understand the *variation* in the phenomena of interest in the setting or group of people studied. As mentioned in Chapter 5, diversity is often underestimated in qualitative research, either by inadequate sampling, by overemphasizing common features or themes and ignoring of minimizing differences, or by imposing uniform theories that don't fit all of the data (Maxwell, 2011b, pp. 64–65). As described previously, the use of numbers to adequately charac-terize such diversity is an important way to check the internal generalizability of your conclusions.

External generalizability poses somewhat different issues for qualitative studies. As noted earlier, external generalization in qualitative research is rather different from generalization in quantitative research, and the imposition of quantitative views of generalization on qualitative research has frequently been criticized (e.g., Donmoyer, 1990; Guba & Lincoln, 1989). Bryman (1988) argued that "The 'problem' of case study generalization entails a misunderstanding of the aims of such research. In particular, the misconception arises from a tendency to approach a case study as if it were a sample of one drawn from a wider universe of such cases" (p. 90).

In fact, the value of a qualitative study may depend on its *lack* of external general-izability in the sense of being representative of a larger population, as discussed in Chapter 5; it may provide an account of a setting or population that is illuminating as an extreme case or ideal type. Freidson's (1975) study of a medical group practice (Example 3.3) made an important contribution to theory and policy precisely because this was a group for whom social controls on practice should have been most likely to be effective. The failure of such controls in this case not only highlights a social process that is likely to exist in other groups, but also provides a more persuasive argument for the unworkability of such controls than would a study of a representative group.

This does not mean that qualitative studies are never generalizable beyond the setting or informants studied. The most important reason for this is that the generalizability of qualitative studies is usually based not on explicit sampling of some defined population to which the results can be extended, but on the development of a theory of the *processes* operating in the case studied, ones that may well operate in other cases, but that may produce different outcomes in different circumstances (Becker, 1991; Ragin, 1987; Yin, 1994). Becker (1991) provided an example of how a theory of the process by which prisoners' deprivations create a distinctive prison culture can be generalized from men's to women's prisons, despite the fact that the actual prison culture is quite different in the two cases. He argued that "generalizations are not about how all prisons are just the same, but about a process, the same no matter where it occurs, in which variations in conditions create variations in results" (p. 240).

In addition, qualitative studies often have what the statistician Judith Singer (personal communication) called "face generalizability"; there is no obvious reason *not* to believe that the results apply more generally. Finally, Hammersley (1992, pp. 189–191) and Weiss (1994, pp. 26–29) listed a number of features that lend plausibility to generalizations from case studies or nonrandom samples, including respondents' assessments of generalizability, the similarity of dynamics and constraints to other situations, the presumed depth or universality of the phenomenon studied, and corroboration from other studies. All of these characteristics can provide credibility to generalizations from qualitative studies, but none permits the kinds of precise extrapolation of results to defined populations that probability sampling allows.

NOTES

1. I present the philosophical argument that informs these statements elsewhere (Maxwell, 1992, 2002, 2004c, 2011b). I also think that the concept of validity presented here is compatible with some postmodern approaches to validity (e.g., Kvale, 1989; Lather, 1993; see Maxwell, 1995, 2004b).

2. Some qualitative researchers refer to these sorts of data as *thick description*, a phrase coined by the philosopher Gilbert Ryle (1949) and applied to ethnographic research by Geertz (1973). However, this is not what either Ryle or Geertz meant by the phrase. Thick description, as Geertz used it, is description that incorporates the intentions of the actors and the codes of signification that give their actions meaning for them, what anthropologists call an *emic* account—one that represents the meanings and perspectives of the participants, not simply those of the researcher (Fetterman, 2008). It has nothing to do with the amount of detail provided. For a more detailed discussion of this concept, see Maxwell and Mittapalli (2008b).

7

Research Proposals

Presenting and Justifying a Qualitative Study

Catherine the Great of Russia once decided to take a cruise down the Danube to view that part of her empire. Her prime minister, Grigory Potemkin, knowing that the poverty of the region would not be pleasing to the empress, allegedly built fake villages along the banks of the river and forcibly staffed these with cheering peasants to impress the empress with how prosperous and thriving the area was. The term "Potemkin village" has since come to be used to refer to "an impressive facade or show designed to hide an undesirable fact or condition" ("Potemkin Village," 1984).

You don't want your proposal to be a Potemkin village—one that does not reflect what you actually believe or plan to do, but is simply fabricated to get approval or money for the study or to fit what you think a proposal should say. Aside from the fact that reviewers are usually fairly good at detecting such facades, the most serious danger of a Potemkin village proposal is that you may be taken in by your fabrication, thinking that you have, in fact, solved your design problems, and thus ignoring your actual theories, goals, questions, and situation and the implications of these—your real research design.

Such proposals are often the result of the writer not having worked out (or worse, not having understood the *need* to work out) the actual design of the study, and thus having to substitute a fake design for this. An ignorance of, or refusal to acknowledge, this real design and the conditions that affect it are certain to cause problems when you actually try to do the study. For this reason, you need to have a fairly clear idea of your design before you attempt to write a proposal for the study. Attempting to create a proposal before you have your design at least tentatively worked out will not only make the task of writing the proposal much more difficult (as I argued previously, in the Preface to the first edition of this book), it may lock your thinking into a Potemkin village design, one that will hinder your development of a workable real design for your study.

Of course, as discussed in previous chapters, your research design will evolve as you conduct the study, and therefore a proposal for a qualitative study can't present an exact specification of what you will do. However, this is no excuse for not developing the design for your study in as much detail as you can at this point, or for failing to clearly communicate this design. In your proposal, you simply need to explain the kinds of flexibility that your study requires, and indicate, as best you can, how you will go about making future design decisions. For dissertation proposals, your committee often wants to see that you have demonstrated the *ability* to design a coherent and feasible study, providing evidence that you are aware of the key issues in your proposed research and ways of dealing with these, rather than requiring a completely worked-out design.

In this chapter, I explain the connections between a study's research design and an effective proposal for that study, and provide some guidelines and advice on how to accomplish the transition from design to proposal. I believe that the model that I have presented in this book simplifies and facilitates this transition, and provides a useful framework for thinking about proposal structure and content. Much more detailed and specific advice on proposal writing is provided by Locke, Spirduso, and Silverman (2007).

I will begin with the purposes and structure of a research proposal, and then take up the ways in which the design of your study connects to these purposes and structure. Finally, I will discuss the specific parts of a proposal and the key issues that a proposal for qualitative research needs to address.

THE PURPOSE OF A PROPOSAL

The structure of a proposal shouldn't follow an arbitrary format or set of rules; it's closely tied to the purpose of a proposal. This purpose is so fundamental that when you are working on a proposal, you should post it above your desk or computer: *The purpose of a proposal is to explain and justify your proposed study to an audience of nonexperts on your topic.*

There are four key concepts in this statement:

1. *Explain.* You want your readers to clearly understand what you plan to do. Locke, Spirduso, and Silverman (2000) emphasized that "advisors and reviewers misunderstand student proposals far more often than they disagree with what is proposed" (p. 123). This observation is abundantly supported by my experience, both with advising and reviewing student proposals and with submitting and reviewing grant proposals. In writing and editing your proposal, clarity is a primary goal.

2. *Justify.* You want the readers of your proposal to understand not only what you plan to do, but *why*—your rationale for how you plan to conduct the study. Proposals are often not accepted, even when the study is clearly described, because it isn't clear why the author wants to do the study a certain way. Your readers may not understand how your proposed methods will provide valid answers to your research questions, or how the questions address important issues or purposes. They may also question whether you have a good reason for doing the study this way, or if you are simply using "boilerplate" language that you've borrowed from other studies.

3. *Your proposed study.* Your proposal should be about your study, not the literature, your research topic, or research methods in general. You should ruthlessly edit out anything in

the proposal that does not directly contribute to the explanation and justification of your study. A proposal is no place to display your general knowledge of the literature on your topic,[1] your theoretical or methodological sophistication, or your political views on the issues you plan to investigate;[2] this will generally annoy your reviewers, who are trying to determine if your proposed study makes sense.

Students sometimes focus their proposal on their planned dissertation, rather than on the research that they propose to do. They provide lengthy, chapter-by-chapter descriptions of what the dissertation will cover, and use language such as "In my dissertation, I will discuss . . ." While it can occasionally be helpful, in explaining and justifying aspects of your study, to refer to how you intend to present these in the dissertation, these references to your dissertation more often are red herrings, interfering with your presentation of the actual research and its design.

4. *Nonexperts.* You can't assume any particular specialized knowledge on the part of your readers. Grant proposals in the social sciences and related fields are generally *not* assigned to readers based on their expertise on your specific topic, and students often will have faculty reviewing their proposals who are not knowledgeable about the specific area of the proposed study. You need to carefully examine your proposal to make sure that everything in it will be clear to a nonspecialist. (The best way to do this is generally to give the proposal to some nonspecialists and ask them to tell you what isn't clear.)

THE PROPOSAL AS AN ARGUMENT

Another way of putting the points made previously is that your proposal is an argument *for* your study. It needs to explain the logic behind your proposed research, rather than simply describe or summarize the study, and to do so in a way that nonspecialists will understand. (It should not, however, attempt to defend your anticipated conclusions; doing so may raise serious questions about your biases. You want to demonstrate that you are open to having your prior beliefs overturned by your data.) Each piece of your proposal should form a clear part of this argument.

The essential feature of a good argument is *coherence*, and a proposal needs to be coherent in two different senses of this term. First, it has to *cohere*—flow logically from one point to the next, and hang together as an integrated whole. The connections among different components of your design are crucial to this coherence. You need to understand why you're doing what you're doing, rather than blindly following rules, models, or standard practice. Examples 7.1 and 7.2, Exercise 7.1, and Appendices A and B can help you to achieve this.

Second, your argument has to *be* coherent—to make sense to the reviewers. You need to put yourself in your readers' shoes, and think about how what you say will be understood by them. This requires avoiding jargon, unnecessarily complex style, and what Becker (2007) called "classy writing." A failure to achieve these two aspects of coherence is the source of the most common problems with proposals: Either they have inconsistencies or gaps in their reasoning, or they don't adequately communicate to the reviewers what the author wants to do and why, or both. Both of the two example proposals (Appendix A and B) are good examples of clear, straightforward language that largely avoids these problems.

THE RELATIONSHIP BETWEEN YOUR RESEARCH DESIGN AND YOUR PROPOSAL ARGUMENT

Reviewers will be asking many questions while reading your proposal, questions that the argument of your proposal needs to address. According to Locke et al. (2007),

The author must answer three questions:

1. What do we already know or do?
2. How does this particular question relate to what we already know or do?
3. Why select this particular method of investigation? (p. 17)

These questions emphasize the connections along one axis of my model of research design, the axis consisting of your conceptual framework, research questions, and methods (see Figure 7.1).

In contrast, Przeworski and Salomon (1988), in their suggestions for applicants seeking funding from the Social Science Research Council, stated that

Every proposal reader constantly scans for clear answers to three questions:

• What are we going to learn as the result of the proposed project that we do not already know?
• Why is it worth knowing?
• How will we know that the conclusions are valid? (p. 2)

These questions, in contrast to those of Locke et al. (2007), emphasize the connections along the other axis of the model, the one consisting of your goals, research questions, and validity.

Thus, the relationships among the components of your research design constitute a crucial part of the argument of your proposal. These relationships provide the coherence that your argument depends on. Above all else, your proposal must convey to the readers your answers to the previous questions, and what the connections are between these answers.

A MODEL FOR PROPOSAL STRUCTURE

The model of research design that I have presented in this book can be directly mapped onto one way of organizing a qualitative proposal. This format is not the only way to

Figure 7.1   Relationship Between Research Design and Questions About Research Proposals

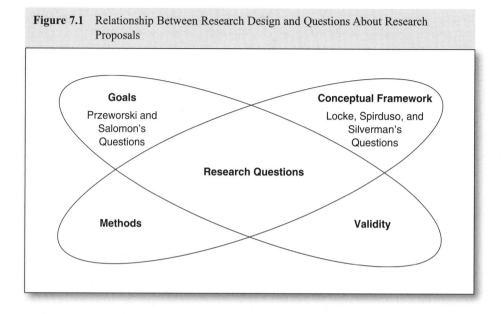

structure a proposal, but it is a fairly standard and generally understood format, and one that lends itself particularly well to communicating the design of a qualitative study. However, every university and funding source has its own requirements and preferences regarding proposal structure, and these must take precedence for your official proposal if they conflict with what I present here. I still recommend, though, that you use the structure I describe here as a first step in writing the proposal, even if you will eventually convert it into a different format. I have seen too many students become lost by trying to use a traditional or required proposal structure to *develop* their design, producing a repetitive, incoherent argument that fails to convey the real strengths of their research.

I will first display the relationships between research design and proposal structure in diagram form (Figure 7.2), and then go through each part of the proposal structure in detail, explaining how it relates to my model of research design. This explanation will make more sense if it is read in conjunction with the two example proposals, (Appendix A and B) and my commentary that I've included in the first proposal. What is important about the structure I describe isn't having separate sections with these names; this is simply a useful organizational tool that can be modified if it conflicts with the structure you are required to follow. The point is to organize the issues in a way that clearly communicates your research design and its justification.

In many universities and departments, there is a standard, three-chapter format to which dissertation proposals must conform. (There is also a widespread belief that these three chapters should constitute the first three chapter of your dissertation, an idea that I think is particularly inappropriate and unhelpful for qualitative dissertations. In your

Figure 7.2   Relationship Between Research Design and Proposal Structure

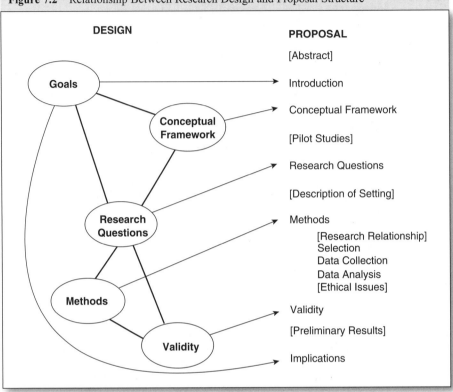

dissertation, all of these chapters, but particularly the methods chapter, will need substantial revision based on what actually happens in your research.) Elizabeth Riddle's proposal (Appendix B) illustrates how the different components I describe can be incorporated into this format.

1. Abstract

Not all proposals will require an abstract, but if you need to have one, this is the place to provide an overview and "road map," not just of the study itself, but also of the argument of your proposal. Your abstract should present in abbreviated form the actual argument for your research, not simply provide placeholders that will later be filled in with real content (Becker, 2007, pp. 50–53). Regan-Smith's abstract (see Appendix A) is a model for how to do this. A useful tool in developing this argument is the argument outline exercise presented later (Examples 7.1 and 7.2 and Exercise 7.1).

2. Introduction

The introduction to your proposal "sets the stage for your research, explaining . . . what you want to do and why" (Peters, 1992, p. 202). It should clearly present the goals of your study and the problem(s) it addresses, and give an overview of your main research questions and of the kind of study you are proposing. (A full presentation of your research questions is often better reserved until after the conceptual framework section, when the theoretical grounding of the questions will be clearer, but this is not an absolute rule.) It should also explain the structure of the proposal itself, if this could be confusing.

3. Conceptual Framework

This section is often called the "literature review"; this term is misleading, for reasons that I explained in Chapter 3, but you may need to use it, depending on whom the proposal is written for. This section of the proposal has two key functions. First, it needs to show how your proposed research fits into what is already known (its relationship to existing theory and research) and how it makes a contribution to our understanding of your topic (its intellectual goals). Second, it needs to explain the theoretical framework that informs your study. These functions are usually accomplished by discussing prior theory and research, but the point is not to *summarize* what's already been done in this field. Instead, it is to *ground* your proposed study in the relevant previous work, and to give the reader a clear sense of your theoretical approach to the phenomena that you propose to study.

Thus, the essential characteristic of a good literature review is *relevance*; each work discussed should be relevant to your proposed study, and you need to explain *how* it is relevant—how it informs, or has implications for, your study—if this is not obvious. The American Psychological Association's *Publication Manual* (2010), a widely used guide for dissertations, proposals, and publications in the social sciences and applied fields, says, "Cite and reference only works pertinent to the specific issue and not those that are of only tangential or general significance . . . avoid nonessential details; instead, emphasize pertinent findings, relevant methodological issues, and major conclusions" (p. 28). (For an extended discussion of this issue, see Maxwell, 2006.) Remember the point made in Chapter 3: Sometimes the most relevant theory or research for your study may come from outside the specific field of your topic. [3]

One qualification to this principle is needed for the literature review in a dissertation proposal. Some advisors and committee members believe that this review should demonstrate that you know the literature in the field of your study, whether it is relevant to your specific study or not. If you are in this situation, your literature review will need to be more comprehensive than I describe; check with your committee about this. However, you *still* need to identify the work that is most relevant to your study and the specific ideas that you can use in your conceptual framework (and other aspects of your design), because doing this is essential to creating a coherent presentation of, and argument for, your research plans, as well as for actually publishing your results. (For more on these two conceptions of a dissertation literature review, and their consequences, see Maxwell, 2006).

Insofar as your personal experience and knowledge form an important part of your conceptual framework, these should be discussed somewhere in your proposal; both Martha Regan-Smith and Elizabeth Riddle devote a separate part of their conceptual framework sections to these. The key issue, again, is *relevance*; the connection of the experience and views discussed in this section to your study must be clear.

Any pilot studies that you have done also need to be discussed in the proposal, explaining their implications for your research. This can be done in any of three places: at the end of the conceptual framework section; in a separate section immediately following the conceptual framework section; or, in some cases, after the presentation of your research questions, if a detailed grasp of these questions is important to understanding the pilot studies. Unless an important purpose of the pilot study was to try out the methods that you plan to use in your research, you should focus your discussion of your pilot studies on what you *learned* from them, rather than on the details of what you did.

4. Research Questions

As in my model of research design, the statement of your research questions is central to your proposal. Although you will usually present a brief statement of your main research questions in the introduction, I recommend putting a detailed discussion and explanation of these after the conceptual framework section. This is because the reasons for focusing on these particular questions may not be clear until the context of prior research, theory, and experience has been described. While you can create a short section just for your research questions, as Regan-Smith did, you can also put them at the end of the conceptual framework section, as Riddle did, or at the beginning of the methods section.

The research questions section, in addition to stating your questions, should clarify two key points, if the answers to these are not obvious:

1. How your questions relate to prior research and theory, to your experience and exploratory research, and to your goals.
2. How these questions form a coherent whole, rather than being a random collection of queries about your topic. Generally, a small number of clearly focused questions is far better than a larger number of questions that attempt to "cover the waterfront" on your topic. If you have more than two or three major questions, you need to think about whether some of these are best seen as subquestions of a broader question, or if your study is, in fact, attempting to do too much.

5. Research Methods[4]

Your proposal probably doesn't need to justify qualitative methods in general, unless you have reasons to think that this could be a concern for some readers.[5] You do need to explain and justify the particular methodological decisions you've made; for every decision, it should be clear why this is a reasonable choice. If you can't specify certain parts of your methods in advance (e.g., how many interviews you'll do), explain the basis on which you'll make your decision.

A description of the setting or social context of your study can be helpful in clarifying and justifying your choice of questions and methods. This description can be placed at the beginning of the methods section, or it can be a separate section just before or after the research questions. A proposal for funding will also need to explain what resources you already have and what ones you are requesting money for, your qualifications and experience, and your timetable and budget; some of this can be included in the methods section, but you will probably need additional sections as well.[6]

The methods section normally has several parts:

a. *Research design in the typological sense.* What kind of a study is this? This can include the particular type of study (e.g., a qualitative interview study) and, if relevant, the particular philosophical or methodological approach you will take (e.g., phenomenology, participatory action research, etc.; see my discussion of such approaches in Chapter 3, under Research Paradigms). This is not always necessary in a qualitative study, but it can sometimes be helpful to describe and justify the overall approach taken—for example, to explain why you have chosen to conduct a case study, or a comparison of two settings. If this doesn't require a detailed explanation, it can often be addressed in the introduction; if your research questions are closely tied to the kind of study you are doing (e.g., if you are comparing two settings and your questions focus on this comparison), this may be best addressed in the section on research questions.

b. *The research relationships you plan to establish with those you are studying.* This is an important part of your design, as argued previously, but it is not usually an explicit part of a proposal. My advice is to discuss this relationship, particularly if it is an important and nonobvious source of information or insights, or if it raises potential data collection difficulties, ethical problems, or validity threats for the study. (See the concise description by Regan-Smith of her relationships with her participants, under Site Selection, and Riddle's discussion of the relationships she planned to establish, in the Research Relationship section of Methods.)

c. *Setting and participant selection.* It is important not simply to describe these, but also to explain why you have decided to study these particular settings or to interview this particular selection (and number) of people.

d. *Data collection.* How you will get the information you need to answer your research questions. This should include a description of the kinds of interviews, observations, or other methods you plan to use, how you will conduct these, and why you have chosen these methods. For both selection and data collection, practical considerations are often important, and your proposal should be candid about these, rather than ignoring them or concocting bogus theoretical justifications for decisions that are, in fact, practically based. If any of your decisions *are* based mainly on practical considerations (such as studying an institution where you have contacts and easy access), you need to deal, at some point, with any potential validity threats or ethical risks that this raises.

e. *Data analysis.* What you will do to make sense of the data you collect. Be as explicit as you can be about how your data will be analyzed; specific examples are generally more useful than abstract descriptions. Also, be clear about how these analyses will enable you to answer your research questions; you may want to include a version of your questions and methods matrix (Example 5.1) to illustrate this.

Issues of ethics can be dealt with as part of the methods section, but if there are significant ethical questions that could be raised about your study, it may be better to have a separate ethics section, as Martha Regan-Smith does.

6. Validity

Validity issues are often dealt with under methods, but I recommend a separate validity section, for two reasons. The first is clarity—you can explain in one place how you will use different methods to address a single validity threat (a strategy discussed previously, known as triangulation), or how a particular validity issue will be dealt with through selection, data collection, and analysis decisions. The second reason is strategic: Devoting a separate section to validity emphasizes that you're taking validity seriously. For this and other issues in a proposal, it is often more important that your reviewers realize that you are aware of a particular problem, and are thinking about how to deal with it, than that you have an airtight plan for solving the problem.

A crucial issue in addressing validity is demonstrating that you will allow for the examination of competing explanations and discrepant data—that your research is not simply a self-fulfilling prophecy. Locke et al. (2007, pp. 87–89) provided a cogent discussion of the scientific state of mind, and of the importance of developing alternative explanations and testing your conclusions. In my view, this issue is just as important for qualitative proposals as for quantitative ones.

7. Preliminary Results

If you have already begun your study, this is where you can discuss what you have learned so far about the practicality of your methods or tentative answers to your research questions. This discussion is often valuable in justifying the feasibility of your study and clarifying your methods, particularly your data analysis strategies; see Regan-Smith's proposal for an example of this.

8. Conclusion

This is where you pull together what you've said in the previous sections, remind your readers of the goals of the study and what it will contribute, and discuss its potential relevance and implications for the broader field(s) that it is situated in. This section should answer any "so what" questions that might arise in reading the proposal. It is normally fairly short, a page or two at most. Martha Regan-Smith's proposal provides a particularly concise, one-paragraph conclusion (not even labeled as such) that nonetheless accomplishes these tasks. Elizabeth Riddle's proposal doesn't have such a conclusion, but it could have used one (my fault for not catching this).

9. References

This section should normally be limited to the references actually cited; unless you are directed otherwise, it should *not* be a bibliography of relevant literature.

10. Appendices

These may include any of the following:

- A timetable for the research
- Letters of introduction or permission

- Questionnaires, interview guides, or other instruments
- A list of possible interviewees
- A schedule of observations
- Descriptions of analysis techniques or software
- A matrix of relationships among questions, methods, data, and analysis strategies (see Figure 5.1)
- Examples of observation notes or interview transcripts from pilot studies or completed parts of the study

The appendixes can also contain detailed explanations of things (e.g., a particular data collection or analysis technique, or background information about your informants or setting) that would require too much space to include in the body of the proposal.

The structure that I present here was originally developed for proposals of about 5,000 words (roughly 20 double-spaced pages). Different universities and funding sources have differing length requirements, some shorter and some longer than this. However, even if your submitted proposal needs to be shorter than this, I still recommend writing an initial draft of about 20 pages, because this is a good test of how well you have worked out your design. One student, whose 10-page proposal was approved by his committee, later said,

> I think it would have been better if I had done a more complete proposal. Even though I wasn't sure what form my research was going to take, I still should have spent more time planning. Then I would have had a greater feeling of confidence that I knew where I was going. (Peters, 1992, p. 201)

Once you are confident of your design and how to present this, you can edit this draft down to the required length. On the other hand, if you need to write a longer proposal than this, I advise starting with a draft of about this length, to help you develop your argument.

I want to emphasize that your research design can't be mechanically converted into a proposal. Your proposal is a document to *communicate* your design to someone else, and requires careful thinking, separate from the task of designing the research itself, about how best to accomplish this communication. To do this, you need take into account the particular audience for whom you are writing. Different universities, review boards, government agencies, and foundations all have their own perspectives and standards, and your design needs to be translated into the language and format required or expected by the people who will be reviewing the proposal. The structure I've presented here will usually be a good first approximation of what you need, but it may still require adjustment to meet the expectations of your reviewers. Discussion with your committee, or with program officers in the funding agency you are approaching, is extremely valuable in accomplishing this.

A useful step in moving from the generic proposal model presented here to a detailed proposal for your specific study is to prepare an outline of the *argument* of your proposal, to develop the sequence of points that you need to make to explain and justify your study. (Exercise 7.1 is an exercise in doing this.) This allows you to work specifically on the *logic* of the proposal, free from the constraints of style and grammatical structure. (For more on how to do this, see Becker, 2007, Chapter 3.) As with concept maps, you can use this exercise in either of two ways—working to develop the logic from scratch and then converting this into a proposal, or taking a draft of your proposal, analyzing this to abstract the argument, and using this argument to revise the proposal. I've provided two examples of such outlines. Example 7.1 is my own outline of the argument of Martha Regan-Smith's proposal; it's fairly brief, but illustrates the basic idea. Example 7.2 is an outline that was actually written by Sherry Steeley in planning her dissertation proposal.

As with my generic model for a proposal structure, I caution you not to use these example outlines as *templates* for your argument. Every study needs a different argument to adequately justify the research, and in developing this argument, you will need to work primarily from your *own* thinking about your study, not borrow someone else's. In particular, as I discuss in more detail in my comments on this, Martha Regan-Smith's study is investigating a topic on which little prior work has been done; your argument (and proposal) will almost certainly need to say more about existing theory and research, as Elizabeth Riddle's does.

Example 7.1   The Argument of a Dissertation Proposal

Following is an outline of the argument of Martha Regan-Smith's proposal, which is presented in full in Appendix A. I have developed this outline from the proposal itself, so it's not a good example of the tentativeness that your outline will probably display initially, but my main purpose here is to illustrate one way to outline your argument. Some of the points in this outline are implicit in the proposal, rather than explicit; the extent to which parts of your argument need to be explicitly stated in your proposal depends on what you can assume that your reviewers will easily infer or take for granted. Similarly, the outline itself is only a sketch of what would be necessary to completely justify the study; even in a full proposal, you will not be able to address every possible question about your research, and will have to focus on those issues that you think are most important for your audience.

Argument for a Study of How Basic Science Teachers Help Medical Students Learn

1. We need to better understand how basic science teachers in medical school help students learn.

   a. There has been an explosion in the amount of information that needs to be transmitted, with no increase in the time available to teach this.

   b. Medical students' performance on the basic science parts of licensing exams has declined.

   c. These facts have led to student disillusionment and cynicism, and to faculty concern.

2. We know little about how basic science teachers help students learn.

   a. Studies of science teachers in other settings don't necessarily apply to medical schools.

   b. Most research on basic science teaching has been quantitative, and doesn't elucidate how such teaching helps students learn.

   c. No one has asked medical students what teachers do that helps them to learn.

   d. The research I've already done indicates that students can identify what teachers do that helps them learn.

   e. Thus, a qualitative study of basic science teaching, focusing on student perspectives, can make an important contribution.

3. For these reasons, I propose to study four exemplary basic science teachers to understand the following:

   a. What they do that helps students to learn

   b. How and why this is effective

   c. What motivates these teachers

   d. The relationship between the students' and teachers' perspectives

4. The setting and teachers selected are appropriate for this study.

   a. The medical school to be studied is typical, and my relationship with the school, teachers, and students will facilitate the study.

   b. The teachers selected are appropriate and diverse, and adding additional teachers would not contribute anything significant.

5. The methods I plan to use (participant observation and videotaping of lectures, student and teacher interviews, and documents) will provide the data I need to answer the research questions.

   a. Videotaping provides rich data on what happens in classes, and will be used to elicit reflection from the teachers.

   b. Interviews will be open ended, and will incorporate questions based on the observations.

   c. The selection of students is guided by theoretical sampling, rather than statistical representativeness, to best understand how the teacher helps students.

6. Analysis will generate answers to these questions.

   a. My analysis will be ongoing and inductive to identify emergent themes, patterns, and questions.

   b. I will use coding and matrices for comparison across interviews, and interview summaries to retain the context of the data.

7. The findings will be validated by the following:

   a. Triangulating methods

   b. Checking for alternative explanations and negative evidence

(Continued)

(Continued)

    c. Discussing findings with teachers, students, and colleagues

    d. Comparing findings with existing theory

    e. These methods, and others described earlier, will enable me to deal with the major validity threats to my conclusions: bias in the selection of teachers and students, and self-report bias for both.

8. The study poses no serious ethical problems.

    a. Teachers and students will be anonymous.

    b. I have taken measures to minimize the possible effect of my authority.

9. Preliminary results support the practicability and value of the study.

Example 7.2   An Outline of a Dissertation Proposal Argument

Language, Culture, and Professional Identity: Cultural Productions in a Bilingual Career Ladder Training Program

Sherry L. Steeley, March 21, 2004

Argument Memo

An overview of research purposes, framework, questions and methodology follows, with a section on validity.

I. Research Purpose:

This study focuses on the professional identity—defined as ideas, beliefs, goals, and values—of bilingual paraeducators in a career ladder training program designed to address the need for qualified teachers of English for Speakers of Other Languages (ESOL) in a diversifying metropolitan area.

At the theoretical level:

- To extend existing research on career ladder programs which has focused primarily on rates of program completion by providing information on the impact of such programs on the individuals entering the teaching profession;

- To explore whether the effects of the program constitute an effective means of overcoming the social reproduction that has limited broader participation by linguistic and cultural minority groups in the teaching profession;
- To understand how paraeducators becoming teachers use their linguistic and cultural funds of knowledge, and how personal experience, views of the profession, and experiences in teacher training shape their eventual professional identity—notions explored in research on culturally and linguistically diverse teachers educated through traditional programs.

At the practice level:

- To provide rich data on the ideas of an underrepresented group in the teaching profession.
- To provide insights useful for educational policy-makers and schools of education planning for programs and student needs.

At the personal level:

- To understand more deeply the personal experiences of underrepresented groups in a program designed to facilitate their entry into a profession that remains predominantly white (Sleeter, 2001);
- To explore the impact of institutional practices and structures on the lives of individuals who will in turn impact upon the lives of students (e.g. Salinas, 2002; Sleeter, 2002; Zirkel, 2002);
- To further my personal commitment to understanding the function of social justice and equity-oriented programs and their outcomes in the lives of individuals.

II. Conceptual Framework:

This study is informed by two bodies of theory as well as extensive research review on culturally and linguistically diverse students, teachers, and schools.

Culturally and linguistically diverse students and teachers:

- Educators and administrators continue to struggle to adapt instruction and learning environments to the linguistic and cultural needs of diverse learners (e.g. Berman, Aburto, Nelson, Minicucci, & Burkart, 2000; Peña, 1997; Salinas, 2002; Zirkel, 2002).
- Research conducted with existing teachers shows that more than half feel unprepared to deal with linguistic and cultural diversity (Darling-Hammond & Youngs, 2002);
- Research conducted with culturally and linguistically diverse teachers (less than 15 percent of the teaching force) shows a commitment to social justice for students from

(Continued)

(Continued)

       culturally and linguistically diverse backgrounds (Hood & Parker, 1994; Quiocho & Rios, 2000; Sleeter, 2002);

- Research shows that while majority culture teacher identity is based on the role models from their own educational experience in predominantly white, middle class schools, culturally and linguistically diverse teacher identity is rooted in their cultural views of the profession, their experience as culturally and linguistically diverse learners, and their teacher training and early in-service experience (Quiocho & Rios, 2000; Su, 1997).

- Research shows that some culturally and linguistically diverse teachers feel inhibited from using their cultural and linguistic skills in schools; others have reacted differently, determined to help their own students overcome educational obstacles to achieve success (Hood & Parker, 1994; Lima, 2000; McCollum, 1999; Moore, 2003; Nguyen-Lam, 2002; Shannon, 1995; Suarez, 2002; Tellez, 1999).

- Career ladder programs emerged in the early 1990s as researchers acknowledged the numerous barriers to culturally and linguistically diverse individuals interested in pursuing a teaching career (Genzuk, Lavandenz, & Krashen, 1994; Guyton, Saxton, & Wesche, 1996; Salinas, 2002; Yasin & Albert, 1999);

- These programs are designed to assist culturally and linguistically diverse paraeducators working in schools to overcome the academic, economic, and/or socio-cultural barriers that have heretofore prevented them from aspiring to or completing higher education and teacher licensure programs (Genzuk & Baca, 1998; Genzuk, Lavandenz, & Krashen, 1994; Gonzalez, 1997; Salinas, 2002; Yasin & Albert, 1999);

- Research on such programs to date has focused on outcomes measured by attrition rate and successful entry into fully-qualified teaching positions (Shen, 1998; Villegas & Clewell, 1998) and on the measures necessary to facilitate such transitions (Genzuk & Baca, 1998; Gonzalez, 1997; Steeley, 2003);

- A recent research review (Sleeter, 2002) noted the importance of examining the role of career ladder graduates to the teaching profession;

- Understanding their ideas about teaching, culture, language is a first step toward understanding that role.

Social Reproduction and Cultural Productions

- Social reproduction theory focuses on how individuals are shaped by societal forces that preserve a position of privilege for dominant classes through subtle practices that shape institutional culture, policies, creating barriers to individuals from subordinate groups (Borman, Fox, & Levinson, 2000; Bourdieu & Passeron, 1977/1970; Erikson, 1996; Levinson & Holland, 1996);

- This theory frames the experiences of many culturally and linguistically diverse teachers described in existing research (Levinson & Holland, 1996);

- Cultural production refers to the reaction of an individual or group to the structural barriers erected by the dominant culture; while many studies have focused on the negative reactions of such groups vis a vis aspirations, others have highlighted the positive reactions in the construction of new meanings or resistance that shapes a positive outcome, allowing for coexistence with the dominant culture while preserving individualized or group values (Cummins, 2000; Eriksen, 1992; Erikson, 1996; Levinson & Holland, 1996);
- Aurolyn Luykx's (1999) study of Aymara preservice teachers in a Bolivian "nationalist-oriented" normal school illustrates the degree of agency of such individuals, although it does not explore their ultimate classroom identity;
- Research conducted as case study or ethnographic research essentially depict a range of other cultural productions, providing an apt model for understanding the experience of culturally and linguistically diverse teachers and teacher-candidates in U.S. schools (Ernst-Slavit, 1997; Escamarilla, 1994; Lima, 2000; McCollum, 1999; Moore, 2003; Nguyen-Lam, 2002; Shannon, 1995; Suarez, 2002; Tellez, 1999).

Identity Theory:

- Proceeds from the acknowledgement that in a post-modern world, individuals are no longer members of easily labeled cultural groups, and that instead they draw from a wealth of symbolic and material resources to construct an identity in accordance with the historical context—broadly, the socioeconomic and cultural conditions—in which they live (Eisenhart, 2001);
- This identity construction is ongoing, reflecting the dynamic of an individual in perpetual negotiation with her surroundings (Eisenhart, 2001);
- Teacher identity and use of cultural and linguistic resources can impact upon student academic experiences (Bartolomé, 2000; Benjamin, 1997; Cassidy, 2002; Clark & Flores, 2001; Escamarilla, 1994; Galindo, 1996; Lima, 2000);
- Because culturally and linguistically diverse teachers draw from diverse spheres of ideas and experience to construct a professional identity, this theory provides an operational orientation to exploring the professional identity of culturally and linguistically diverse teachers in a career ladder program.

My Theory:

- The career ladder program will impact upon the development of professional identity as individuals already possessing educational insights gleaned from their experience as paraeducators develop a reflective stance toward the messages from their education;
- Educational and life experience could retain a strong influence, although it may be mediated by experiences in the career ladder program;

(Continued)

(Continued)

- Individuals may be empowered to serve as advocates and change agents on behalf of their students;

- Messages from the current educational policy context with its emphasis on standardized testing could impact upon teacher beliefs;

- Understanding how the career ladder program impacts upon developing beliefs and practices will provide insight into the professional identity of bilingual bicultural teachers trained through the career ladder program;

III. Research Questions:

1. How do participants in a career ladder program characterize their professional identity, including their beliefs about teaching ELLs and their sense of agency in schools and in the lives of their students?

2. How did participating in the career ladder program modify their understanding of themselves as becoming educators?

IV. Methods:

Data Collection:

- In-depth interviewing with four career ladder participants, two graduates who are practicing teachers, two who are still enrolled in the program;

- Field notes on observation of situations recommended by participants related to participant identity (classroom, community);

- Artifacts from teacher education coursework and/or professional context provided by participants to depict their identity.

Data Analysis: the data will be analyzed in the following manner:

- Interviews will be transcribed, coded, and categorized, and analyzed on an ongoing basis as a source for further questions, the emergence of themes, and as an eventual source for organizing patterns of response across categories and individuals;

- Artifacts will serve as a further basis of discussion in interviews according to themes, providing a source to compare and contrast beliefs, practices, thinking, and identity;

- Field notes will further serve as a basis for discussion, coding, and categorizing, reflection, and member checking.

- Interview transcripts will be coded according to:

  o Theoretical categories emerging from the conceptual framework: cultural production, barriers, source of assistance in overcoming barriers;

- o Sources of messages impacting upon beliefs: educational experience, cultural views of teaching, teacher training, the career ladder program.

- o Substantive categories which emerge as themes in participant interviews: school leadership, standardized testing.

- o Direct beliefs: Statements of belief or ideas participants use to understand their experience and position.

- To verify findings and themes, I will undertake extensive member checking of my findings and transcripts on an ongoing basis.

- To further contrast and compare interview data with other sources, I will attempt to collect and inventory relevant artifacts on an ongoing basis throughout the study.

- To deepen the understanding of my data, I will discuss field observations extensively.

V. Validity

- To deal with "reactivity" I will emphasize that I support them as learners and teachers and am interested in learning more about their views and experiences;

- To deal with bias, I will exercise extensive reflection and reflexivity as I proceed through interviews, observation, and artifact collection, bringing to my own awareness.

Verification Techniques:

- Member-checks of interview transcripts, artifacts, and field notes;

- Actively seek discrepant evidence by using informed interviewing techniques, emphasizing discrepant evidence in member checks;

- Seeking informed input from colleagues and committee members while undertaking reflection and analysis of interview transcripts, artifacts, and field notes.

Generalizability:

- This study is not intended to be generalizable, although some themes may resonate in similar contexts.

- Findings are intended to provide rich description and insights for policy makers, practioners in the fields of linguistic and cultural education and teacher education rather than to identify a generalizable phenomenon.

[The references were omitted because of their length]

Exercise 7.1   Developing a Proposal Argument

The purpose of this exercise is for you to outline the *argument* of your proposal, not its detailed content or structure. You want to present the main substantive points that you need to make about your study, and to organize these so there is a clear logic that leads to a justification for the study. These arguments do not have to be developed in the full form that they will have in the proposal itself, but they should provide the essence of the latter, and should form a coherent sequence.

If you are in the beginning stages of planning your proposal, the outline can be very hypothetical and tentative; the purpose of the exercise is for you to start working on developing your argument, not for you to commit yourself to anything. At this point, it's not important whether you have any evidence or citations to back up your claims; after you have developed an outline of your argument, you can then assess where the holes are in your logic and evidence, and what you need to do to fill them in. This is a come-as-you-are party; construct the best argument you can with your present knowledge.

You should address all of the issues listed, although not necessarily in the order presented—sometimes explaining your research relationships depends on knowing your methods or setting, and sometimes the reverse. Don't try to write well-developed prose at this stage; bulleted points will be easier to do and more useful for this exercise.

1. *Research goals.* What intellectual, practical, and personal goals will doing this study accomplish, or attempt to accomplish? What problem(s) will the study address, and why is it important to address this (if this isn't obvious)?

2. *Conceptual framework.* What are the most important theories, ideas, and knowledge (personal as well as research) that inform this study? *How* have these shaped the study? What is your conceptual framework for the study, and how does it use and incorporate these? What do we *not* know that your study will address?

3. *Research questions.* What do you want to learn by doing this study? How (if it isn't obvious) will answering these questions address the study's goals? How are the questions connected to your conceptual framework?

4. *Research relationships.* What sorts of research relationships do you plan to establish with the participants in your study or setting, or with those controlling access to your setting or data, and why? How will you go about this, and how will this be influenced by any existing relationships you have with them?

5. *Site and participant selection.* What setting(s) will you study, and/or what individuals will you include in your study? (If you haven't made these decisions yet, explain *how* you expect to make them, along with the criteria you plan to use.) What theoretical and practical considerations have influenced these choices? How are these choices connected to your research questions (if this isn't obvious)?

6. *Data collection.* How do you plan to collect your data, and what data will you collect? Why have you chosen these methods, rather than other possible alternatives? How will these data enable you to answer your research questions (if this isn't obvious)?

7. *Data analysis.* What strategies and techniques will you use to make sense of your data? Why have you chosen these? Indicate *how* you will use these analyses to answer your research questions; don't just give boilerplate descriptions of analysis strategies.

8. *Validity.* What do you see as the most important potential threats to the validity of your conclusions? What will you do to address these? What limitations on the generalizability of your results do you see?

Harry Wolcott (1990) provided a useful metaphor to keep in mind as you develop your proposal: "Some of the best advice I've ever seen for writers happened to be included with the directions I found for assembling a new wheelbarrow: *Make sure all parts are properly in place before tightening*" (p. 47). Like a wheelbarrow, your proposal not only needs to have all the required parts; it also has to *work*—to be put together so that it functions smoothly and conveys to others your research design and the justification for this. This requires attention to the connections between the different parts of the proposal (and your design), and to how well the proposal, as a written document, can be understood by your intended audience. As described previously, these are two aspects of what I call coherence. A coherent proposal depends on a coherent design, but it also needs its own coherence, to flow clearly from beginning to end without gaps, obscurities, confusing transitions, or red herrings. As I've emphasized, there isn't one right way to do this; I've tried to give you the tools that will enable you to put together *a way* that works for you and your research.

NOTES

1. Some university departments and dissertation committees *do* want a comprehensive review of the literature on your topic, as a demonstration that you are familiar with prior work in this area. See my discussion of this issue in A Model for Proposal Structure, under Conceptual Framework.

2. This doesn't mean that you should *conceal* your political views; these are an appropriate part of the discussion of your goals, and may be a possible validity threat that you want to address. However, the discussion should focus on how these views inform your design, rather than being political polemic or irrelevant self-display.

3. Locke et al. (2007, pp. 68–73) provide an excellent discussion of the purposes and construction of a literature review.

4. The term "methodology" is often used for this section of a proposal. Despite its prevalence, this is an inaccurate and pretentious usage, a good example of what Becker (2007) called classy writing. Methodology is the theory or analysis of methods, not what you actually do in a particular study. The *Publication Manual of the American Psychological Association* (2010, p. 29), a commonly used guide for both dissertations and research publications, uses the term "method" for this section of a manuscript.

5. For some suggestions on how to justify a qualitative study to a potentially ignorant or hostile audience, see Maxwell (1993).

6. Locke et al. (2007, pp. 178–219) and Robson (2011, pp. 387–397) discussed the specific requirements of funding proposals.

Appendix A

A Proposal for a Study of Medical School Teaching

No single proposal can adequately represent the diversity of qualitative research designs and ways of communicating these. For this edition, I've included two proposals, to emphasize that there is no one right way to structure either a qualitative study or a proposal. Martha Regan-Smith's proposal for her dissertation, a study of exemplary medical school teachers, provides a clear, straightforward, and very concise explanation and justification for the proposed study, and raises many of the key issues that most qualitative proposals will have to address. In my comments, which are set off and indented, I try to identify and clarify the connections between these issues and my model of research design, and to present alternative ways of handling these issues. The proposal appears here just as Martha submitted it, with only a few additions (marked by brackets) or corrections of typos or punctuation for greater clarity; the appendices have been omitted.

The most serious danger in presenting exemplary proposals such as these is that you might use one as a *template* for your own proposal, borrowing its structure and language and simply "filling in the blanks" with your study. This is a sure recipe for disaster. Your proposal needs to fit the study that you are proposing, and an argument that works well for one study may totally fail to justify a different study. Construct your proposal around your *own* design, not someone else's.

HOW BASIC SCIENCE TEACHERS HELP
MEDICAL STUDENTS LEARN

The Students' Perspective

Dissertation Proposal
Martha G. Regan-Smith
March 6, 1991
Harvard Graduate School of Education

ABSTRACT

Medical school consists of two years of basic science and two years of clinical training. The sciences taught in the first two years include Anatomy, Biochemistry, Physiology, Pathology, Microbiology, and Pharmacology. As a result of the biomedical information expansion which has occurred in the last eighty years with no increase in the time available to teach this information, the teaching of basic science has become content heavy. In addition, the teaching has become increasingly rapid paced as most schools over the past twenty years have decreased the number of hours spent in laboratories and demonstrations while increasing reliance on lecturing as the way to teach. Medical student performance on the basic science examinations used for licensure has decreased, and, as a result, medical school faculty feel medical student learning of basic science is less than desired.

As a member of medical school faculties for eighteen years, I want to improve medical student learning of basic science by improving the teaching of basic science in medical school. No qualitative studies of basic science teaching in medical school exist. What works for student learning and how it works is not known. In order to understand how teachers can help medical students learn basic science, I propose to do a qualitative study of four exceptional basic science teachers to answer the following research questions: How do these basic science teachers help medical students learn? What do these teachers do to help students learn? How and why do these techniques help students learn? What motivates the teachers to do what they do? Is what students feel teachers do to help them learn what teachers intend? How do student understandings of what helps them learn differ from teacher understandings?

Each of the four teachers studied teaches a different basic science at a typical private medical school in the northeastern United States. The school has a traditional curriculum in which the two years of basic science is taught predominantly using the lecture format. Each teacher is a winner of the student-selected "Best Teacher Award" and each teacher uses the lecture format for his teaching.

Participant observation of the teacher's lectures and teacher and student interviews are the primary data sources. Classes, in addition, are audiotaped for transcription and videotaped. Videotapes are analyzed as well as used as prompts for dialogue when shown to teacher or students. Interviews are tape-recorded, transcribed and coded. Analytic memos are written and coded for each class observation and interview. Matrices are constructed to identify themes and to check evolving concepts. Both teacher and student collaboration is obtained by getting their opinions of my analysis and conclusions. Each teacher's teaching is analyzed separately followed by comparative analysis of all four teachers' teaching. Generated theory will be compared to existing theory which is primarily based in other educational settings or on personal experience. The goal is to identify teaching techniques and behaviors that help students learn and to gain understanding of how and why these techniques help students learn. This knowledge about practice in context can be taught to teachers in faculty development workshops designed to teach teachers how to improve their teaching. By teaching teachers how to better help students learn, it is hoped improved student learning will result.

> This abstract is a concise summary, not just of the components of the research design, but of the connections between these—the argument of the proposal. Standards and requirements for abstracts vary, and this one is relatively long. However, conveying the basic argument of your proposal should be a major goal of your abstract, regardless of the length.

TABLE OF CONTENTS

INTRODUCTION

Since the Flexner Report in 1910, the four-year medical school curriculum has comprised two years of teaching the sciences basic to medicine followed by two years of training in the clinical disciplines. The basic sciences include Anatomy, Microbiology, Biochemistry, Pharmacology, Pathology, and Physiology, and the clinical disciplines include Surgery, Medicine, Pediatrics, Psychiatry and Obstetrics/Gynecology. Because of the information explosion in biomedical science during the past eighty years, the basic science curriculum has become "overstuffed" (Eichna, 1980). Usually three to four sciences are taught simultaneously, using predominantly the lecture format. As a result, students are in class 25–33 hours per week throughout the first two years of medical school. This, combined with the student perception of ineffective teaching (Eichna, 1980; Jonas, 1978; Konner, 1987; Awbrey, 1985), has led to student disillusionment with science (Eichna, 1980) and student cynicism about the educational process (Petersdorf, 1987). In addition, the national failure rate on the basic science portion of the National Board of Medical Examiners examinations has risen over the past six years (NBME letter to Deans, Appendix A) without a demonstrable decrease in student undergraduate grade point averages or admission examination scores.

In an effort to improve the teaching of basic science in medical school, I want to study what teachers of basic science actually do to help medical students learn. I propose to conduct a qualitative study of four exceptional basic science teachers' teaching, from the students' perspective, to answer the question, "How do these teachers help medical students learn?" The goal is to identify teaching techniques and behaviors which help students learn, which can then be taught to teachers in faculty development workshops designed to teach teachers how to improve their teaching and hence better assist student learning.

> In this brief introduction, Martha sets the stage for what follows by concisely presenting the practical problem that motivates the study and the historical context of this problem (first paragraph), and briefly stating the goals and nature of the proposed study (second paragraph). The abstract has already given some information about the problem and the study, and further details are left for later. Different studies will require different amounts of information to adequately orient the reader to the research problem and study.

Conceptual Framework

To increase medical student enthusiasm for and learning of basic science, several scholars have called for critical examination of the teaching of basic sciences (Bishop, 1984; Neame, 1984; Beaty, 1990). A small number of schools, such as McMaster and Harvard, have been able to replace lectures with small group tutorials during which students participate in problem-based learning by independently solving paper patient cases (Neufeld and Barrows, 1974; Schmidt, 1983). Most medical schools, however, because of financial and faculty constraints, must continue to rely on lectures as a major method of teaching basic sciences. Therefore investigation of how the lecture method can be effective in assisting student learning is worthwhile.

> This paragraph justifies studying the lecture method of teaching basic science. It works well here, but it could also have been included in the introduction.

Existing Literature on Basic Science Teaching in Medical School

Studies of science teaching in secondary or undergraduate schools do not necessarily apply to the medical school setting. The teaching of science through the use of lectures in medical school is unlike the teaching of science in any other educational setting. The rapid pace of medical school and the vast quantity of material needed to be learned by students with varying science backgrounds makes the teaching of science and the learning by the students unique. Effective teaching through the use of lectures in nonmedical school educational settings has been well described and studied (Katona, 1940; McKeachie, 1969; Hyman, 1974; Eble, 1976), but whether the teaching techniques recommended are appropriate in the medical school setting or whether other techniques are helpful is unknown. Qualitative study asking students what works for their learning is needed.

The medical education and health professions education literature on lecturing is limited. Some prescriptive works on how to give effective lectures (Miller, 1962; Bughman, 1973) are based on implicit theory derived from personal experience as students and as faculty (Cook, 1989). Others have been written by educators working in the medical school arena (Jason, 1982), but these are based on educational theory derived from educational settings other than medical school. Schwenk and Whitman (1987) prescribe effective lecturing techniques related to existing educational theory and relate these techniques to communication theory and negotiation theory inherent in effective doctor/patient relationships.

Quantitative studies of lecturing in medical school, usually utilizing student ratings of lecturing techniques, depend on the researchers' prior understanding and assumptions about what helps students learn. Because no qualitative studies of medical student learning of basic science exist, this understanding is based on theory derived from study of or experience with nonmedical school settings. The few quantitative studies in the literature looking at basic science teaching in medical school (Naftulin, 1973; Ware, 1975; Mendez, 1984; Russell, 1984) are limited in scope and contribute little to the research question, "How do basic science teachers help medical students learn?"

Naftulin (1973), looking at teaching delivered in a "seductive charismatic manner," showed that students could give high ratings of such teaching, however, the audience's perception of learning was not included in the study. In response, Ware (1975) concluded that "seductive, charismatic lecturers" assist student learning by showing that students attending lectures with high seduction (characterized by enthusiasm, humor, friendliness, expressiveness, charisma, personality) and low content have similar examination scores as students attending low seduction high content lectures. How these teacher characteristics contribute to student learning of content was not addressed. Mendez (1984) surveyed year I and II medical students for the factors contributing to lecture attendance and found that students attend lectures which they perceive to have clearly defined objectives and which covered material tested on the final examination. How the objectives help student learning and which lecture techniques helped learning were not investigated. Russell (1984) looked at medical student retention of basic material immediately after and fifteen days following lectures with varying amounts of content and found that increasing information density of lectures reduced retention of the basic information. The reasons for this effect were not a part of the study.

Slotnick (1975) and Irby (1976), using quantitative methods, demonstrated that teaching criteria presumed by the researchers to be important for student learning were in fact important to students for their learning. Slotnick (1975) showed that faculty-student rapport, student work required outside of class, pace of class, overall workload, understandability of lecture material, lecturing activities (e.g. summarizes material, concise explanation, organization of material in a logical way), student ability to organize material, and professor knowledge of students' knowledge level are interrelated rather than univariate factors in effective teaching. How these factors affect student learning and why was not a part of the study. Irby (1976) showed that teachers could improve their teaching when given immediate feedback about student ratings of their teaching. The rating variables were derived from education literature and whether the list of teaching techniques rated by the students included all the techniques helpful for student learning could not be determined from the study.

No one has asked medical students what teachers do to help them learn. Existing research has asked students to rate particular teaching techniques or to state whether a technique works or not. These studies depend on the researchers' understanding of what works for student learning. What works to help students learn science in other educational settings may not work in medical school. Quite possibly basic science teachers in medical school have happened upon or developed teaching techniques that are unique to medical school or are unintentionally assisting learning in ways they do not appreciate. Qualitative study is needed to generate a theory of effective nonclinical teaching in medical school.

> This section of the proposal argues that we know very little about how basic science teachers in medical school help their students learn. This point is important in justifying a qualitative study of this phenomenon. As a result, however, the proposal says little about what will be the focus of the conceptual framework section of most proposals: existing theory about, and research on, the phenomenon studied. Martha briefly reviews several theories about what constitutes effective teaching in medical school lectures, but her main point is that these studies address neither how such teaching methods work nor the students' perspective. If your study is of a topic for which there exists a substantial literature of theory and research, your conceptual framework section will need to address this literature, as well as your experience (which Martha discusses in the next section) and pilot research (which she deals with both in the next section and later, in the preliminary findings section).

Personal Interest

I am a physician, an internist and rheumatologist. I was a chemistry major in college, and, prior to this study, I had not participated in a science class since I was a medical student 21 years ago. I have taught how to diagnose adult disease in clinical medicine for 18 years. Approximately six years ago I realized I was also trying to teach both critical thinking skills and the communication skills needed to enable others to understand the reasoning behind a diagnosis. I also realized that I did not know much about critical thinking or communication, let alone how to effectively teach these skills. In 1987 I entered the [Harvard Graduate School of Education] master's program to learn about these skills and how they can be taught. I felt these skills should be a part of a physician's education, and I quickly learned that effective learning of these skills necessitated teaching of these skills throughout medical school, not just in clinical medicine courses.

In 1988, for a course on perspectives of teaching, I was required to study a teacher, classroom or school. I chose to study a teacher. As the Assistant Dean for Clinical Education, whose responsibility is to oversee all clinical teaching, I anticipated I could more easily gain entry into a teacher's classroom if I chose to study a basic science teacher rather than a clinical teacher. In addition, I chose to study a winner of the student awarded "Best Teacher Award." I reasoned that I could learn more about teaching from a winner of such an accolade than a nonwinner, and that a winner would be more likely (i.e. have more confidence) to allow my presence in his classroom than a nonwinner.

I expected the teacher to be skillful; however, I was awed by the extent of his skill as a teacher. Equally surprising was how articulate the students were at describing how he helped them learn. Although I appreciated how he helped me learn in the classroom, I needed student input to appreciate all the aspects of what he did and why it worked for them. Curiosity about how other teachers help medical students learn basic science, and my desire to improve medical education, led to my application in 1988 to the doctoral program with plans to pursue study of how basic science teachers help students learn. By finding out, from the students' perspective, what works to help students learn, I want to discover how teachers can help their students learn and why. Two more teachers have been studied as part of methods courses: the most recent was written up as my qualifying paper entitled "Relevance in Teaching." Each teacher has exemplified all the teaching characteristics that I identified as helping students learn; however, each teacher has best exemplified a different teaching characteristic. The information gleaned from these teacher studies can be used in faculty development workshops designed to teach teachers how to better help their students learn.

> In this section, Martha describes how the study originated, presenting her personal goals and how these connect to the practical and theoretical goals described in the introduction. She also describes her background as the "research instrument" of the study. In doing these, she also begins to build her justification for the selection of exemplary teachers as the focus of the study, and for using students as a major source of data.

Proposed Research

Research Goals

I want to learn what teachers do to help students learn. The teaching techniques gleaned from teachers in practice which I identify as helping students learn will be useful for other teachers to improve their teaching. Quantitative researchers define the problems of practice in their own terms, not the terms of the practitioners, and tend to generate knowledge that is not useful to the practitioner (Bolster, 1983). Quantitative research often does not cause change in practice, whereas qualitative research, which strives to understand the meaning of action to the participants, can offer improvement of arguments for practice and hence can have greater effect on practice (Fenstermacher, 1986). Knowledge generated by quantitative educational research is often not useful to practitioners who are swayed more by practical arguments, experience and faith (Buchmann, 1984). To improve practice, educational research needs to emphasize the context within which the activities studied occur and the meanings of activities studied for the participants. Qualitative research methods meet these needs (Abrahamson, 1984).

The unique teaching/learning situation in the first two years of medical school merits a qualitative research design which (1) takes into account the contextual elements which makes medical education different from other science education settings and (2) allows for inductive hypothesis generation. What works for basic science lectures is unknown. What helps medical students learn may well be different than what works for students of science in other settings. There is a need for students to define and explain what works. Understanding how particular methods work will require understanding of the context. Using qualitative research methods to study teachers and their students in basic science lecture-format classrooms, I intend to learn from the students and their teachers how basic science teachers help students learn.

For my dissertation I propose to study four basic science teachers. Recognizing that students can be valid, reliable, and useful evaluators of teaching (Costin, 1971; Rippey, 1975; Palchik, 1988; Irby, 1977), I decided to continue to study student selected "Best Teacher Award" winners. I will analyze each teacher's teaching individually, and then comparatively analyze the data collected from all four teacher studies. The theory generated about basic science teaching will be compared to existing effective teaching theory generated from other educational settings.

In this section, Martha reviews the main question and goals of the study, and uses these to justify a qualitative study. In the process, she brings in two additional pieces of the conceptual framework, which relate particularly to methods: the relatively greater impact of qualitative research on practice, and the validity of student ratings of teaching. This discussion could just as easily have been included in the conceptual framework section.

Research Questions

The research questions to be answered are: How do these basic science teachers help their students learn? What do these teachers do to help students learn? How and why do these techniques help students learn? What motivates teachers to do what they do? Is what students feel teachers do to help them learn what teachers intend? How do student understandings of what helps them learn differ from teacher understandings?

> In this section, Martha expands on the single, main question she stated in the introduction, specifying the range of questions and subquestions that she will address. In many proposals, more explanation or justification of the questions would be desirable, but because of the clear rationale that Martha provides for these questions in previous sections, it seems unnecessary here. For clarity, it is often better to number your research questions, and to indicate which of these are subquestions of particular main questions.

Research Site

I chose to study teachers at a private Northeastern medical school where I have been on the faculty for ten years (I was a winner of the "Best Teacher Award" for clinical teaching in 1987) and I have been the Assistant Dean for Clinical Education for four years. The school is a typical private medical school of slightly less than average student body size. It has a traditional curriculum with two years of basic science followed by two years of clinical experience.

The students are fifty to sixty-five per cent males and thirty-five to fifty per cent females and come from over 50 different public and private schools throughout the United States. Passage of the National Board of Medical Examiners examinations is not required for promotion or graduation; however, most students take the examinations to obtain licensure to practice. The school's matriculating students' admission grade point averages and admission examination scores are near or slightly above the national mean. During the past five years, the school's students' failure rate on the basic science portion of the National Board of Medical Examiners examinations has been at or near the national failure rate and has risen as the national failure rate has. The only differentiating features of this school from other U.S. medical schools are its rural location and its close, friendly faculty/student rapport.

I have professional relationships of considerable mutual respect with the teachers I have chosen to study. All have worked with me as colleagues on Dean's Advisory, Curriculum and/or Student Performance Committees. We see each other as education advocates in an environment which does not reward education program development or teaching achievement. The four teachers chosen from the "Best Teacher" list to be studied each teach at least twenty hours of different basic science discipline courses (Appendix B) and primarily use the lecture format. The basic science teacher winners that will not be studied either teach the same discipline as another studied teacher or teach using a non-lecture method (see Appendix B).

Three teacher observations and interviews have been completed. The teacher remaining to be studied is to be included because he has passion for his subject, which is a recognized dimension of effective teaching (Eble, 1976). Students participating in my previous studies of medical school basic science teaching have recommended study of this professor, who teaches Pathology, because they perceive him as best exemplifying love of subject, which they feel is very important for their learning.

> In this section, Martha accomplishes two purposes. First, she describes the setting of her proposed study (supporting the generalizability of her results) and the kind of study she plans to do, and further justifies her choice of teachers. Second, she explains some aspects of her research relationship with the teachers she will be studying. The proposal would have been stronger if she had said more about this, and about her relationship with the students.

Methods of Data Collection

Qualitative research methods were selected for this study both because I did not know a priori what I would find, and because I wanted to generate data rich in detail and embedded in context. Classroom participant observation, student interviews, and teacher interviews are the primary sources [methods] of data collection. In addition, course outlines, syllabi, quizzes, examinations and examination results, paper cases, slides, and other handouts are collected as data. Student evaluations of the course and of the teacher's teaching are also used if available.

For all case studies I attend all possible scheduled lectures given by the teacher throughout a four month course. This will be no less than 2/3's of the teacher's teaching. Two to four lectures are audiotaped to record exactly what was said by the teacher and students in the classroom and later transcribed. As discussed below I videotape teachers teaching and interview both students and teachers. I take field notes while in class unless I am videotaping, and write analytic memos and contact summaries (Miles and Huberman, 1984) following each class as well as each interview.

> These two paragraphs provide an overview of the methods section as a whole, and explain the selection strategy for her observations. The selection of students is dealt with later, in the student interviews section.

Videotaping

Videotaping, which I first used with the third teacher I observed, produces a rich source of data about what is going on in the classroom. It allows me to see things I could not see otherwise. I will have the opportunity to review classroom action and observe and isolate individual parts of what is going on. Several of the videotapes will also be used to facilitate the teacher discussing his own teaching in depth. By showing the teacher the tapes of his teaching, I can ask about individual components of his teaching in context. In addition, the tapes will be used to stimulate student dialogue. They will be shown to students to facilitate their explaining the effect of what the teacher does in the classroom to help their learning. Since videotaping was not used to study all four teachers, a comparative analysis cannot be done including all teachers.

> Note that videotaping serves two different purposes in this study: ensuring the descriptive validity of her observations, and stimulating recall and reflection as a component of some of the interviews with teachers and students. Videotaping only two of the four teachers would be a serious flaw if the primary purpose of this study were to compare the teachers, but the purpose is to obtain an in-depth understanding of each of the four teachers, and it would be pointless to forego the advantages of videotaping the last two teachers simply to maintain a superficial consistency of method. In a proposal that will be reviewed by readers not familiar with qualitative research, such a decision might need more explicit justification.

Student Interviews

The student interviews begin with an open-ended question such as "What stands out for you?" or "What did you notice?" Subsequent questions are conversational in an attempt to get the interviewee to discuss further something he/she mentioned in an answer. For the first several interviews, the only other preconceived question is "What does the teacher do that helps you learn?" As I observe more classes, questions arise for which I need answers in order to confirm my observation conclusions and to understand what is going on in the classroom, and these are added. Eventually a set of questions (Appendix C) emerges from the evolving data; I ask these questions of all remaining interviewees in addition to the two original set questions.

Out of a class of 84 students, ten to twenty formal student interviews, lasting 20–45 minutes each, are conducted for each teacher study. As many of the student interviews as time will allow are done after the final examination to minimize student fear that what they say will affect their grade. The interviews occur in my office, and are audio-taped and later transcribed. Each interview is preceded by my stating that I am studying what teachers do in the classroom to help students learn, and all interviews are kept anonymous. Analytic memos and contact summary sheets discussing setting, student attitude and demeanor, and content are written for each interview.

The students I interview are selected to contribute student opinion and characteristics that seem important to the context of the study. In the three concluded studies and planned for the fourth study, I seek samples of the student population guided by my emerging theory using theoretical sampling (Strauss, 1987). I do not attempt to get an empirically "representative" sample. As I learn about and make sense of the events in the classroom and its meaning to the participants, I look for negative data as well as positive data for my emerging theory. I determine how many interviews I will do by doing interviews until I find that I am discovering nothing new. I purposely interview students known to be outspoken and critical to be sure I hear negative comments, as well as students known to be outsiders (loners not a member of one of the cliques in the class) to be sure to get different opinions rather than just "the party line." By asking interviewees to tell me who in the class has opinions about class and the teacher different from their own, I find which students are likely to provide contrasting perspectives. In addition, I try to interview students who do not regularly attend class in an effort to understand what informs their decisions to attend or not to attend class.

In this section, Martha presents and justifies both her selection strategy for the student interviews and how she will conduct these. Again, the lack of uniformity of interview questions for all students would be a flaw if the purpose of the study were to compare student responses, but it is not. The number of student interviews could have received more explicit justification, but most readers would feel that this is a more than adequate number. Further justification for her selection decisions is provided in her discussion of validity, and these decisions are supported by her preliminary results.

Teacher Interviews

For all four studies, the teacher is interviewed formally three to six times, and all interviews are audiotaped and transcribed. The interviews occur throughout the course as well as after the course if appropriate. In general, the interview questions are about issues about which I become curious as an observer in class or as the result of student input. I pursue issues raised by the teacher, and ask preconceived questions only if the teacher does not spontaneously address an issue of interest to me.

Formal teacher interviews last at least 30–55 minutes. For two of the teachers, I will use a class videotape as "text for dialogue" about the teacher's teaching for at least one interview. This yields more specific information about the teacher's play-by-play reasoning and strategy than interviews without videotapes, which tend to yield more abstract general teaching strategies and attitudes. Data gathered is analyzed along with the class observations in daily analytic memos and contact sheet summaries.

> Because Martha had already collected much of her data when she wrote this proposal, she has a dilemma with what tense to use. Her decision to use mostly present tense seems to be the best choice; this could be misleading, but she has clearly explained earlier that she has already completed data collection for three of the four teachers. For dissertation proposals, I advise you to be completely candid about how much of your data you have already collected, unless you receive authoritative advice to the contrary.

Methods of Analysis

Single-Case Analysis

Analysis of collected data is ongoing. Analysis of transcribed interviews and classes is coded during data collection as soon as transcriptions are available. Codes are inductively generated using the "grounded" approach of Glaser (1965) and emerge from the participants' descriptions of the teacher's teaching. In addition, coding is done using codes from a "start list" (Miles and Huberman, 1984) generated from previous studies. All interviews and classroom transcripts are reread specifically for codes which emerge from later interviews. As patterns or themes are identified, dimensionalization (Strauss and Corbin, 1990) is carried out accompanied by recoding for the developed dimensions or properties of a given theme.

Matrices are constructed from the data and are used to identify patterns, comparisons, trends, and paradoxes. Further questions and possible routes of inquiry are devised to answer the questions which emerge from matrices. Periodic review of all the collected data as well as all the analytic memos followed by summary construction and formulation of yet to be answered questions is done every two or three weeks throughout the study. In addition, I meet weekly with an education colleague, knowledgeable about qualitative research and the research site, to summarize the status of the research and to discuss emerging themes, concepts and explanations.

In the final phase of data analysis each interview is reread with the objective of writing individual short interview summaries. These summaries allow me to see threads that run through interviews and thereby maintain the context for the quotes which are lifted out of the interviews and used as examples in writing up the research. Using Microsoft Word (Apple, 1988), I then cut and paste quotes from all the interviews creating new separate documents for each code that had emerged from analysis of the interviews. This compilation of quotes for each code is used to appreciate trends, contrasts, and similarities. Matrices are constructed to check the validity of themes which emerge. Finally the data is reviewed to pair up student perspectives with teacher perspectives of the same phenomenon to compare and contrast perspectives as well as to look at whether what the teacher intends is, in fact, what the students perceive as happening.

Validation of data is achieved by triangulation (Denzin, 1970) of methods by comparing student perspectives, teacher perspective, and participant observer perspective of events in the classroom. Theoretical validation is achieved by regular presentation and discussion of emerging conclusions with medical school colleagues familiar with the setting, students and teachers. Further validation is achieved by discussing my analyses and conclusions with the teacher and with students.

Cross-Case Analysis

Once I develop an understanding about how the fourth teacher helps his students learn, I will begin cross-case analysis. The first step will be construction of a conceptual framework (Miles and Huberman, 1984) containing the dominant themes of how these four teachers help students learn. Each theme will be dimensionalized (Strauss and Corbin, 1990) or broken into factors and graphically displayed illustrating the relationships between them.

Patterns and themes will be sought by construction of cross-case displays and matrices. Plausible explanations and metaphors will emerge as the variables are related, split and factored (Miles and Huberman, 1984). The goal will be to build a logical chain of evidence (Scriven, 1974) and to construct a theoretically and conceptually coherent theory by checking for rival explanations and looking for negative evidence. In order to check for theory validation informants will be asked for feedback on generated theory after data collection is completed.

> Martha's description of her analysis strategies is detailed and comprehensive, but rather abstract and boilerplate, and doesn't give a good sense of the actual methods and coding categories she'll use; examples would be helpful here. This weakness is remedied by her discussion of preliminary findings, below, which provides detailed, concrete examples of the content of her analysis. Her discussion of evidence, rival explanations, and feedback also paves the way for the next section, on validity. In this section, she tends to slide into impersonal, passive-voice language, which seems incongruent with the mostly first-person, active-voice language of previous sections.

Validity Issues

1. Teacher selection: After the fourth teacher study, I will have studied the award winners from four different discipline courses who use the lecture method (Appendix B). I will stop at four teachers, unless another important teaching characteristic is identified that I have not already found. Because the study school has no features which make it different from other U.S. medical schools with a traditional curriculum of two years of basic science and two years of clinical experience, I find no reason to study teachers elsewhere. Most teachers of basic science in most schools are male, so I found no validity threat to my study by the teachers being male.

> This is really an argument for the *generalizability* of her results, not their validity.

2. Student selection: Did I interview enough students? Did I bias the data by who I interviewed? I intentionally try to interview students who have different perspectives and opinions of the teacher's teaching. I interview students who are: (1) known to be outspokenly critical of teaching, (2) from all quartiles of the class, (3) from a variety of career choices, (4) whom I know and whom I barely know, (5) who are referred to me by classmates as feeling differently about the class and teacher, (6) who participate in the typical camaraderie of the class and those who do not, and (7) who attend most every class and those who attend only a few. In essence, I try to seek out students who do not feel the teacher helps them learn as well as those who do. Thereby I try to get both negative and positive student input. I stop interviewing when I begin to hear the same things repeated and no new information.

> This paragraph deals with some plausible threats to the validity of her results. The selection strategy described here is an example of purposeful selection; the decision on when to stop interviewing is based on what Strauss (1987) called "theoretical saturation."

3. How do I know what students say is true and not just what I want to hear (i.e. that the teacher helped them learn when he did not)? To make students comfortable being honest with me I assure the students anonymity and interview them in a location distant from the classroom. As often as possible I postpone student interviews until after student grades have been awarded. I also attempt to interview students who are scheduled to finish their third and fourth years at another medical school, thereby eliminating any power I may have as Dean for Clinical Education over them. In the three completed studies, students have not held back from criticizing the teachers nor sharing with me their negative feelings and opinions of the teachers' teaching. I use my presence in the classroom as a learner trying to understand new subjects (e.g. the molecular biology of viruses) to substantiate whether a teacher truly helps students learn. If the teacher helps me learn and the students said he helps them and they pass the course, I believe them. I ask students to give examples of all teaching characteristics they claim help them learn and then I substantiate student examples by being present in class. Collaboration with students (both those in the study and those who were not) by discussing my observations and my conclusions also helps increase my confidence in the validity of my work.

> This paragraph addresses her relationship with the students, which has ethical as well as validity implications, and argues that her relationship to them as Dean is not a validity threat to her conclusions. Someone who didn't know Martha and her reputation among these students might not find this argument completely convincing, but I'm not sure what else she could say. The most persuasive point, for me, is that the students she's interviewed have been critical of their teachers.

4. How do I know what the teacher says he does is true? I substantiate all teacher claims by participant observation and through student interviews. Teacher beliefs and stated reasons for behavior are accepted as true unless I encounter discrepant evidence.

> Here, Martha basically relies on triangulation to deal with the validity threat of self-report bias in the teacher interviews. She could also have used the argument she made in discussing the student interviews: that, having already studied three of the teachers, she *knows* that the observations and student interviews corroborate the teachers' reports.
>
> This section as a whole is organized by particular validity threats—how she might be wrong. In discussing these threats, Martha draws on information previously presented in the methods section, but she reorganizes this information so that it is clear how the data obtained through these methods will help her to deal with these threats.

Ethical Issues

Could my research harm the students or teachers? The teachers risk my finding out that they are not as good a teacher as their award recipience would merit. Even though I do not oversee the basic science part of the curriculum, my administrative colleagues do; and I am a member of the Curriculum Committee. To minimize this fear of risk, each teacher is assured that no one other than specified study school education colleagues with whom I discuss results and conclusions (and my thesis readers) will know of the results of my research unless the teacher gives me permission to do otherwise. I can not eliminate this risk for the teachers.

No harm from teachers can come to the students who participate because the students' identities are kept secret. I can not eliminate the risk that I as the Dean, who writes the student's letter of recommendation for residency after graduation, will form opinions about them as a result of my interview. Those students concerned about such a risk can easily avoid participation. I am aware of no one refusing to participate when asked, hence I do not think student avoidance of participation poses a significant validity threat to my research.

> This section could be placed either before or after the validity section. One point that could have been made explicitly here is that these teachers, as award winners, have less to fear from examination of their teaching than most teachers. Martha could also have dealt more convincingly with the ethical issue of risk to the students. Ultimately, her argument depends on her integrity. The point at the end, about validity, would fit better in the previous section.

Preliminary Findings

To date, preliminary analysis of the data has enabled me to identify a number of teaching characteristics which help students learn: clarity, relevance, knowledge of students' understanding, teaching to different learning styles, and passion for the subject. Each of the three teachers studied so far has been found to best exemplify different teaching characteristics even though the characteristic was found in all the other teachers' teaching. In other words, the characteristics identified that help medical students learn basic science are practiced by all the teachers studied but each teacher is a "master" at one or two different characteristics.

The first teacher teaches heart physiology, anatomy and clinical disease to Year II students as a part of the Scientific Basis of Medicine course. The students felt that his lecture style was "like a conversation" with them; the students felt he understood what they knew and what they did not. In addition, this teacher addressed multiple student learning styles by presenting the course material (e.g. coronary artery disease) in seven different ways (i.e. lecture, reading assignments with clear stated objectives, computer interactive patient cases, student participation in demonstrations, small group discussions, problem solving of paper cases, and student presentations of current articles to small groups).

The second teacher teaches the virology section of the Microbiology course in Year I. The students and the teacher felt that the most important feature of his teaching was clarity. The students perceived him to achieve clarity by (1) limiting the material needed to learn, (2) explicitly defining the material the students need and do not need to know, (3) specifying the meaning of his words, (4) presenting concepts moving from the simple to the complex in a logical progression, (5) including stories about patients, epidemiological problems or medical history to explain concepts, (6) asking the class questions critical to understanding the concepts, and (7) repetition of key concepts and facts. He checks on his clarity by giving weekly quizzes and spending extra time in class to explain any quiz questions missed by a significant number of students. The quizzes promote clarity for the students because they additionally give the students feedback on what they know and do not know as well as force them to learn the material weekly and keep up with learning the material rather than cramming for the final examination.

The third teacher teaches pharmacology and best exemplifies the use of relevance in teaching. He uses relevance in his classroom teaching by structuring each lecture around either a presentation of a patient case of his own or a patient case volunteered by a student. In addition, each week he provides students with paper case problems to solve individually thereby letting students simulate practice as physicians. Relevance is also achieved by having students teach students how to solve the case problems. The ensuing class discussion allows students (and the teacher) to learn and discuss student understanding of the pharmacologic principles. The use of the Socratic method by this teacher as cases are discussed in class gives the students opportunity to privately reflect on their own similar experiences with patients. Relevance is also achieved by students privately conversing during class, relating to a neighbor what they are learning in class to cases they have seen, and sharing the experience with the classmate.

Previously studied teachers were not aware of all they did in the classroom to help students learn. Often a teacher is unable to fully appreciate how he helps students learn without my feedback. From the fourth teacher I expect to learn how a teacher's passion for or love of subject helps students learn. I have heard the fourth teacher speak and he is mesmerizing. His charismatic style of presentation captures the audience's attention and, I suppose, it helps them remember what he says. He may also contribute to their learning by motivating them to learn on their own.

I expect the comparative analysis to reveal that the dimensions of each of the individual teacher's teaching characteristics overlap (e.g., anecdotes used to achieve clarity also achieve relevance). Ongoing analysis of my first three case studies reveals that students feel that student-involved teaching, such as students teaching students, is particularly useful for their learning because it achieves clarity, relevance, a form of student/teacher conversation, and addresses student learning styles.

> This discussion of preliminary findings serves several purposes. First, it supports Martha's argument that the methods she proposes are workable and will allow her to generate interesting and valid answers to her questions. Second, it fleshes out her rather abstract and general discussion of data analysis, clarifying how she is coding her data and integrating themes within each case, and suggesting issues that the cross-case analysis will focus on.

In summary, by using qualitative research methods to study basic science teachers who primarily use the lecture format to teach, I intend to find how these teachers help medical students learn. The theory generated will be compared to existing theory on effective teaching using lectures in other educational settings. This theory will be used to develop faculty workshops to teach teachers how to teach. The ultimate goal of improved basic science teaching in medical school is to improve medical student enthusiasm for, and learning of, the sciences basic to medicine.

> This final paragraph sums up the study by briefly reviewing, in the reverse order from their presentation in the proposal, four components of the design: the methods, the research question, the theoretical framework, and the goals of the study. In doing this, it clearly shows the connections between these components, and links the proposed research to the goals with which the proposal began. However, this is pretty terse for a conclusions section; most proposals will need to say more to summarize the proposal and present the implications of the study.

Appendix B

A Proposal for a Study of Online Learning by Teachers

This is a second dissertation proposal, similar in organization to the first but with rather different content. Unlike Regan-Smith's proposal, it follows the common three-chapter format, based on a five-chapter dissertation model, that I described in Chapter 7 (with caveats). If your department or committee requires this format, Riddle's proposal illustrates how to adapt my design structure to this. However, qualitative dissertation proposals, and dissertations, often don't follow this model; my own dissertation (Maxwell, 1986) had 10 chapters (an introduction, three literature review chapters on different relevant issues, a setting and methods chapter, four results chapters, and a conclusion). For this proposal, I have included three of Riddle's appendices, since they are helpful in clarifying how she actually planned to conduct the research.

Dissertation Proposal

Voluntary Participation and Online Learning

A Research Study Investigating Why K–12 Teachers Participate in Informal Online Learning and How It Influences Their Professional Development

Elizabeth Riddle Hoover
George Mason University
September 3, 2002

Contents

CHAPTER 1: INTRODUCTION

Educators desperately need alternative methods of distributing and receiving professional development. Research reveals that "good professional development" should be
designed around teacher interest, connected to teacher's current knowledge, and sup-
portive and nurturing of teachers' intellectual capacity (Corcoran, 1995; Little, 1993).
In other words, professional development should be learner-centered. However, providing "good professional development" for teachers is extremely challenging for local
school districts. Teacher interest, knowledge, and intellectual capacity vary widely
within and among schools. Offering appropriate professional development requires a
large investment in time and money. This type of investment is often neither a priority
nor a possibility. Therefore, despite research, school districts typically offer professional development opportunities that are irrelevant and uninteresting for teachers.
Professional development is packaged in one-day workshops scattered throughout the
year on isolated, generic topics. As a result, teachers often seek out their own professional development at local universities, summer workshops, and increasingly on the
Internet.

   Since the emergence of the Internet, there has been a proliferation of resources
offered to teachers through websites, discussion boards, and listserves. According to
Zhao and Rop (2001), the underlying belief in the development of such resources is that
they provide a solution to problems of teacher isolation and that they have the potential
to individualize teacher professional development. They also identify three major purposes these resources fall under: sharing information, fostering professional development, or creating communities. These claims have not been rigorously researched
(Zhao and Rop, 2001).

Topic and Purposes of this Study

   Research that identifies reasons for voluntary participation in teacher online learning
is necessary. This research can contribute to the creation of online learning opportunities that provide professional development that meets the needs of teachers. School
districts could offer a wider variety of learning opportunities by merging with other
organizations in the "virtual world". Online learning opportunities can overcome the
current challenges of traditional professional development.

   For my dissertation, I will explore how teachers are accessing and enhancing their
professional development through participation in an online environment. Specifically,
I am interested in teacher participation that is independent of online coursework or any
other credit. I will study why K–12 teachers participate voluntarily, how their participation is sustained, how they believe their participation impacts their professional development, and if their participation fosters "communities of practice" as defined in the
literature on professional development.

   It is important to K–12 schools and universities to understand the reasons behind
voluntary online participation. This knowledge can help districts and universities make

online learning more interesting for teachers and students like myself. Additionally, if teachers' experiences in voluntary online learning reflect the characteristics of good professional development, these environments may provide school districts with an alternative medium for distributing professional development.

CHAPTER 2: CONCEPTUAL FRAMEWORK

My Experiential Knowledge

My interest in the ways technology can provide and assist teachers with their professional development started in fall of 1999 when I was in EDIT 895: Leadership Issues in Educational Technology. Dr. Dede asked us to find and explore a "knowledge network" that used technology as its medium. I chose to write a paper on Teachers.net and how it provides learning environments for professional development. I specifically looked at how a group of teachers involved in a balanced literacy program, called 4Blocks, were using Teachers.net to share information, reflect upon their experiences, support one another and advocate the program. I used Peter Senge et al's *Dance of Change* (1999) and John Bransford et al's *How People Learn* (1999) to guide my analysis. The assessment of Teachers.net focused on its ability to encourage, implement, and support an educational initiative. I concluded that Teachers.net supplies the tools that enable educational leaders to promote their change initiative. However, it is impossible to separate the people behind the technology from the technology. The success of the 4Blocks' community on Teachers. net is equally tied to the medium, as it is to the leadership of its program.

The participation of the teachers involved in the 4Blocks community is entirely voluntary. Teachers do not receive course credits or staff development points from their school districts. Teachers are not there to learn technology. Instead, these teachers are using technology to meet their own learning needs. Voluntary learning motivates their use of technology. When I started the PhD program I was focused on teaching teachers how to use technology with their students. Now my interest has expanded to how and why teachers use technology for their own learning needs. Why are teachers choosing to participate in online learning?

All of my experiences with online learning have been embedded within my graduate work at George Mason University. Mandatory online participation can be exhausting. I often hear students complain about participating on WebCT, TownHall, or BlackBoard. Although online learning fascinates me, I'm not sure I would participate if I weren't involved in a graduate program. However, multitudes of teachers are reaching out to the Internet for knowledge in specific and general areas.

The Need for New Forms of Professional Development

The road from the industrial age in the early 1900s to the information age of the 21st century has been wrought with economic, social, and political changes that have transformed the United States significantly from what it was a hundred years ago. Technological advances have changed the way we conduct business, socialize with others, and decide our local and national leadership. Despite such tremendous change in daily life, schools are still fundamentally organized around the needs of the industrial age. This is evident in the structure of the six-hour school day, the nine- month school year, and often in the delivery of academic instruction.

The diversity of students and their learning needs in today's world demands a different type of education than the industrial age. As a result, educators are increasingly adopting initiatives and mandates that deal with scheduling, curriculum, and instructional strategies to address the learning needs of students. However, these adoptions are usually done quickly and without regard to professional development. It is impossible to expect teachers to acquire new skills and knowledge without providing them the necessary education. This common practice is no different than giving students tests without teaching the material and then holding them accountable for their score.

The need for quality professional development has been recognized. In 1995 U.S. Secretary of Education Richard W. Riley stated, "Schools and students have changed significantly in recent years, but teachers are still at the heart of instruction. If, as a nation, we expect to prepare all students for the 21st century, we must provide teachers with ongoing opportunities to be the most informed, the most capable, and the most inspiring classroom leaders possible" (U.S. Department of Education, 1995). The 1996 Report of the National Commission on Teaching and America's Future, *What Matters Most: Teaching for America's Future* outlines necessary recommendations for educational reform. It emphasizes the need to "reinvent teacher preparation and professional development" (p.11) and calls for the creation of stable high quality sources of professional development

Despite such statements, most school districts continue to ignore the learning needs of teachers. Just as the factory model of schooling is inappropriate for K–12 students, traditional professional development formats are inappropriate for teachers. Professional development for K–12 teachers is usually packaged in one of three forms: after school workshops, designated days scattered throughout the year or annual conferences. They are designed for general populations, often lacking relevance to teachers' interests and daily needs. Workshop attendances and teacher attitudes on evaluation forms usually measure successes. A survey conducted by the National Center for Education Statistics in 1999 revealed that 80% of teachers believed current professional development activities were only "moderately" or "somewhat" helpful (NCES, 1999).

In contrast to traditional professional development, the National Council of Staff Development describes effective professional development as having the following characteristics:

- Focuses on deepening teachers' content knowledge and pedagogical skills
- Includes opportunities for practice, research and reflection
- Is embedded in educators' work and takes place during the school day

- Is sustained over time and
- Is founded on a sense of collegiality and collaboration among teachers and principals in solving important problems related to teaching and learning.(NCSD, 2001).

How People Learn lists the following characteristics of effective learning environments:

- Learner-centered environments (to build on strengths, interests, and needs of learners)
- Knowledge-centered environments (focusing on pedagogical content knowledge)
- Assessment-centered environments (testing ideas, trying them with students, receiving feedback)
- Community-centered environments (communities of practice, with teacher collaborations) (Bransford, Brown, & Cocking, 1999).

Effective professional development not only focuses on the learning needs of teachers but the environments that facilitate learning.

Recent research has linked such professional development to student achievement. In *How Teaching Matters: Bringing the Classroom Back into Discussions of Teacher Quality* (2000), Wenglinsky links sustained teacher professional development to increased subject matter knowledge and the use of effective classroom strategies such as teaching higher order thinking skills through hands-on activities. The increased use of these strategies resulted in increased academic achievement in math and science.

A report on the federally funded Eisenhower professional development program, a three- year longitudinal study, found links between high quality professional development and academic achievement. The report describes high quality professional development as activities such as teacher collaboratives, networks or committees; internships; mentoring; and teacher study groups (U.S. Department of Education, 2000). Such reports have deemed professional development as one of the most important factors in education. Research indicates "the most successful teachers' professional development activities are those that are extended over time and encourage the development of teachers' learning communities" (Bransford et al, 1999, p.192). This type of learning is rooted in educational theory.

Social Learning

Educational theorists John Dewey and Lev Vygotsky addressed the relationship between learning and communities. Both men emphasized the importance of social context in acquiring knowledge (Roschelle, 1992). John Dewey, the father of inquiry learning and activity based education, believed that knowledge is the method by which one makes meaning of one's experiences. He believed these learning experiences were biological and social and that they could not be understood outside a social context (Dewey, 1916).

Similarly, Vygotsky is credited with the creation of social development theory. He focused on the connections between people and the cultural context in which they act and interact in shared experiences (Vygotsky, 1978). According to Vygotsky, humans use tools that develop from a culture, such as speech and writing, to mediate their social environments.

Situated Learning

Current literature discusses knowledge and communities in context of situated learning. Like the works of Dewey and Vygotsky, situated learning theory emphasizes the importance of authentic learning contexts and social interaction. In this view, a learning environment should encompass real-life problems and support collaboration and interaction among learners and their environment (Miao, Fleschutz, & Zentel, 1999). Communities of Practice (CoP) have emerged from this learning theory. In a CoP members are self-selected and share a common goal based on a practice. Members collaborate with one another to not only do their work but also to clarify it, define how it is done and even to change how it is done. Through this mutual engagement, members also establish their identities at work (Wenger, 1998). A CoP has a professional hierarchy ranging from novice to expert. Where a member is "situated" in this hierarchy, describes how learning takes place. Knowledge is part of the organization and participation of the community. Membership is interdependent and there is a social obligation to learn from and learn for the community (Riel & Polin, in press). Therefore, learning is a natural outcome of membership in a community of practice (Brown & Duguid, 1996; Lave & Wenger, 1991; Wenger, 1998).

Communities in Teacher Professional Development

It should not be surprising that communities of practice have become a popular theme in teacher professional development. By definition a CoP focuses on a common need or interest, which is a missing component in traditional forms of professional development. In the effort to design effective professional development based on the theoretical foundation described above, semantics have become particularly confusing. Researchers interchangeably term professional development reforms as: communities of practice (Schlager, Fusco, & Schank, in press), collaboratives (Rosenholtz, 1991, Nias, Southworth, & Yeomans, 1989, Zellermayer, 1997), professional communities (Louis & Kruse, 1995), discourse communities (Putnam & Borko, 2000), teacher networks (Lieberman, 2000), and professional learning communities (Dufour & Eaker, 1998).

Regardless of the specific term used, early educational theorists and recent research emphasize the effectiveness of learning in a community. Research shows that "a self-conscious professional community was a salient characteristic of those schools most successful with students. Professional community meant that teachers pursued a clear and shared purpose for all student learning, engaged in collaborative activity to achieve that purpose, and took collective responsibility of their students' learning" (Lieberman, 2000, p. 222).

Despite such positive impact of community learning in teacher professional development, traditional challenges such as teacher isolation, lack of time for collaboration or reflection, varied interest among teacher populations, and lack of resources remain as paralyzing obstacles in implementing such communities in schools and school districts. Educators who understand the importance of quality professional development are frustrated by the reality of providing, implementing, and receiving it.

New Electronic Tools Can Support Professional Development

Since Vygotsky's work in the first half of the twentieth century, technology has expanded the number of tools we use in the physical world and the growing virtual world. In order to expand our professional and social environments into the virtual world, it is important that we have the necessary tools to interact in shared experiences. Without the appropriate tools, it will be impossible to mediate the virtual world and take advantage of its potential. New electronic tools can help overcome traditional challenges to even the best models of teacher professional development. They can provide continuity and optimize communication in the process of distributing information, knowledge and best practices among wide audiences (Trenton, 2001). Specifically, research shows that online forums provide (1) freedom from time constraints; (2) time for reflection; (3) opportunities to research and back up assertions; and (4) support for cost effective global communication (Anderson & Kanuka, 1997).

Tools like web-based conferencing that provide real-time communication (synchronous) and discussion boards and listserves that provide reflective discourse (asynchronous communication) facilitate professional development by optimizing time for learning, places for learning, opportunities for learning, and designs for learning (NCSD, 2001). Asynchronous tools allow users to participate in learning twenty-four hours a day, seven days a week. Email and discussion boards enable communication and collaboration among teachers with differing schedules due to job, family, or region. Places to learn are only limited by computer access. With technology tools, opportunities to learn are expanded beyond one's geographical region to the entire world. Equally important to these exponentially increased opportunities, is the ability for teachers to communicate in the modality that best suits their learning style (Rose, 1999). If teachers prefer immediate interaction, they can choose synchronous mediums for collaboration. However, if teachers prefer a more reflective approach to collaboration, they can choose to utilize asynchronous mediums.

Online Learning Communities

Online communities of practice usually emerge from two different needs: the need to follow up on some type of course and the need to create communities of professionals based on the concepts of knowledge sharing (Trenton, 2001). They differ from face-to-face communities of practice in their intensity of participation, representation of members, and accessibility to resources, information, and expertise (Hung & Chen, 2001). Online communities can have larger memberships that increase their intensity of participation. Participation can be seen in three main patterns: communicative learning in which learners actively express their views and respond to others; quiet learning in which learners read the content but rarely post their own ideas; and finally, non-participation in which the learner drops out of the community for periods at a time (Hammond, 2000).

The presence of technology tools that mediate constructions of knowledge do not necessarily foster learning or create a community of practice. It is the understanding of the desired outcome and the use of appropriate tools to achieve a goal that impacts learning (Blanton, Moorman & Trathen, 1998; Schlager et al, in press). Roschelle describes a community of practice as "[arising] through the coordinated use of technologies (broadly defined to include language) to arrive at mutually intelligible resolutions to shared problematic experience" (Roschelle, 1992, p.40). Participants in an online community of practice should see themselves as working towards a common goal. Their use of synchronous and asynchronous mediums should enable them to accomplish tasks that are appropriate for their level of participation. Their growth is not dependent on a specific course or learning path, but on "experience-sharing, the identification of best practices, and reciprocal support for tackling day-to-day problems in the workplace" (Trenton, 2001, p.5) Although explicit knowledge, discrete units that can be easily distributed such as definitions or data charts, are valued, equally important is tacit knowledge, "know how" convictions, ideals, or emotions about the topic (Trenton, 2001).

There are many projects focused on supporting online learning communities such as those described here.

PBS TeacherLine

In collaboration with International Society for Technology in Education (ISTE) and the National Council of Teachers of Mathematics (NCTM), PBS has developed an online professional development for teachers in mathematics and technology integration. TeacherLine offers self-paced learning opportunities, facilitated modules, which are like mini-courses, and a Community Center with synchronous tools and web-based resources for teachers to use.

Classroom Connect

Classroom Connect provides professional development for K–12 teachers and online resources to facilitate the use of the Internet in education. It is a business unit within Harcourt, Inc. The site offers a database of resources, listserves, discussion boards and live meetings organized around special interest. Beyond the web-based learning opportunities, Classroom Connect offers onsite training, conferences and newsletters.

Teachers.net

Teachers.net provides K–12 teachers with web-based resources and tools for synchronous and asynchronous communication. In March 1996, Dr. Tony Bott, then a doctoral candidate at UCLA, founded Teachers.net, an online learning community for teachers. Bott's purpose in creating Teachers.net was to provide teachers information, resources, and networking tools in a mentoring community on the web at no cost (B. Reap, a personal interview, October, 13, 1999).

A survey administered on Teachers.net revealed over 100,000 hits daily, over 400,000 unique user sessions monthly, and over 30,000 mail list subscribers. It was started by a doctoral student, Tony Bott, in 1996. Bob Reap, who joined Dr. Bott at Teachers.net in 1998, says that although he does not have the numbers to prove it, Teachers.net is probably one of the busiest sites for teachers on the Internet. According to Reap, Teachers.net cultivates a strong sense of community for teachers, and in return, teachers provide the site with a tremendous amount of information and resources. The site is more successful than Bott ever imagined. (B. Reap, a personal interview, October, 13, 1999)

Tapped In

Tapped In (TI), sponsored by the National Science Foundation, SRI International, Sun Microsystems, and the Walter S. Johnson Foundation, is a platform independent, web-based, multi-user virtual environment (MUVE) that provides teachers a professional development workplace. Through synchronous and asynchronous communication, educators collaborate with each other in Tapped In on a large spectrum of topics from different locations around the world.

The goal of Tapped In "is to learn how to grow a self-sustaining on-line community of education professionals that supports and enhances the professional growth of its members over the length of their careers" (Schlager, Fusco & Schank, 1998, p.15). Membership, which has reached beyond 14,100 as of November, 2001, is comprised of teacher professional development schools, educational organizations, and individual teachers. It functions as a community for communities. TI is one of the more ambitious online teacher professional development communities because it actively seeks to embody the characteristics of a true community of practice.

In developing an online community Schlager et al. (2002) warns against the "build it and they will come" attitude. Nichani also warns against this attitude, cautioning that it ignores the fundamentals of human interaction (Nichani, 2001). There are also arguments against the potential for online learning communities. Cohen and Prusak (2001, p.163) list the following arguments:

- The inability of online environments to replicate important nuanceses of social meetings. These include gestures, grimaces, looks, tones, etc. that convey nonverbal communication.
- The brevity of virtual connections do not foster close human relationships that require time.
- Serendipity is limited. Chance conversations are more limited online than in face-to-face relationships. These conversations often lead to new ideas and thoughts.
- The challenge of building trusting relationships purely through virtual connections.

Although these concerns may be valid in assessing what online learning communities cannot provide learners, it is more important to focus on how it can provide solutions that are desperately needed. Traditional forms of professional development are ineffective. New designs for professional development demonstrate success but cannot be easily distributed in traditional environments. Online learning is emerging as a viable and potentially successful mode for professional development. In order to understand how to design an online learning community for K–12 teachers and promote it as a useful, if not preferred, environment for teachers, it is essential to understand what motivates teachers to participate in one and how it influences their professional development.

Research Questions

My research questions include:

- Why do teachers voluntarily participate in online learning?
- In what ways do teachers voluntarily participate in online learning?
- How do their reasons for participation affect their level of participation?
- How do they believe their participation impacts their development as teachers?
- Does voluntary online learning foster "communities of practice" as defined in the literature?

These questions focus on understanding why teachers voluntarily participate in informal online learning and how this type of participation models/reflects/fosters good professional development practices as defined in the literature.

CHAPTER 3: METHODS

Site Selection

In order to study K–12 teacher's voluntary and sustained participation in online learning, my research site must be an established environment with a high level of voluntary teacher participation. I believe that Teachers.net is an appropriate choice because participation is not associated with structured courses or workshops promising credit or certification. The groups in Teachers.net have emerged as a grassroots effort. Voluntary teacher interest, rather than corporate initiatives, has driven the community. This voluntary initiative in Teachers.net is a critical aspect for my research site.

Organization and Design of Teachers.net

Dr. Bott, the founder of Teachers.net, designed Teachers.net so that all of its resources can be accessed through the Internet and an email account. Presently, there are over 45 different forums for K–12 educators in the areas of general interest, special interest, career support, technology, and language. Each forum has a listserv, called a mailring, and a chatboard that publishes the listserv's recent postings. Other posted resources include lesson plans, online projects, and curriculum resources. In addition to these asynchronous modes of communication, Teachers.net also provides educators with 4 meeting rooms for synchronous discussions. Educators meet in these rooms for formal and informal meetings. Although forums normally schedule formal meetings at night, educators meet informally twenty-four hours a day.

Forums with larger memberships exchange more information, both synchronously and asynchronously than smaller ones. They also tend to meet synchronously more often than the smaller forums. Whereas some forums use Teachers.net to casually share information from their experiences, others use the tools of Teachers.net to advocate and implement specific learning initiatives. Membership size, participation, focus, and the use of Teachers.net's tools vary in each forum. As a result, forums have created different learning environments.

Group and Participant Selection

I will ask for research participants from four groups from Teacher.net: Special Education Teachers, 4-Blocks Literacy group, the National Board for Professional Teaching Standards Certification group and the Middle School group. These groups were chosen because they represent different interests and have active chatboards, large mailrings, and archived and scheduled formal synchronous meetings. Although there are other groups with similar characteristics, I am only focusing on four because it is more time efficient to recruit participants in a limited number of groups. In addition, I have the possibility for finding unique trends within groups. Three of the four groups are specific interest groups. I have chosen to focus more on these types of groups rather than general ones because general groups, such as elementary, primary, math or language arts, do not seem to have as many members. However, by including one general group, middle school, I have more of an opportunity to compare trends and generalize findings.

My interview sample will come out of my survey sample. I would like to interview twelve participants, three from each forum. The interviews will further explore the survey questions and ask additional questions.

Research Relationship

Although I will be entering the relationship as "the researcher," I will emphasize my role as an elementary teacher. I will introduce myself as a full time teacher and a part time doctorate student. I will do this when I recruit participants and at the beginning of each interview. I hope that this will help establish more of a colleague/colleague relationship than a researcher/researchee relationship that may be viewed as more intimidating.

In addition, the virtual environments I am using for the interviews will allow me to enhance our communication beyond text. Tools such as file sharing and web browsing will allow me to share more information about myself and give the research participant more options to express him or herself. For example, I can post my picture with additional information about myself in my workspace. Knowing what the person looks like that you are conversing with can help personalize the relationship.

Data Collection

I will collect data through a survey and online synchronous interviews. My first step in data collection is to solicit research participants for my survey. A description of the research project will be posted on each group's discussion board, within each listserv and at synchronous meetings. (See Appendix A.) It is important to advertise in each of these modes so that members who only use one or two of these tools will have the opportunity to participate. Interested participants will be asked to email the researcher or go directly to the survey by clicking on the URL within the advertisement. An email will be sent to volunteers, thanking them for their participation.

An informed consent form will be embedded in the survey. At the beginning of the survey participants will be asked to read the letter of consent and check a box indicating they have read it and are willing participants. (See Appendix B.)

The survey addresses all of my research questions. (See Appendix C.) It is mostly quantitative with the opportunity to clarify any question with qualitative data. It is quantitative because I want to obtain a "snapshot" of how a larger group believes their participation is related to their own professional development. Having this quantitative data will help me know if my interview data is representative of the larger group. This web-based survey will be designed around the principles outlined by Don Dillman in Mail and Internet Surveys: The Tailored Design Method (2000).

By following these principles I hope to avoid problems such as browser limitations, length of time required for taking it, and accessibility. The survey will also help me identify interviewees.

This survey will be developed with Response-O-Matic, a web-based tool, and hosted on the GMU server. This forty-question survey will take about 15 minutes to answer. A question at the end of my survey asks participants if they are willing to be contacted for a follow-up online interview. When participants click on submit, a Thank You page is displayed with the contents of the completed survey, so the participant can review what was entered. The contents of the survey are also emailed directly to me. A follow-up email will be sent to participants, thanking them for their time. I am considering offering some type of incentive for interviews. One possibility would be a gift certificate for the online Teachers.net catalog that offers books and teacher supplies.

If a participant indicated a willingness to be interviewed, an interview will be scheduled. Through email, participants will receive further explanation of how the interview will be conducted. Interviews will be conducted in TappedIn. Tapped In (TI) is sponsored by the National Science Foundation, SRI International, Sun Microsystems, and the Walter S. Johnson Foundation, is a platform independent, web based, multiuser virtual environment (MUVE) and provides teachers a professional development workplace. A private office space has already been setup within TI. Participants will enter TappedIn and go directly to the researcher's office space. Interviews will last approximately an hour. Phone numbers will be exchanged before the interviews so that we can make contact if there are technical difficulties. I will offer to accept any collect calls.

Participants will receive step-by-step instructions on logging onto TI and going directly to my office space. I will schedule an hour and fifteen minutes for each interview. I want to provide some time for the participant to explore and become comfortable in the virtual environment. After the participant has had time to ask any questions or explore, I will begin the interview using an interview guide. (See Appendix D.) The interview will be captured by TI's automatic transcription tool. When a user logs out of TI, she receives an email documenting her actions and conversations while in TI. This will automatically provide an interview transcription for the participant and me.

Below is a table that shows which questions address my research questions.

Table 2 Matrix of Research and Interview/Survey Questions

Why do teachers voluntarily participate in online learning?	In what ways do teachers participate in online learning?	How do their reasons for participation affect their level and kind of participation?	How do they believe their participation impacts their development as teachers?	Does voluntary online learning foster "communities of practice" as defined in the literature?
What influenced you to participate?	Describe how you participate?	How long do you think you will continue participating?	How does your participation influence your teaching?	What kinds of knowledge do you share with other participants in your forum?
What are some benefits to your participation?	How often do you participate?	Has the frequency of your participation changed? If so how and why?	How is your participation different than collaboration within your school or school district?	Do you have common practices and beliefs about best practices with other participants?
How did you become involved with TI?	How do you use the different tools (mailring, discussion board, meetings)?	Is your participation different on Teachers.net than it is in other professional development opportunities? How?	How does your participation influence your own professional development? Can you describe an example of this?	Are you aware of others' competencies, strengths, shortcomings and contributions?

(Continued)

(Continued)

Is your participation different with (4 Blocks/ Spec. Ed Teachers/ Nat'l Board) on Teachers. net than in other professional development opportunities? How?	How do these tools influence your participation?			Do members in your group have common tools, methods, and techniques such as forms, job aids, etc?
What is the purpose of your participation? Do you think others in your forum share the same purpose?				Do members in your group have a shared, evolving language (e.g. special terms, jargon, shortcuts such as acronyms, etc.)?
What do you hope to achieve through your online participation?				Do members depend on each other's educational/ instructional expertise?
How is your participation sustained? Why do maintain your participation? How long do you think you will continue participating?				Is there a quick diffusion of innovation among members in your group (e.g., rapid transfer of best practices)?

Data Analysis

The qualitative data will be analyzed with memos and with categorizing and contextualizing strategies. Memos will be written after each interview to facilitate analytical thinking about the data and to help remember details that may not necessarily be included in the transcripts. Predetermined, open, and emic coding will "fracture" the data so that themes around the reasons for participation can be determined. In addition, narrative analysis may be used to help understand the following questions: what is going on for a specific issue or person; how specific people sustain their participation; and identify examples of how their participation impacts professional development. Although I have not used NVivo before, I am considering using this data analysis software for ordering data, generating coding categories, and cross-linking data and generated memos.

The quantitative data from the online survey will be entered and analyzed using SPSS software. This data will provide information on the research questions from a larger sample of participants than interviewed. I will use descriptive statistics to describe characteristics of the sample. Collected data will be nominal or ordinal and that will determine the statistical procedure to be used. I will use a Chi-square test with nominal level data to test the statistical independence of two variables. When using this test the P value will be set at .05.

Validity

In order to avoid possible threats and to test the validity of my conclusions, I will employ the following strategies suggested by Maxwell (1996): triangulation, feedback, "rich data" and quasi-statistics.

Triangulation requires a variety of methods to be used when collecting data. By using interviews, surveys and memos, I am counterbalancing flaws that may be inherent in a single method. Throughout the study I will solicit feedback from my committee when forming theories or generalizations from my data. This can help identify and deter biases or skewed logic that could threaten the conclusions.

The qualitative aspect of this study inherently provides rich data. Interview transcripts capture details that can be found and referred to long after the interview has taken place. Writing memos creates additional "rich data" because reactions and initial theories and/or conclusions are documented before the actual analysis of the data.

Finally, the qualitative survey functions as quasi-statistics, which better inform the qualitative data. Although one would expect the statistics and the qualitative data to support each other, discrepancies help reveal possible flaws in the study. It is essential to use all of these strategies to protect the data, and ultimately the conclusions, from validity threats.

TIMELINE OF PROCEDURES

Activity	Task Analysis	Timeline
1: Recruit research participants	1) Join Teacher.net mailrings 2) Post requests on discussion boards 3) Attend formal and informal synchronous meetings	September, 2002– November, 2002
2: Send follow-up emails to willing participants	1) Send participants URL of survey 2) Thank participants for time	September, 2002– November, 2002
3: Conduct online interviews	1) Schedule interviews 2) Conduct interviews	September, 2002– December, 2002
4: Analyze survey results.	1) Enter data into SPSS. 2) Developing coding categories from qualitative data using Nvivo. 3) Extract data.	November/December, 2002
5: Review and analyze memos and interview transcripts.	1) Review transcripts. 2) Developing coding categories from transcripts using Nvivo. 3) Extract data from transcripts.	September, 2002– January, 2003
6: Write chapters 4 and 5.	1) Draft and submit versions to committee members.	December, 2002– February, 2003
7: Prepare for defense		February/March, 2003
8: Defend dissertation		March, 2003
9: Graduate		May 17, 2003

REFERENCES

(Omitted because of length)

APPENDICES

APPENDIX A–Project Description/Advertisement

Educators desperately need alternative methods of distributing and receiving professional development! If you are participating in Teachers.net, you probably already know this. Help solve the problem by participating in a research study that identifies why teachers like you voluntarily participate in informal online learning and how it influences your professional development.

As a fellow teacher and part-time doctoral student I know that your time is scarce. However, with only 15 minutes you can answer a web-based survey and be a part of research! The ultimate goal of this research is to help school districts design online learning opportunities that are effective for K–12 teachers' professional development. If you are a willing participant, please email me or click on the link below to go directly to the survey. Thank you!

APPENDIX B–Informed Consent Letter

Dear Teachers,

This letter is to request your permission for participation in a research project that explores how teachers are accessing and enhancing their professional development through participation in an online environment. I am specifically, interested in teacher participation that is independent of online coursework or any other credit. This study the investigates why K–12 teachers voluntarily participate in informal online learning and how it influences their professional development. The ultimate goal of this research is to help school districts develop or invest in online learning opportunities that will be successful for their teachers.

This research project is based on survey data and twelve to fifteen hour long interviews with teachers who participate in various groups on Teachers.net. Participants who take the survey may indicate on the survey whether or not they would like to be interviewed. All participants who indicate a willingness to be interviewed may not be interviewed. Surveys will be developed with the web-based tool, Response-O-Matic and hosted on the GMU server. Interviews will be conducted in an online environment. While it is understood that no computer transmission can be perfectly secure, reasonable efforts will be made to protect the confidentiality of your transmission.

I will be the only one who has access to these transcriptions. If at any time during the interview, you choose to withdraw from the project, survey and interview data will be destroyed immediately. Your participation is voluntary. Although there are no foreseeable risks in participation of this study, you may withdraw from the study at any time and for any reason. There is no penalty for not participating or withdrawing. Research data will be collected between September and December of 2002. Participation and records of participation will be confidential. To ensure that data collected cannot be linked back to participants, data will be kept in a secure location. In addition, names and identifiable information will not be included in the dissertation.

I am a doctoral student at George Mason University in Fairfax, VA. This research is part of my dissertation. I am working under the direction of my advisor, Dr. Debra Sprague (dspragu1@gmu.edu) at the Graduate School of Education. If you have questions regarding this project, please contact me at (703)931-2391 or at eriddle@acps. k12.va.us. You may also contact the George Mason University Office of Sponsored Programs at (703) 993-2295. This project has been reviewed according to the George Mason University procedures governing your participation in this research.

A check in the box below indicates your willingness to participate in the study. Please return the signed letter to me within three days, if possible. Thank you.

Sincerely,
Elizabeth M. Riddle

I have read the consent form above. I understand the parameters of this research study and I am a willing participant.

APPENDIX C–Survey

(Omitted because of length)

APPENDIX D–Interview Guide

Interview Guide

Tell my how you became involved with the (specific group) on TN?
What influenced you to participate?
Describe how you participate?
What are the benefits to your participation?
Is your participation different with (4 Blocks/Spec. Ed Teachers/ Nat'l Board) on Teachers.net than in other non-mandatory professional development opportunities? How?
Is your participation different than it is in mandatory professional development opportunities? Why?

How do you use the different tools (mailring, discussion board, meetings)?
How do these tools influence your participation?
How often do you participate?
Why do you maintain your participation? How long do you think you will continue participating?
How does your participation influence your teaching?
How is your participation different than collaboration within your school or school district?
Do you share similar beliefs about best practices with other participants?
Can you think of an example of how members depend on each others' educational/ instructional expertise?
In what ways does this group seem like a community?

References

Abbott, A. (2001). *Chaos of disciplines.* Chicago, IL: University of Chicago Press.

Abbott, A. (2004). *Methods of discovery: Heuristics for the social sciences.* New York, NY: W. W. Norton.

Abu-Lughod, L. (1986). *Veiled sentiments: Honor and poetry in a Bedouin society.* Berkeley: University of California Press.

Agar, M. (1991). The right brain strikes back. In N. G. Fielding & R. M. Lee (Eds.), *Using computers in qualitative research* (pp. 181–194). Newbury Park, CA: Sage.

American Psychological Association. (2010). *Publication manual of the American Psychological Association* (6th ed.). Washington, DC: Author.

Anderson, G. L., & Scott, J. (in press). Toward an intersectional understanding of causality and social context. *Qualitative Inquiry 18*(8).

Atkinson, P. (1992). The ethnography of a medical setting: Reading, writing, and rhetoric. *Qualitative Health Research, 2,* 451–474.

Bazeley, P. (2007). *Qualitative data analysis with NVivo.* Thousand Oaks, CA: Sage.

Becker, H. S. (1970). *Sociological work: Method and substance.* Chicago: Aldine.

Becker, H. S. (1991). Generalizing from case studies. In E. Eisner & A. Peshkin (Eds.), *Qualitative inquiry in education: The continuing debate* (pp. 233–242). New York, NY: Teachers College Press.

Becker, H. S. (2007). *Writing for social scientists: How to start and finish your thesis, book, or article* (2nd ed.). Chicago, IL: University of Chicago Press.

Becker, H. S., & Geer, B. (1957). Participant observation and interviewing: A comparison. *Human Organization, 16,* 28–32.

Becker, H. S., Geer, B., Hughes, E. C., & Strauss, A. L. (1961). *Boys in white: Student culture in medical school.* Chicago, IL: University of Chicago Press.

Berg, D. N., & Smith, K. K. (1988). *The self in social inquiry: Researching methods.* Newbury Park, CA: Sage.

Berger, B. (1981). *The survival of a counterculture: Ideological work and everyday life among rural communards.* Berkeley: University of California Press.

Bernstein, R. J. (1992). *The new constellation: The ethical-political horizons of modernity-postmodernity.* Cambridge, MA: MIT Press.

Bhattacharjea, S. (1994). *Reconciling "public" and "private": Women in the educational bureaucracy in "Sinjabistan" Province, Pakistan.* Unpublished doctoral dissertation, Harvard Graduate School of Education.

Bhattacharya, H. (2008). Interpretive research. In L. Given (Ed.), *The SAGE encyclopedia of qualitative research methods* (pp. 464–467). Thousand Oaks, CA: Sage.

Bloor, M. J. (1983). Notes on member validation. In R. M. Emerson (Ed.), *Contemporary field research: A collection of readings* (pp. 156–172). Prospect Heights, IL: Waveland Press.

Blumer, H. (1969). The methodological position of symbolic interactionism. In H. Blumer, *Symbolic interactionism: Perspective and method* (pp. 1–60). Berkeley: University of California Press.

Bogdan, R. C., & Biklen, S. K. (2003). *Qualitative research for education: An introduction to theory and methods* (4th ed.). Boston, MA: Allyn & Bacon.

Bolster, A. S. (1983). Toward a more effective model of research on teaching. *Harvard Educational Review, 53,* 294–308.

Bosk, C. (1979). *Forgive and remember: Managing medical failure.* Chicago, IL: University of Chicago Press.

Bredo, E., & Feinberg, W. (1982). *Knowledge and values in social and educational research.* Philadelphia, PA: Temple University Press.

Bricolage. n.d. In *Wikipedia.* Retrieved from http://en.wikipedia.org/wiki/Bricolage

Briggs, C. (1986). *Learning how to ask.* Cambridge, England: Cambridge University Press.

Briggs, J. (1970). *Never in anger: Portrait of an Eskimo family.* Cambridge, MA: Harvard University Press.

Brinberg, D., & McGrath, J. E. (1985). *Validity and the research process.* Beverly Hills, CA: Sage.

Britan, G. M. (1978). Experimental and contextual models of program evaluation. *Evaluation and Program Planning, 1,* 229–234.

Brown, L. M. (Ed.). (1988). *A guide to reading narratives of conflict and choice for self and moral voice.* Cambridge, MA: Harvard University, Center for the Study of Gender, Education, and Human Development.

Brydon-Miller, M., Kral, M., Maguire, P., Noffke, S., & Sabhlok, A. (2011). Jazz and the banyan tree: Roots and riffs on participatory action research. In N. K. Denzin & Y. S. Lincoln (Eds.), *The SAGE handbook of qualitative research* (4th ed., pp. 387–400). Thousand Oaks, CA: Sage.

Bryman, A. (1988). *Quantity and quality in social research.* London, England: Unwin Hyman.

Burman, E. (2001). Minding the gap: Positivism, psychology, and the politics of qualitative methods. In D. L. Tolman & M. Brydon-Miller (Eds.), *From subjects to subjectivities: A handbook of interpretive and participatory methods* (pp. 259–275). New York, NY: New York University Press.

Campbell, D. T. (1984). Foreword. In R. Yin, *Case study research: Design and methods* (pp. 7–8). Beverly Hills, CA: Sage.

Campbell, D. T. (1988). *Methodology and epistemology for social science: Selected papers.* Chicago, IL: University of Chicago Press.

Campbell, D. T., & Stanley, J. (1963). Experimental and quasi-experimental designs for research on teaching. In N. L. Gage (Ed.), *Handbook of research on teaching* (pp. 171–246). Chicago, IL: Rand McNally.

Cannella, G. S., & Lincoln, Y. S. (2011). Ethics, research regulations, and critical social science. In N. K. Denzin & Y. S. Lincoln (Eds.), *The SAGE handbook of qualitative research* (4th ed., pp. 81–90). Thousand Oaks, CA: Sage.

Christians, C. G. (2011). Ethics and politics in qualitative research. In N. K. Denzin & Y. S. Lincoln (Eds.), *The SAGE handbook of qualitative research* (4th ed., pp. 61–80). Thousand Oaks, CA: Sage.

Coffey, A., & Atkinson, P. (1996). *Making sense of qualitative data.* Thousand Oaks, CA: Sage.

Cohen, J. (1994). The Earth is round (p<.05). *American Psychologist 49*(12), 997–1003.

Cook, T. D., & Campbell, D. T. (1979). *Quasi-experimentation: Design and analysis issues for field settings.* Boston, MA: Houghton Mifflin.

Corbin, J., & Strauss, A. (2007). *Basics of qualitative research: Techniques and procedures for developing grounded theory.* Thousand Oaks, CA: Sage.

Creswell, J. W. (1994). *Research design: Quantitative and qualitative approaches.* Thousand Oaks, CA: Sage.

Creswell, J. W. (2002). *Educational research: Planning, conducting, and evaluating quantitative and qualitative research.* Upper Saddle River, NJ: Merrill Prentice Hall.

Creswell, J. W. (2006). *Qualitative inquiry and research design: Choosing among five traditions* (2nd ed.). Thousand Oaks, CA: Sage.

Croskery, B. (1995). *Swamp leadership: The wisdom of the craft.* Unpublished doctoral dissertation, Harvard Graduate School of Education.

Cumming, G. (2011). *Understanding the new statistics: Effect sizes, confidence intervals, and meta-analysis.* London, England: Routledge.

Denzin, N. K. (1970). *The research act.* Chicago, IL: Aldine.

Denzin, N. K., & Lincoln, Y. S. (2000). Introduction: The discipline and practice of qualitative research. In N. K. Denzin & Y. S. Lincoln (Eds.), *handbook of qualitative research* (2nd ed., pp. 1–28). Thousand Oaks, CA: Sage.

Denzin, N. K., & Lincoln, Y. S. (2005a). Introduction: The discipline and practice of qualitative research. In N. K. Denzin & Y. S. Lincoln (Eds.), *SAGE handbook of qualitative research* (3rd ed., pp. 1–42). Thousand Oaks, CA: Sage.

Denzin, N. K., & Lincoln, Y. S. (2005b). *SAGE handbook of qualitative research* (3rd ed.). Thousand Oaks, CA: Sage.

Denzin, N. K., & Lincoln, Y. S. (2011). *SAGE handbook of qualitative research* (4th ed.). Thousand Oaks, CA: Sage.

Dere, E., Easton, A., Nadel, L., & Huston, J. P. (Eds.). (2008). *Handbook of episodic memory.* Amsterdam: Elsevier.

Design. (1984). In F. C. Mish (Ed.), *Webster's Ninth New Collegiate Dictionary* (p. 343). Springfield, MA: Merriam-Webster.

Dexter, L. A. (1970). *Elite and specialized interviewing.* Evanston, IL: Northwestern University Press.

Dey, I. (1993). *Qualitative data analysis: A user-friendly guide for social scientists.* London, England: Routledge.

Diamond, J. (2011). *Collapse: How societies choose to fail or succeed.* New York, NY: Penguin.

Donmoyer, R. (in press). Can qualitative researchers answer policymakers' what-works question? *Qualitative Inquiry 18*(8).

Dressman, M. (2008). *Using social theory in educational research: A practical guide.* London, England: Routledge.

Elbow, P. (1973). Appendix essay. The doubting game and the believing game: An analysis of the intellectual process. In *Writing without teachers* (pp. 147–191). London, England: Oxford University Press.

Elbow, P. (2006). The believing game and how to make conflicting opinions more fruitful. In C. Weber (Ed.), *Nurturing the peacemakers in our students: A guide to teaching peace, empathy, and understanding.* Portsmouth, NH: Heinemann.

Emerson, R. M., Fretz, R. I., & Shaw, L. L. (1995). *Writing ethnographic fieldnotes.* Chicago, IL: University of Chicago Press.

Erickson, F. (1986). Qualitative methods. In M. C. Wittrock (Ed.), *Handbook of research on teaching* pp. 119–161. New York, NY: Macmillan.

Erickson, F. (1992). Ethnographic microanalysis of interaction. In M. D. LeCompte, W. L. Millroy, & J. Preissle (Eds.), *The handbook of qualitative research in education* (pp. 201–225). San Diego, CA: Academic Press.

Festinger, L., Riecker, H. W., & Schachter, S. (1956). *When prophecy fails.* Minneapolis: University of Minnesota Press.

Fetterman, D. M. (2008). Emic/etic distinction. In L. Given (Ed.), *The SAGE encyclopedia of qualitative research methods* (p. 249). Thousand Oaks, CA: Sage.

Fielding, N., & Fielding, J. (1986). *Linking data.* Beverly Hills, CA: Sage.

Fine, M., Weis, L., Weseen, S., & Wong, L. (2000). For whom? Qualitative research, representations, and social responsibilities. In N. K. Denzin & Y. S. Lincoln (Eds.), *Handbook of qualitative research* (2nd ed., pp. 107–131). Thousand Oaks, CA: Sage.

Finley, S. (2008). Community-based research. In L. Given (Ed.), *The SAGE encyclopedia of qualitative research methods* (pp. 97–100). Thousand Oaks, CA: Sage.

Flick, U. (2000). Episodic interviewing. In M. W Bauer & G. Gaskell (Eds.), *Qualitative researching with text, image and sound* (pp. 75-92). London, England: Sage.

Flick, U. (2007). *Managing quality in qualitative research.* London, England: Sage.

Freidson, E. (1975). *Doctoring together: A study of professional social control.* Chicago, IL: University of Chicago Press.

Galilei, G. (2008). Extracts from *Discorsi e demonstrazioni matematiche* (M. A. Finocchairo, Trans.). In M. A. Finocchairo (Ed.), *The essential Galileo* (pp. 301–302. Indianapolis, IN: Hackett. (Original work published 1628)

Galileo's Leaning Tower of Pisa experiment. n.d. In *Wikipedia.* Retrieved from http://en.wikipedia .org/wiki/Galileo%27s_Leaning_Tower_of_Pisa_experiment

Gee, J. P. (2005). *An introduction to discourse analysis: Theory and method.* New York, NY: Routledge.

Gee, J. P., Michaels, S., & O'Connor, M. C. (1992). Discourse analysis. In M. D. LeCompte, W. L. Millroy, & J. Preissle (Eds.), *The handbook of qualitative research in education* (pp. 227–291). San Diego, CA: Academic Press.

Geertz, C. (1973). *The interpretation of cultures.* New York, NY: Basic Books.

Geertz, C. (1974). From the native's point of view: On the nature of anthropological understanding. *Bulletin of the American Academy of Arts and Sciences, 28*(1), 27–45.

Gilligan, C., Spencer, R., Weinberg, M. C., & Bertsch, T. (2003). On the listening guide: A voice-centered relational method. In P. M. Camic, J. E. Rhodes, & L. Yardley (Eds.), *Qualitative research in psychology: Expanding perspectives in methodology and design* (pp. 157–172). Washington, DC: American Psychological Association.

Given, L. (Ed.). (2008). *The SAGE encyclopedia of qualitative research methods.* Thousand Oaks, CA: Sage.

Glaser, B., & Strauss, A. (1967). *The discovery of grounded theory.* Chicago, IL: Aldine.

Glesne, C. (2011). *Becoming qualitative researchers: An introduction* (4th ed.). Boston, MA: Pearson.

Glesne, C., & Peshkin, A. (1992). *Becoming qualitative researchers: An introduction.* White Plains, NY: Longman.

Goldenberg, C. (1992). The limits of expectations: A case for case knowledge of teacher expectancy effects. *American Educational Research Journal, 29,* 517–544.

Grady, K. A., & Wallston, B. S. (1988). *Research in health care settings.* Newbury Park, CA: Sage.

Greene, J. (2007). *Mixed methods in social inquiry.* San Francisco, CA: Jossey-Bass.

Groenewald, T. (2008). Memos and memoing. In L. Given (Ed.), *The SAGE encyclopedia of qualitative research methods* (pp. 505-506). Thousand Oaks, CA: Sage.

Guba, E. G., & Lincoln, Y. S. (1989). *Fourth generation evaluation.* Newbury Park, CA: Sage.

Guilbault, B. (1989). *The families of dependent handicapped adults: A working paper.* Unpublished manuscript.

Hacking, I. (1999). *The social construction of what?* Cambridge, MA: Harvard University Press.

Hallaj, D. (2006). *Caught between culture and conflict: Palestinian refugee women's perceptions of illiteracy and education.* Unpublished doctoral dissertation, George Mason University.

Hammersley, M. (1992). *What's wrong with ethnography?* London, England: Routledge.

Hammersley, M. (2008). Bricolage and bricoleur. In L. Given (Ed.), *The SAGE encyclopedia of qualitative research methods* (pp. 65–66). Thousand Oaks, CA: Sage.

Hammersley, M., & Atkinson, P. (1995). *Ethnography: Principles in practice* (2nd ed.). London, England: Routledge.

Hammersley, M., & Atkinson, P. (2007). *Ethnography: Principles in practice* (3rd ed.). London, England: Routledge.

Hannerz, U. (1992). *Cultural complexity: Studies in the social organization of meaning.* New York, NY: Columbia University Press.

Harlow, L. L., Mulaik, S. A., & Steiger, J. H. (Eds.). (1997). *What if there were no significance tests?* Mahwah, NJ: Lawrence Erlbaum.

Heider, E. R. (1972). Probability, sampling, and ethnographic method: The case of Dani colour names. *Man, 7,* 448–466.

Heinrich, B. (1979). *Bumblebee economics.* Cambridge, MA: Harvard University Press.

Heinrich, B. (1984). *In a patch of fireweed.* Cambridge, MA: Harvard University Press.

Hoover, E.R. (2002). *Voluntary participation and online learning: A research study investigating why K–12 teachers participate in informal online learning and how it influences their professional development.* Dissertation proposal. Fairfax, VA: George Mason University.

Howard, V. A, & Barton, J. H. (1988). *Thinking on paper.* New York, NY: William Morrow.

Howe, K. R. (2011). Mixed methods, mixed causes? *Qualitative Inquiry, 17,* 166–171.

Huberman, A. M. (1993). *The Lives of Teachers* (J. Neufeld, Trans.). New York, NY: Teachers College Press. (Original work published 1989)

Huck, S. (2009). *Statistical misconceptions.* New York: NY: Taylor & Francis.

Huck, S. W., & Sandler, H. M. (1979). *Rival hypotheses: "Minute mysteries" for the critical thinker.* London, England: Harper & Row.

Irwin, S. (2008). Data analysis and interpretation: Emergent issues in linking qualitative and quantitative evidence. In P. Leavy & S. Hesse-Biber (Eds.), *Handbook of emergent methods*, pp. 415–435. New York, NY: Guilford Press.

Jackson, B. (1987). *Fieldwork.* Urbana: University of Illinois Press.

Janesick, V. J. (1994). The dance of qualitative research design: Metaphor, methodolatry, and meaning. In N. K. Denzin & Y. S. Lincoln (Eds.), *Handbook of qualitative research* (pp. 209–219). Thousand Oaks, CA: Sage.

Jansen, G., & Peshkin, A. (1992). Subjectivity in qualitative research. In M. D. LeCompte, W. L. Millroy, & J. Preissle (Eds.), *The handbook of qualitative research in education* (pp. 681–725). San Diego, CA: Academic Press.

Jordan, S. (2008). Participatory action research (PAR). In L. Given (Ed.), *The SAGE encyclopedia of qualitative research methods* (pp. 601–604). Thousand Oaks, CA: Sage.

Josselson, R., Lieblich, A., & McAdams, D. P. (2007). *The meaning of others: Narrative studies of relationships.* Washington, DC: American Psychological Association.

Kaffenberger, C. (1999). *The experience of adolescent cancer survivors and their siblings: The effect on their lives and their relationships.* Unpublished doctoral dissertation, George Mason University.

Kaplan, A. (1964). *The conduct of inquiry.* San Francisco, CA: Chandler.

Kidder, L. H. (1981). Qualitative research and quasi-experimental frameworks. In M. B. Brewer & B. E. Collins (Eds.), *Scientific inquiry and the social sciences.* San Francisco, CA: Jossey-Bass.

Kincheloe, J. L., & Berry, K. S. (2004). *Rigour and complexity in educational research: Conceptualizing the bricolage.* Maidenhead, England: Open University Press.

Kincheloe, J. L., McLaren, P., & Steinberg, S. L. (2011). Critical pedagogy, and qualitative research: Moving to the bricolage, In N. K. Denzin & Y. S. Lincoln (Eds.), *The SAGE handbook of qualitative research* (4th ed., pp. 163–177). Thousand Oaks, CA: Sage.

Kirk, J., & Miller, M. (1986). *Reliability and validity in qualitative research.* Beverly Hills, CA: Sage.

Koro-Ljungberg, M. (2004). Impossibilities of reconciliation: Validity in mixed theory projects. *Qualitative Inquiry 10,* 601–621.

Kuhn, T. (1970). *The structure of scientific revolutions* (2nd ed.). Chicago, IL: University of Chicago Press.

Kvale, S. (Ed.). (1989). *Issues of validity in qualitative research.* Lund, Sweden: Studentlitteratur.

Kvarning, L. Å. (1993, October). Raising the *Vasa. Scientific American,* 84–91.

Lather, P. (1993). Fertile obsession: Validity after poststructuralism. *Sociological Quarterly, 34,* 673–693.

Lave, C. A., & March, J. G. (1975). *An introduction to models in the social sciences.* New York, NY: Harper & Row.

Lawrence-Lightfoot, S., & Hoffman Davis, J. (1997). *The art and science of portraiture.* San Francisco: Jossey-Bass.

LeCompte, M. D., & Preissle, J. (1993). *Ethnography and qualitative design in educational research* (2nd ed.). San Diego, CA: Academic Press.

LeGuin, U. K. (2000). Introduction. *The left hand of darkness.* In New York, NY: Ace Books.

LeGuin, U. K. (2003). *Changing planes.* Boston, MA: Houghton Mifflin Harcourt.

Levi-Strauss, C. (1968). *The savage mind.* Chicago, IL: University of Chicago Press.

Light, R. J., & Pillemer, D. B. (1984). *Summing up.* Cambridge, MA: Harvard University Press.

Light, R. J., Singer, J., & Willett, J. (1990). *By design: Conducting research on higher education.* Cambridge, MA: Harvard University Press.

Lincoln, Y. S. (1990). Toward a categorical imperative for qualitative research. In E. Eisner & A. Peshkin (Eds.), *Qualitative inquiry in education: The continuing debate.* New York: Teachers College Press.

Lincoln, Y. S., & Guba, E. G. (1985). *Naturalistic inquiry.* Beverly Hills, CA: Sage.

Lincoln, Y. S., Lynham, S. A., & Guba, E. G. (2011). Paradigmatic controversies, contradictions, and emerging confluences, revisited. In N. K. Denzin & Y. S. Lincoln (Eds.), *SAGE handbook of qualitative research* (4th ed. pp. 97–128). Thousand Oaks, CA: Sage.

Linde, C. (1993). *Life stories: The creation of coherence.* New York, NY: Oxford University Press.

L. L. Bean (1998). *October classics catalog.* Freeport, ME: Author.

Locke, L., Silverman, S. J., & Spirduso, W. W. (2009). *Reading and understanding research.* Thousand Oaks, CA: Sage.

Locke, L., Spirduso, W. W., & Silverman, S. J. (1993). *Proposals that work* (3rd ed.). Newbury Park, CA: Sage.

Locke, L., Spirduso, W. W., & Silverman, S. J. (2000). *Proposals that work* (4th ed.). Thousand Oaks, CA: Sage.

Locke, L., Spirduso, W. W., & Silverman, S. J. (2007). *Proposals that work* (5th ed.). Thousand Oaks, CA: Sage.

Malinowski, B. (1954). *Magic, science and religion and other essays.* Garden City, NY: Doubleday.

Manning, H. (Ed.). (1960). *Mountaineering: The freedom of the hills.* Seattle, WA: The Mountaineers.

Margolis, J. S. (1990). *Psychology of gender and academic discourse: A comparison between female and male students' experiences talking in a college classroom.* Unpublished doctoral dissertation, Harvard Graduate School of Education.

Marshall, C., & Rossman, G. (1999). *Designing qualitative research* (3rd ed.). Thousand Oaks, CA: Sage.

Maxwell, J. A. (1971). *The development of Plains kinship systems.* Unpublished master's thesis, University of Chicago.

Maxwell, J. A. (1978). The evolution of Plains Indian kin terminologies: A non-reflectionist account. *Plains Anthropologist, 23,* 13–29.

Maxwell, J. A. (1986). *The conceptualization of kinship in an Inuit community.* Unpublished doctoral dissertation, University of Chicago.

Maxwell, J. A. (1992). Understanding and validity in qualitative research. *Harvard Educational Review, 62,* 279–300.

Maxwell, J. A. (1993). Gaining acceptance for qualitative methods from clients, policy-makers, and participants. In D. Fetterman (Ed.), *Speaking the language of power.* London: Falmer Press.

Maxwell, J. A. (1995). Diversity and methodology in a changing world. *Pedagogía,* 30, 32–40.

Maxwell, J. A. (1996). *Qualitative research design: An interactive approach.* Thousand Oaks, CA: Sage.

Maxwell, J. A. (2002). Realism and the role of the researcher in qualitative psychology. In M. Kiegelmann (Ed.), *The role of the researcher in qualitative psychology* (pp. 11–30). Tuebingen, Germany: Verlag Ingeborg Huber.

Maxwell, J. A. (2004a). Causal explanation, qualitative research, and scientific inquiry in education. *Educational Researcher, 33*(2), 3–11.

Maxwell, J. A. (2004b). Re-emergent scientism, postmodernism, and dialogue across differences. *Qualitative Inquiry, 10,* 35–41.

Maxwell, J. A. (2004c). Using qualitative methods for causal explanation. *Field Methods, 16*(3), 243–264.

Maxwell, J. A. (2006). Literature reviews of, and for, educational research: A commentary on Boote and Beile's "Scholars before researchers." *Educational Researcher 35*(9), 28–31.

Maxwell, J. A. (2008). The value of a realist understanding of causality for qualitative research. In N. K. Denzin (Ed.), *Qualitative research and the politics of evidence* (pp. 163–181). Walnut Creek, CA: Left Coast Press.

Maxwell, J. A. (2010). Using numbers in qualitative research. *Qualitative Inquiry, 16*(6), 475–482.

Maxwell, J. A. (2011a). Paradigms or toolkits? Philosophical and methodological positions as heuristics for mixed method research. *Mid-Western Educational Researcher 24*(2), 27–30.

Maxwell, J. A. (2011b). *A realist approach for qualitative research.* Thousand Oaks, CA: Sage.

Maxwell, J. A. (in press). The importance of qualitative research for causal explanation in education. *Qualitative Inquiry 18*(8).

Maxwell, J. A., & Loomis, D. (2002). Mixed methods design: An alternative approach. In A. Tashakkori & C. Teddlie (Eds.), *Handbook of mixed methods in social and behavioral research* (pp. 241–271). Thousand Oaks, CA: Sage.

Maxwell, J. A., & Miller, B. A. (2008). *Categorizing and connecting as components of qualitative data analysis.* In S. Hesse-Biber and P. Leavy (Eds.), *Handbook of emergent methods,* pp. 461-477. New York, NY: Guilford Press.

Maxwell, J. A., & Mittapalli, K. (2008a). Theory. In L. Given (Ed.), *The SAGE encyclopedia of qualitative research methods* (pp. 878–879). Thousand Oaks, CA: Sage.

Maxwell, J. A., & Mittapalli, K. (2008b). Thick description. In L. Given (Ed.), *The SAGE encyclopedia of qualitative research methods* (p. 880). Thousand Oaks, CA: Sage.

McGinn, M. K. (2008). Researcher-participant relationships. In L. Given (Ed.), *The SAGE encyclopedia of qualitative research methods* (pp. 767–771). Thousand Oaks, CA: Sage.

McMillan, J. H., & Schumacher, S. (2001). *Research in education: A conceptual introduction.* New York, NY: Longman.

Menzel, H. (1978). Meaning: Who needs it? In M. Brenner, P. Marsh, & M. Brenner (Eds.), *The social contexts of method* (pp. 140–171). New York, NY: St. Martin's Press.

Merriam, S. (1988). *Case study research in education: A qualitative approach.* San Francisco, CA: Jossey-Bass.

Metzger, M. (1993, June). Playing school or telling the truth? *Harvard Graduate School of Education Alumni Bulletin, 37*(3), 14–16.

Miles, M. B., & Huberman, A. M. (1984). *Qualitative data analysis: A sourcebook of new methods.* Beverly Hills, CA: Sage.

Miles, M. B., & Huberman, A. M. (1994). *Qualitative data analysis: An expanded sourcebook* (2nd ed.). Thousand Oaks, CA: Sage.

Mills, C. W. (1959). On intellectual craftsmanship. In C. W. Mills, *The sociological imagination* pp. 195–212. London, England: Oxford University Press.

Mishler, E. G. (1986). *Research interviewing: Context and narrative.* Cambridge, MA: Harvard University Press.

Mishler, E. G. (1990). Validation in inquiry-guided research: The role of exemplars in narrative studies. *Harvard Educational Review, 60,* 415–442.

Mohr, L. (1982). *Explaining organizational behavior.* San Francisco, CA: Jossey-Bass.

Morgan, D. L. (2008a). Sample size. In L. Given (Ed.), *The SAGE encyclopedia of qualitative research methods* (p. 798). Thousand Oaks, CA: Sage.

Morgan, D. L. (2008b). Sampling. In L. Given (Ed.), *The SAGE encyclopedia of qualitative research methods* (p. 799–800). Thousand Oaks, CA: Sage.

Norris, S. P. (1983). The inconsistencies at the foundation of construct validation theory. In E. R. House (Ed.), *Philosophy of evaluation* (pp. 53–74). San Francisco, CA: Jossey-Bass.

Novak, J. D., & Gowin, D. B. (1984). *Learning how to learn.* Cambridge, England: Cambridge University Press.

Olsson, M. R. (2008). Postmodernism. In L. Given (Ed.), *The SAGE encyclopedia of qualitative research methods* (pp. 655–659). Thousand Oaks, CA: Sage.

Organic architectural. n.d. In *Wikipedia.* Retrieved   from http://en.wikipedia.org/wiki/Organic_architecture

Palys, T. (2008). Purposive sampling. In L. Given (Ed.), *The SAGE encyclopedia of qualitative research methods* (pp. 697–698). Thousand Oaks, CA: Sage.

Patton, M. Q. (1990). *Qualitative evaluation and research methods* (2nd ed.). Newbury Park, CA: Sage.

Patton, M. Q. (2001). *Qualitative research and evaluation methods* (3rd ed.). Thousand Oaks, CA: Sage.

Pawson, R., & Tilley, N. (1997). *Realistic evaluation.* London, England: Sage.

Pelto, P., & Pelto, G. (1975). Intra-cultural diversity: Some theoretical issues. *American Ethnologist, 2,* 1–18.

Peshkin, A. (1991). *The color of strangers, the color of friends: The play of ethnicity in school and community.* Chicago, IL: University of Chicago Press.

Peters, R. L. (1992). *Getting what you came for: The smart student's guide to earning a master's or a Ph.D.* New York, NY: Noonday Press.

Pfaffenberger, B. (1988). *Microcomputer applications in qualitative research.* Thousand Oaks, CA: Sage.

Phillips, D. C. (1987). *Philosophy, science, and social inquiry.* Oxford, England: Pergamon Press.

Phillips, D. C., & Burbules, N. (2000). *Postpositivism and educational research.* Lanham, MD: Rowman & Littlefield.

Pitman, M. A., & Maxwell, J. A. (1992). Qualitative approaches to evaluation. In M. D. LeCompte, W. L. Millroy, & J. Preissle (Eds.), *The handbook of qualitative research in education* (pp. 729–770). San Diego, CA: Academic Press.

Platt, J. R. (1964). Strong inference. *Science, 146,* 347–353.

Poggie, J. J., Jr. (1972). Toward control in key informant data. *Human Organization, 31,* 23–30.

Polit, D. F., & Beck, T. B (2010). Generalization in quantitative and qualitative research: Myths and strategies. *International Journal of Nursing Studies 47*, 1451–1458.

Potemkin village. (1984). In F. C. Mish (Ed.), *Webster's Ninth New Collegiate Dictionary* (p. 343). Springfield, MA: Merriam-Webster.

Przeworski, A., & Salomon, F. (1988). *On the art of writing proposals: Some candid suggestions for applicants to Social Science Research Council competitions.* New York, NY: Social Science Research Council.

Pushor, D. (2008). Collaborative research. In L. Given (Ed.), *The SAGE encyclopedia of qualitative research methods* (pp. 91–94). Thousand Oaks, CA: Sage.

Putnam, H. (1987). *The many faces of realism.* LaSalle, IL: Open Court.

Putnam, H. (1990). *Realism with a human face.* Cambridge, MA: Harvard University Press.

Rabinow, P. (1977). *Reflections on fieldwork in Morocco.* Berkeley: University of California Press.

Rabinow, P., & Sullivan, W. M. (1979). *Interpretive social science: A reader.* Berkeley: University of California Press.

Ragin, C. C. (1987). *The comparative method: Moving beyond qualitative and quantitative strategies.* Berkeley: University of California Press.

Ravitch, S., & Riggan, M. (2011). *Reason and rigor: How conceptual frameworks guide research.* Thousand Oaks, CA: Sage.

Reason, P. (1988). Introduction. In P. Reason (Ed.), *Human inquiry in action: Developments in new paradigm research.* Newbury Park, CA: Sage.

Reason, P. (1994). Three approaches to participative inquiry. In N. K. Denzin & Y. S. Lincoln (Eds.), *Handbook of qualitative research* (pp. 324–339). Thousand Oaks, CA: Sage.

Regan-Smith, M. G. (1991). *How basic science teachers help medical students learn.* Unpublished doctoral dissertation, Harvard Graduate School of Education.

Richardson, L. (1997). *Fields of play: Constructing an academic life.* New Brunswick, N. J.: Rutgers University Press.

Riessman, C. K. (1993). *Narrative analysis.* Newbury Park, CA: Sage.

Robson, C. (2011). *Real world research* (3rd ed.). Oxford, England: Blackwell.

Rosenau, P. M. (1992). *Post-modernism and the social sciences.* Princeton, NJ: Princeton University Press.

Rudestam, K. E., & Newton, R. R. (2007). *Surviving your dissertation* (3rd ed.). Thousand Oaks, CA: Sage.

Ryle, G. (1949). *The concept of mind.* London, England: Hutchinson.

Sandelowski, M. (2008). Member check. In L. Given (Ed.), *The SAGE encyclopedia of qualitative research methods* (pp. 501–502). Thousand Oaks, CA: Sage.

Sankoff, G. (1971). Quantitative aspects of sharing and variability in a cognitive model. *Ethnology, 10,* 389–408.

Sayer, A. (1992). *Method in social science: A realist approach* (2nd ed.). London, England: Routledge.

Schram, T. H. (2003). *Conceptualizing qualitative inquiry.* Upper Saddle River, NJ: Merrill Prentice Hall.

Schwandt, T. A. (1997). *Qualitative inquiry: A dictionary of terms.* Thousand Oaks, CA: Sage.

Scriven, M. (1967). The methodology of evaluation. In R. E. Stake (Ed.), *Perspectives of curriculum evaluation* (pp. 39–83). Chicago, IL: Rand McNally.

Scriven, M. (1991). Beyond formative and summative evaluation. In M. W. McLaughlin & D. C. Phillips (Eds.), *Evaluation and education at quarter century* (pp. 19–64). Chicago, IL: National Society for the Study of Education.

Seale, C. (1999). *The quality of qualitative research.* London, England: Sage.

Seidman, I. E. (1998). *Interviewing as qualitative research* (2nd ed.). New York, NY: Teachers College Press.

Shadish, W. R., Cook, T. D., & Campbell, D. T. (2002). *Experimental and quasi- experimental designs for generalized causal inference.* Boston, MA: Houghton Mifflin.

Shavelson, R. J., & Towne, L. (Eds.). (2002). *Scientific research in education.* Washington, DC: National Academy Press.

Shubin, N. (2008). *Your inner fish: A journey into the 3.5-billion-year history of the human body.* New York, NY: Random House.

Shweder, R. A. (Ed.). (1980). *Fallible judgment in behavioral research.* San Francisco, CA: Jossey-Bass.

Smith, L. (1979). An evolving logic of participant observation, educational ethnography, and other case studies. *Review of Research in Education, 6,* 316–377.

Smith, M. L., & Shepard, L. A. (1988). Kindergarten readiness and retention: A qualitative study of teachers' beliefs and practices. *American Educational Research Journal, 25,* 307–333.

Somekh, B. (2008). Action research. In L. Given (Ed.), *The SAGE encyclopedia of qualitative research methods* (pp. 4–7). Thousand Oaks, CA: Sage.

Spradley, J. (1979). *The ethnographic interview.* New York, NY: Holt, Rinehart & Winston.

Stake, R. (1995). *The art of case study research.* Thousand Oaks, CA: Sage.

Starnes, B. (1990). *"Save one of those high-up jobs for me": Shared decision making in a day care center.* Unpublished doctoral dissertation, Harvard Graduate School of Education.

Strauss, A. (1987). *Qualitative analysis for social scientists.* Cambridge, England: Cambridge University Press.

Strauss, A. (1995). Notes on the nature and development of general theories. *Qualitative Inquiry, 1,* 7–18.

Strauss, A., & Corbin, J. (1990). *Basics of qualitative research: Grounded theory procedures and techniques.* Newbury Park, CA: Sage.

Tashakkori, A., & Teddlie, C. (Eds.). (2003). *Handbook of mixed methods in social and behavioral research.* Sage.

Tashakkori, A., & Teddlie, C. (Eds.). (2010). *Handbook of mixed methods in social and behavioral research* (2nd ed.). Thousand Oaks, CA: Sage.

Tolman, D. L., & Brydon-Miller, M. (2001). *From subjects to subjectivities: A handbook of interpretive and participatory methods.* New York, NY: New York University Press.

Tukey, J. (1962). The future of data analysis. *Annals of Mathematical Statistics, 33,* 1–67.

Tulving, E. (2002). Episodic memory: From mind to brain. *Annual Review of Psychology 53,* 1–25.

Weiss, R. S. (1994). *Learning from strangers: The art and method of qualitative interviewing.* New York, NY: Free Press.

Werner, O., & Schoepfle, G. M. (1987). *Systematic fieldwork.* Newbury Park, CA: Sage.

Wievorka, M. (1992). Case studies: History or sociology? In C. C. Ragin & H. S. Becker (Eds.), *What is a case?* (pp. 159–172). Cambridge, England: Cambridge University Press.

Wimsatt, W. (2007). *Re-engineering philosophy for limited beings: Piecewise approximations to reality.* Cambridge, MA: Harvard University Press.

Wolcott, H. F. (1990). *Writing up qualitative research.* Newbury Park, CA: Sage.

Yin, R. K. (1994). *Case study research: Design and methods* (2nd ed.). Thousand Oaks, CA: Sage.

Index

scientific method and, 52
spotlight metaphor for, 49–50,
    50–51 (example)
thought experiments and, 69
underuse/uncritical overuse of, 53
variance theory, 99
See also Concept maps;
    Conceptual framework
Theory-in-use, 30, 103
Thought experiments, 65, 68–69,
    69 (example), 70–71 (exercise)
Tolman, D. L., 92
Topic selection, 24, 25–26 (example)
    research goals, flexibility in,
        32–34 (example)
    See also Methods; Qualitative
        research design
Triangulation:
    and validity, 128
    data collection methods and,
        102–104, 128
    See also Methods
Trust building, 92, 93
Tukey, J., 81
Tulving, E., 103

Validity, 4, 5, 19 (figure), 121–122
    causal explanations and, 31
    data, interpretation of, 88
    design map strategy and, 11
    ethics issues and, 7
    generalizability and, 137–138
    qualitative research and, 122
    realist research questions and, 81
    rival hypotheses and, 123

testing theories and, 53
validity matrix and, 129, 130–134 (figure),
    135–136 (example)
validity testing and, 122–123, 125
See also Interactive model; Validity test
    checklist; Validity threats
Validity test checklist, 125
See also Validity; Validity threats
Validity threats, 122, 123
    identification/management of,
        136 (exercise)
    reactivity and, 124–125
    researcher bias and, 124
    triangulation of data collection
        methods and, 128
    See also Validity; Validity test checklist
Variance orientation, 29, 31, 99
    variance concept maps, 56 (figure),
        58 (figure), 64
    variance research questions, 82–83
Voice, 112

Wahl, B., 83
Wallston, B. S., 46
Weiss, R. S., 31, 73, 91, 97, 103, 138
Wievorka, M., 98
Willett, J., 66, 83, 96, 97
Wimsatt, W., 42
Wolcott, H. F., 159
Wright, F. L., 3
Writing. *See* Memo tool; Research proposals

Yin, R. K., 3

Zinsser, K., 58

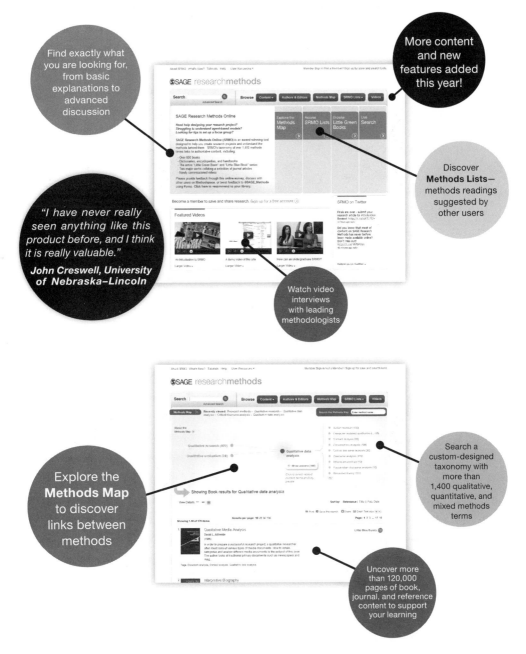

SSAGE researchmethods

The essential online tool for researchers from the world's leading methods publisher

Find exactly what you are looking for, from basic explanations to advanced discussion

More content and new features added this year!

"I have never really seen anything like this product before, and I think it is really valuable."

John Creswell, University of Nebraska–Lincoln

Discover **Methods Lists**— methods readings suggested by other users

Watch video interviews with leading methodologists

Explore the **Methods Map** to discover links between methods

Search a custom-designed taxonomy with more than 1,400 qualitative, quantitative, and mixed methods terms

Uncover more than 120,000 pages of book, journal, and reference content to support your learning

Find out more at
www.sageresearchmethods.com